An Anatomy
of Values

An Anatomy of Values

Problems of Personal and Social Choice

Charles Fried

Harvard
University Press
Cambridge
Massachusetts
1970

Distributed in Great Britain by Oxford University Press, London

Library of Congress Catalog Card Number 78–111483
SBN 674–03151–2

Printed in the United States of America

To my mother and father

Acknowledgments

I owe a very great debt to the friends and colleagues who have discussed the material in this book with me and have read some or all of the manuscript in various stages of completion. Some of my colleagues at the Harvard Law School, Paul Bator, Derek C. Bok, Alan M. Dershowitz, Lon L. Fuller, Frank I. Michelman, Robert E. Keeton, Charles R. Nesson, Lawrence H. Tribe, and the late Henry M. Hart, read large parts of the manuscript. I am particularly grateful to Stephen G. Breyer for his painstaking and relentless criticism.

The Harvard colleagues outside of the Law School to whom I am grateful for suggestions and encouragement are Kenneth J. Arrow, Edward C. Banfield, Stephen A. Marglin, Howard Raiffa, Richard H. Rosen, Thomas C. Schelling, and Richard J. Zeckhauser. The last two particularly devoted considerable time to reading a large part of earlier versions of this manuscript.

An earlier version of Part Three was distributed to the members of The Society for Ethical and Legal Philosophy, and I received many useful suggestions from that group; I am particularly grateful to Saul Kripke, Judith Jarvis Thomson, Gerald Dworkin, Thomas Nagel, and Robert Nozick. The last three read earlier versions of the whole manuscript and were helpful and generous with their time in many respects. I am particularly grateful to Thomas Nagel not only for many important suggestions and criticisms but also for the considerable encouragement I drew from the fact that his own forthcoming book *The Possibility of Altruism* in many ways attempts a similar task, makes some similar arguments, and generally draws its inspiration from similar sources.

Herbert Morris of the University of California, Los Angeles, read this manuscript with meticulous care and made many useful criticisms.

My greatest debt is to John Rawls. I have been discussing philosophy and learning with him over the past nine years. Many of the ideas in this book arose out of conversations between us, and my thinking has been enriched and clarified by him. My debt extends, of course, to his published and unpublished works, particularly his "Chapters on Justice" and his lectures on Kant and Hegel delivered at Harvard in 1963.

Chapter Nine appeared, in part, under the title "Privacy" in *The Yale Law Journal*, 77 (1968): 475, and portions of that article are reprinted here with the permission of the Yale Law Journal Company and Fred B. Rothman and Co. The editors of the Journal, and particularly Thomas G. Grey, provided valuable editorial and substantive assistance. A portion of Chapter Twelve appeared in *The Harvard Law Review*, 82 (1969): 1415. The editors, and particularly J. Lawrence Schultz, made useful contributions both of substance and form.

James B. Moore, of the Harvard Law School, did extensive research in the preparation of the notes and criticized the text as well. Lorne Tepperman, of the University of Toronto, criticized the text of Chapter Seven.

Contents

An Anatomy
of Values

". . . May God us keep
From Single vision and Newton's sleep!"
— William Blake, letter to Thomas Butts

Chapter I
Introduction

This essay analyzes the ends men pursue, and the ways in which these ends are ordered in some kind of system. The driving force behind the analysis is the attempt to present ends, or at least some important ends, as complex entities having a discernible and significant structure, and then to present the priorities, preferences, and relationships that men impose on their ends as themselves constituting a complex, coherent structure, whose principles of ordering may be discerned and criticized.

I propose an analysis of ends as they may appear to persons who have those ends. It is not an account like that of the psychologist, biologist, or neurophysiologist, which treats ends as external theoretical entities. This contrast must seem quite obscure; it will I hope become clear. For the present, I am content to say that the analysis should make the ends considered more perspicuous to the persons who have those ends. Those persons should recognize in a deeper way what it is to have these ends or to order ends as we do. That is why this essay is primarily a philosophical and critical account of ends, rather than a descriptive or scientific account. There is no new knowledge here, and the account begins from the perspective of persons who have at least an intuitive sense of what it is to have an end, to value something for its own sake. It is that experience which I seek to analyze, criticize, and rationalize.

My main aim is understanding and appreciation. I do not pretend that at any point I will completely lay bare the essence of some particular end and even less of any system of ends. If I succeed in displaying at least partially the complexity and structure of some ends, then to that extent an aspect of what it is to be a person has been captured by rational analysis and statement. For it is our ends, that which we pursue and are gratified in attaining, that make us what we are. As I will consider ends in respect to notions like love, friendship, trust, knowledge, beauty, life and death, as well as in respect to institutional notions like justice, society, and law, I am quite clear that much — most, perhaps — of what makes these ends most vivid and crucial to us will escape this statement and analysis. But this too is a gain for understanding and appreciation, since these most elusive aspects of significant ends are at least picked out negatively; they are the unstated residuum which defies analysis, or at least has defied my analysis.

A second aim is moral and didactic. In presenting a particular analysis I am putting forward an account of how our ends may coherently be regarded. And to that extent I offer a criticism not only of inconsistent accounts, but also of ends and systems of ends which do not accord with it. Such discordant ends and orderings are asserted to be inconsistent with a particular conception of what it is to be a person, as the notion of human personality emerges from our system of ends. Thus, for instance, I argue that to be a person capable of love, trust, and friendship entails certain constraints on the possible range of ends and orderings of ends one may have. So also to have a conception of one's own identity over time implies a certain ordering of ends, and to be a person is to have such a sense of identity. But the moral and didactic aspect of this essay is not prescriptive. It does not say you must embrace this or that end, this or that ordering. Rather it works out the entailments of doing so, and not doing so. Morality, after all, cannot be commanded; it can only be chosen. So that by explicating certain ends and systems which might be chosen, I seek to expose what it is to choose in one way or another; to lay bare the entailments of choice.

Finally, it is the purpose of this essay to influence through understanding the kinds of social systems and social values we take up. This purpose is not in truth different from its general moral and didactic aim. It is only that where social, institutional forms are involved we are readier, perhaps, to accept the guidance of analysis. Our intuitions about our ends or values are often so attenuated when we come to embody them in institutional forms that we are used to looking to analysis and argument to draw out the implications of our intuitive premises for the complex choices that institutional design requires. We are used in this realm to offering and accepting arguments which have the form of telling us what it is we really want to do. Where I take up these social and institutional entailments of ends and value systems, the didactic aspect of the analysis is plainest, and includes concrete criticisms of social and legal institutions.

The Plan

In Chapter Two I explore the notion of an end. I show that some ends have a complex structure, and I try to show something about the nature of this structure. An analysis of ends as ends must proceed, it is argued, from an appreciation of their complexity as well as their diversity. Ends differ from each other not just because they consist each one of them of some one single, simple, different unanalyzable element — although this may sometimes be the case — but because they are complex. A particular end may consist of a number of elements, and these elements are arranged in specific ways. It is this ordering of elements that makes many ends what they are, and it is the uncovering of this structure which an analysis of ends must produce.

Chapter Three considers a particular class of ends, which is called the class of rational ends. This is the class to which the holding of certain beliefs and the acceptance of certain principles is necessary. Not only do these beliefs and principles determine the ordering of the elements in the ends, but a person who pursues these ends must in some way have it as part of his end to order his conduct by such principles. These principles are called rational principles, and the ends are thus called rational ends. The ordering principle of an end is said to be constitutive of the end, and there is introduced the metaphor of the musical score which arranges the elements of a musical piece. The kinds of constituting principles and the ways in which they constitute ends are then considered.

Chapter Four examines a family of these constituting principles that are all related to a single more general principle, which is called the principle of morality. These principles, which are constitutive of the ends which involve relations with other persons, include the principles of right and of justice.

Chapter Five considers relations of love, friendship, and trust, and shows how these relations are important because they refer to a range of significant ends. The discussion shows how the analysis of ends can illuminate significant human ends and relations. It also elaborates a particular conception of a human person, which is a person having certain ends, involved in certain relations, subject to certain emotions, and therefore accepting those principles which are constitutive of those ends, relations, and emotions.

The concluding chapter of Part One looks briefly at certain other classes of rational ends and their constituting principles, and then goes on to introduce the notion of a more general rational principle which orders the whole repertoire of ends and principles. Such an overriding principle is more general than the rational principles considered earlier. It is a principle which can be specified in a large number of different ways. In choosing a specification of this general principle, a person chooses a life plan which determines in a general way the sort of person that he is.

Part Two carries the implications of the theories and concepts developed in Part One to an analysis of social institutions. I argue that social institutions can be more completely understood if we see them as complex structures of rational ends mutually pursued, rather than just as instruments for the attainment of other ends.

Part Three focuses on questions of life and death. In examining how persons might approach decisions involving the risk of death, the problem of the ordering of ends and the concept of the life plan are more fully elaborated. These notions are then applied to choices involving risks of death for others.

Part One
The Structure
and Ordering
of Ends

Chapter II
Means and Ends

A Straw Man

The analysis of ends and their structure can be approached by considering a model of ends and of the relation of activity to ends which is in direct contrast to the conception I shall develop. By this contrasting model — I am perfectly prepared to concede it is a straw man — all activity, all striving, whether mental or physical, is instrumental. The end of all striving and activity lies outside of it as a distinct, separately describable and conceivable goal. The extreme version of this account holds that some state, say pleasure as in one form of hedonism, is the true goal of all activity, that this end state can be understood and experienced entirely apart from the pursuits which bring it about, so that the sole entity having intrinsic value is that end state. Nor is this view of the relation of means to ends necessarily limited to hedonism, as we shall see. Hedonism is only a familiar example. To cast the point in linguistic terms, by this extreme model there is always only one terminus for the string of questions beginning with the question "why are you doing this," and that terminus is: "because it gives me (pleasure) (produces X)." Moreover, when that final answer is given, it is not given — as one might suspect from ordinary usage — simply to stop the flow of questions. The answer is conceived as an informative explanation of what the actor expects to get by so acting. When the actor says that finally he does something because it gives him pleasure (or produces X), this is not to be taken as the equivalent of saying "I do so, just because I want to." Rather, his answer is of the same logical form as "I am turning the switch in order to put on the light."

There is a further aspect of this extreme view which needs to be developed so as to provide the contrast against which I can put forward my account of the structure of ends. On the extreme view, ends, or rather the single and ultimate end, is entirely simple. It is a single state whose instances may vary in intensity and duration, but these variations are not at all variations in structure; they are matters of more or less of the same, single entity. The structure of pleasure — or whatever this end state is called — is entirely simple and invariant. Moreover, the time dimension is as extrinsic to an understanding of this single, sovereign value as are the means by which this end state is attained. That is to say, it may be important to understand how pleasure is attained, but that understanding does not contribute to our understanding — on this view — of what pleasure is. And also on some occasions pleasure may be experienced intensely for a brief time or over a longer period, but these differences also do not go to our understanding of what it is to experience pleasure. They tell us only that the simple ultimate value may be multiplied in two dimensions, as it were, horizontally over time and vertically in terms of intensity. In either case, however, it is a matter of piling up identical units of the same thing.

For this kind of extreme view the analysis of value can take only two forms. One might consider the ways in which the desired end state can be brought about, prolonged, or intensified. Or one might investigate the physiological and neurological processes and states corresponding to that end state. Neither of these inquiries tells us, or is intended to tell us, more about the end itself, for it is the premise of this view that apart from postulating the end, there is nothing more to be said.

It may be doubted whether any philosopher has ever espoused such an extreme form, say, of hedonism. At the very least, entities are multiplied by most hedonist philosophers to include a negative element, pain. And with the introduction of that second element come very great difficulties for a theory which would maintain a simple and consistent instrumental relation between all activity and the end (or ends) of that activity. The introduction of a second albeit negative element necessitates an account of how these two elements are to be compared to each other, how they are to be ordered. And the theory becomes even more complicated when there is introduced — as for instance in Mill's theory — the possibility of several different distinct pleasures. What account is to be given of the differences?

It is not at all my intention to elaborate or criticize these or any form of hedonism. Rather, by sketching the outlines of one possible extreme view of the relation of means to ends, I wish only to bring out some issues that are important to the positive thesis I shall be presenting. These issues are: First of all, it is assumed that ends as such (indeed, the single end) cannot be the subject of analysis. The end or value appears as a simple, primitive, unanalyzable term in the theory. Second is the assumption that the consideration of value (or the end or ends) must therefore be limited either to the analysis of the means by which the end is attained, or perhaps to the physiological-neurological substratum of the end state, where the theory admits of this. Third, it is assumed that therefore all activity and striving can only have an instrumental value in relation to the valued end state. No activity or striving can have intrinsic value, since its sole value inheres in the contingent fact that it is in fact productive of the single valued end state. Fourth, there is entailed a characteristic approach to the complexity of elements in ordinary pursuits and goals: eating, sex, listening to music, solving a problem. This complexity is interesting only insofar as it is the case that such and such a combination and arrangement of elements is likely to be productive of the valued end state. Fifth, there is also a characteristic approach to time and change. Since the valued end state (or states) are unanalyzable simples, they are not subject to change, and their deployment in time is only a matter of temporal location or of quantity as located in time. Finally, there is a characteristic conception of reason, for reason can only make us more successful in attaining the simple end state. Since the end state is simple and unanalyzable, reason can tell us nothing about it, only how to attain it.

There are, of course, numerous puzzles and objections about

9

each of these propositions, but I would assert that together they make up a frequently encountered ensemble of implicit philosophical and methodological assumptions about questions of ends and values. Thus, for instance, modern utility theory — with which I have no necessary quarrel — is often understood and treated as if it accepted some or all of this ensemble of assumptions, although in truth there is no need for utility theory to accept a single one of them. In general, much vulgar theorizing about matters of value, of personal and social choice, implicitly departs from some such set of assumptions. Nor is this set of assumptions about the nature of ends necessarily restricted to forms of hedonism. There are certain theological systems, for instance, which I believe posit exactly the same set of assumptions, mutatis mutandis, with ultimate celestial bliss standing in place of pleasure as the sole, simple end.

The view which I shall put forward assumes, by contrast, that at least some ends and values have a structure; that this is a structure of an ordered complexity of elements which constitutes the end or value; that these elements are sometimes deployed in time, so that the end is a structure of elements arranged in a particular way over time; and that not only does reason have a special role in revealing these structures but that in certain cases the structure is consciously rational. It is because of this notion of some ends as structured that I believe that it makes sense to speak of an analysis of ends as such, and to assert that such an analysis can make more perspicuous to a person having such an end what it is to have that end, hold that value. It is because of this view that it becomes possible to think clearly of activities as sometimes being ends in themselves, for these activities can be conceived of as a structured complex of elements constituting an end. And it is because we can see how activities and other complex structures are ends in themselves that we are brought to see that there is a multiplicity of ultimate ends, things valued for their own sakes, and not just as instruments to the attainment of some other end.

I hope that by sketching the contrasting set of assumptions, I have been able to show that something of significance is at stake in the task I undertake, that an important balance may be redressed, and that useful and illuminating views on actual activities and striving may be attained. I shall refer to this contrasting conception from time to time in developing my own account, for I believe the assumptions behind it go deep, and it will serve to make more pointed what I wish to say.

I am concerned about human ends and their explication, and the question therefore arises in what sense is this a work about morals. I have, for instance, equated the concept of end and that of value. My concern is to elucidate the structure of human ends, and I assume that what is an end in itself is a value also. The difference in terms has no significance in my account. Now morals will enter into this account in two ways. I shall assert that morality is incorporated in a whole set of important ends as a structuring principle. And also I shall assert that to have certain ends, which I call moral ends, and to give these moral ends a certain prominence in one's system of values is necessary to being a certain sort of person — a moral person.

The Complexity of Ends

Consider a simple example, eating an ordinary meal. Usually this would be done for nourishment, whether or not one was hungry, or for pleasure. One can, of course, easily imagine other reasons, such as a wish to be sociable or to win a bet, but I will ignore these. If one eats for nourishment the means-end analysis is applicable, in the sense that nourishment may be conceived of as an end state — the state of being nourished — which is conceivable apart from any particular activity which procures that state, and which indeed is temporally subsequent to that activity.

But this is not the only reason for eating a meal, and I wish to consider the case of eating for pleasure. If once the search is abandoned for a single sensation of "pleasure" which is attained in eating for pleasure, the experience is obviously a complex one. It may begin with the thought of eating, then pass to the sight and the smell of food. After that come various sorts of handling, cutting, lifting to the mouth — and finally eating itself. This too has very many constituents. There is biting, chewing, and swallowing. There are various sensations of taste and smell, of texture and kinesthetic sensations of different sorts associated with biting, chewing, and swallowing foods of different consistencies. And finally there is the sensation and awareness of food reaching the stomach, and sometimes of hunger being assuaged. The complex of experiences is, to be sure, compounded largely of sensations: taste, texture, and consistency are experienced through various senses. But the pleasure in eating will often consist also of attitudes and beliefs. An obvious example would be the belief that a dish had been prepared according to the recipe of a great chef invented for some historic state occasion. There may be memories, associations, and expectations surrounding even the humblest meal. But even abstracting from these complications, as from the complications arising from the almost inevitable functional aspect of eating, the pleasure of eating is evidently a most complex entity: it is compounded of sensations of various sorts, perceptions, and movements, all disposed in a partially variable but not indifferent order in time.

This familiar activity illustrates several aspects of the conception of ends as complex entities. To be sure, a person eats in order to maintain his health, to be sociable, perhaps to win a contest. Thus eating may be an example of an instrumental activity in the sense that it is a means to an end external to the activity, separately identifiable from it. If the activity is purely instrumental, then every element in it must be determined by its aptness to that external end. But it may be and often is an end in itself as well, in that no further end can be adduced as determining that activity.* The answer to the question "why did you do that" is then only something of the form "because I wanted to." Nor do we feel that any further information has been supplied, any further end identified if that answer takes the form "for pleasure."

This much is obvious and well understood. What I wish to draw attention to is that such an end is not at all simple. It is complex in several ways. The end consists of a number of elements, such as the various sensations, beliefs, and attitudes identified in the example. It is doubtful if any one of them in isolation would be pursued as an end in itself, and it is clear that even if some single element did have such intrinsic value, it would be quite a different

---

* A hard case, but one which offers no difficulty in principle, is the mixed case, of which eating is probably frequently an instance: the activity is pursued both for its own sake and for the sake of an outside end, here to assuage hunger. Indeed, it may be that the intrinsic end of the activity in eating cannot be attained — or fully attained — unless it performs also its instrumental function. Of course, that instrumental end does not determine the details of the activity, especially when hunger could be assuaged more quickly and easily in other ways.

value from that of the end constituted by the whole ensemble. Nor is the complex end simply the sum of the particular ends which might be associated with the particular elements of it. This is so because some of those elements, though necessary to the complex, in isolation have no value. Even those elements that might have some intrinsic value in isolation take on a different significance from this context. Finally, the end is complex not only because of the multiplicity of its elements, but also because the order, the arrangement of the elements is important. Thus the temporal sequence, rhythm, and tempo of the constituting elements are important to the pleasure of eating. This becomes evident if one imagines all the sensations being experienced contemporaneously, or all separately, or in alphabetically arranged pairs, or grouped as they normally are but each separated by a period of twenty minutes, and so on. There may be substitutions and omissions, but past a certain point these might spoil the pleasure — or invent a new one; smoking might be an example.

The example of eating illustrates, then, that an end in itself may be a complex entity, made up of several elements, of different sorts, arranged in a particular, only partially variable order. And thus it stands in contrast to the assumption made in my straw-man model that the intrinsically valuable, the end in itself (or ends in themselves), is necessarily simple. Throughout this discussion I shall say of such complex ends that they are constituted by their elements and by the particular arrangement of these elements. I use this term, constitution, because it points up that the entity constituted by the elements is a distinct entity, not just the sum of its constituting parts. The analogy might be drawn to a complex molecule, whose chemical properties are a function of its constituting elements, their proportions and arrangement; it does not make sense to say that the properties of the molecule are the sum of the properties of its constituting elements.

This example illustrates, as against the straw man, also a different possible significance of the temporal dimension. For the straw man the temporal dimension can have no intrinsic significance: the simple units of pleasure (or whatever) may be piled up horizontally in time or vertically in intensity; their significance is not thereby altered. Also time is the dimension in which means precede the end which they are instrumental in producing. Once it is appreciated, however, that ends may be complex in the ways I have been discussing, the temporal dimension becomes a possible element in that complexity. Not only the sequence of elements is important, but also their rhythm and spacing in time. And, of course, the relation of temporally prior elements to subsequent elements is not that of means to end, just as the relation of all the constituting elements to the end they constitute is not that of means to end.

The Concept of Rational Ends

The example of eating, like many other more or less "instinctual" physical actions, while showing the complexity of ends and of the actions in which they are attained, does not exemplify clearly the notion of an end having a rational structure.

In the example of eating I did no more than to demonstrate the complexity of the end, and to demonstrate also the constitutive relation between an action and an end. I asserted that it is necessary to the end that the elements of the complex whole be ordered in a particular way, but I said little or nothing about that ordering. Indeed the implication of the preceding account is that beyond describing the end and its constituting ordering, nothing more can be said. Or if something further could be said about the ordering, it would be in terms of psychological or biological factors. But to account for ends in terms such as these is not to fulfill the promise of this work, which is to present an analysis of values and ends which makes those ends and values more perspicuous as ends. The promised analysis is intended to illuminate what it is to have such values. Now while a description of the ordering of instinctual ends such as those I have been discussing goes a certain way in that direction, it fails to show why that ordering is necessary or appropriate. Every analysis, every account, must stop somewhere, but this account seems to stop too soon. In discussing rational ends and rational actions in this section, I shall attempt to push the account further to an analysis of the structure of the ordering itself. I shall do this by reference to some clear examples of rational ends and actions. Eventually the question will be raised whether even such instinctual ends as eating or sex do not have a significant rational element, but at this point that claim seems implausible. Indeed I concede that these remarks as a whole must appear obscure, and so I proceed to the examples.

A person makes a gift to another. Now just as with eating, one may do this as a means to some ulterior end, such as to curry favor, but also as with eating it would seem this is an action that may be performed for its own sake, with no ulterior motive. There is, to be sure, a difficulty about this: the question "why did he make that gift" might in such pure cases still receive the answer "out of kindness," or "out of generosity," or (more difficult) "to make him happy," or (more difficult yet) "out of friendship." But, as I shall argue later, these answers do not imply an ulterior motive in the way that ends such as currying favor do. When a person gives a gift out of kindness or generosity, this does not mean that he is doing so to attain some more remote end to which this act is just a means. Indeed, giving a gift out of kindness and giving a gift to curry favor are not even on the same categorical level. The correlate to giving a gift out of kindness is rather giving a gift out of flattery or duplicity. More of this later; for the time being let us consider giving a gift for its own sake, no further consequences being taken into account or expected.

Giving a gift is a complex act, exemplifying the concepts not only of complex action but also of rational action. In giving a gift certain overt events are caused to occur: property is transferred, either physically or by some legal or conventional formality which stands in the place of such a transfer. In the simplest notion I just seize hold of the item to be given and hand it over to you, releasing my physical hold on it. But in addition to the overt events, there must also be a whole complex of beliefs. To make a gift to you I cannot believe that what I am giving you is rightfully yours to begin with. And perhaps — though this is less clear — I must believe that it is in some sense mine to give. Further, I must believe that the gift will be pleasing to you. There are gifts — the white elephant, the box of poisoned chocolates — which seem to contradict this, but I think they bear me out. They are gifts only in an ironical sense: they start out by pleasing (and that is why they are gifts) but end up not pleasing. Finally, it may be that a gift must be pleasing as a gift. Thus if I give you something in such a way that you think you have found it, or you think that I am repaying a debt, you may be pleased but you are not pleased with the thing as a gift.

Another similar example is that of a person who has acquired property unjustly and wishes to perform an act of restitution. Here too I shall assume that a person has made restitution at least partially just for the sake of doing so: he would have done so even if the act were deprived of all consequences which might operate as a motive for it — say if both the agent and the beneficiary knew they were to die the moment after the restoration had been effected. In order to attain this end it is not only necessary to perform certain overt gestures; they must be performed in the appropriate context. One cannot make restitution simply by any means at all that returns the property to the owner. Cases where the property is given as a gift or sold to the owner must be excluded. Perhaps the restoration must be accompanied by some acknowledgment of wrongdoing, if only to oneself, so that it would not do when the property is no longer needed to abandon it where the owner will find it. Here, then, is an end that can be accomplished only if the agent has certain beliefs and attitudes. Further, these attitudes and beliefs can be entertained only if the actor understands certain principles or arguments, such as arguments of morality and fairness. What in detail this understanding consists of and what these principles and arguments are I will develop subsequently.

A less complex but related set of examples are games. Games are played for many reasons — to exercise one's mind, to display skill, to win money — but generally they are played for pleasure, just for fun. To play a game of chess not only must the appropriate moves be made, but they must be made in the appropriate context: the context of playing a game, which is a context of beliefs and attitudes. One must, for instance, believe one is playing a game, intend to play a game, perhaps intend to win. And these beliefs and attitudes depend on an understanding of certain principles and arguments. In general these are the rules of the particular game and the conception of playing games of that sort.

In spite of many differences and distinctions, all three of these examples bring out what I mean by a rational end. In all three cases there will be certain overt gestures, movements, words, physical sensations. In this respect the actions and the ends pursued in them are like those in the eating example. Moreover, again as in eating, these elements must be arranged in a certain order if a gift is to be given, restoration made, or a game played. This order is not invariant, but there are limits; not any order will do. In these examples, however, it is clear that there is involved also a different class of elements. It is necessary that the actors have certain beliefs and attitudes; one must understand certain rules or arguments; and in the case of gifts or restitution one must understand and accept certain principles about what is rightfully due another and what is one's own, what is fair treatment, and the like. Without these additional elements one cannot be said to be making a gift, effecting restitution, or playing a game. Now perhaps even in the category of actions and ends I have loosely called instinctual there are also necessarily involved beliefs and attitudes of various sorts. I am not concerned to deny this — on the contrary, it seems to me to be the case. It may well be, after all, that every voluntary action is to a greater or lesser degree a rational action. What I wish to bring out by the three examples of gifts, restitution, and games is a special feature, which cannot at least plainly be attributed to complex actions and ends in general.

Giving a gift, restoration, and games belong to a class of actions and ends that are complex and have ordered elements, including certain mental elements: attitudes, beliefs, understanding, and acceptance of rules and principles. The crucial feature that makes these ends rational is that the ordering of the elements is intimately related in various ways to these mental elements. It is something of an oversimplification, as we shall see, but for the moment it might be said that these mental elements *are* the ordering of the other elements in the action or end. In the case of a game there are the various overt moves, there is the understanding and acceptance of the rules, the motive to win, and a strategy or plan for winning. But what is crucial is that the acceptance and understanding of rules, the strategy, and the plan are the ordering of the overt moves. Thus what is distinctive about rational actions and ends is their reflexive quality: the actor is conscious of the ordering of the constituent elements of his end, and that consciousness is necessary to that end's being what it is, so that he consciously orders the elements in accordance with the plan, principles, or rules which are necessary to the end.

It is when a complex end or action is ordered in this way by a rule or principle or plan, the acceptance and understanding of which are necessary to the end, that I shall speak of a rational end or action, and the ordering element I shall call the rational principle or rational plan of that action or end. At times I shall also refer to such a principle as the score — using an analogy to a musical score — according to which the action is played.

There are difficult issues about what it means to accept a principle, to be guided by an attitude, to understand and follow a rule, and the like. I shall go into these questions — though not exhaustively — in the next section. Also there are important questions and distinctions to be made about rational principles of various sorts at different logical levels, and this and the next chapters will go into these in some detail. At this point I would hope that the reader will accept the possibility that distinctions, clarifications, and answers can be supplied sufficient to give the concepts of rational action and end coherence. At this point I wish to point out why those concepts permit an analysis of ends and values of the sort I promised at the outset of this essay.

First, if an end is ordered by a rule which one knows and follows, if such a rule not only orders the elements in the sense of arranging them in time and space, but also dictates what those elements should be, then if we can arrive at a coherent and adequate statement of that ordering principle, we shall have stated the very thing which determines the content and form of the end, and thus given an account of why that end is what it is. Moreover, we shall have done this by reference to an entity which is experienced as an aspect of the value by those who hold or might hold that value. The revelation of the structure of the end by articulating its ordering rational principle makes that end more perspicuous to a person who has it or could imagine having it. There is at this point an objection which I would like to mention: if the rational ordering principle is (by definition) a principle of the actor so that in some sense he knows and understands it, why does it help understanding to state that which must be known and understood already. A simple answer to this objection is that it is a way of explaining the value to someone else who has values and ends, but not these values and ends. But that is too simple, since the account should be illuminating also — indeed primarily — to the very person whose end is thus accounted for. And for that case I shall at this point simply allude to the difference between implicit and explicit understanding, between grasping a principle so you can operate with it and grasping a principle so you can give a full and coherent statement of it.

Second, as we shall see in concrete detail in succeeding chapters, there are relations between rational principles. The principle ordering a particular act, say the making of a gift, involves complex reference to whole systems of often more general principles which govern concepts like right and title, free relinquishment of title, or friendship. Through these more general principles, the relationship can be shown between a particular end and whole systems of other ends. This leads to an appreciation of the coherence that exists between the discrete ends we pursue. Here too, of course, it is important to become clearer about the sense in which a principle or system of principles can be attributed to a person. It is to a discussion of that issue that we proceed.

Explicit and Implicit Principles

It is a central notion of this essay that significant ends are ordered ("scored" to use the musical metaphor) by plans or principles which are the plans or principles of the actor, and not just theoretical entities posited to explain or describe behavior. Putting the point loosely, these are principles in terms of which the actor orders his ends.

A clear case of a rational end, as I have defined that term, would seem to be a person playing a game according to rules and a strategy which he had constantly in mind as he played, or a musician playing a piece according to a score which he had in mind as he played, or a priest performing a ceremony in a prescribed form, or a dancer following the steps and gestures of a choreographic score, or a mathematician solving a problem by reference to rules, axioms, and definitions. In all of these cases the plan, principle, or score is imagined to be before the consciousness of the actor as he acts, directing his execution of the action, his pursuit of the end. In each of these cases, also, the ordered action can be conceived as an end in itself. At the other end of the spectrum are actions like swimming, doing arithmetic, improvising a dance or a piece of music. In such cases the difficulty is less in discovering the principles of performance than in determining in what sense, if any, the actor can be said to follow such principles in his performance. Yet even at the clear end of the spectrum questions can be raised.

Even in the clearest cases there are a host of philosophical questions about what it means to follow a perfectly explicit rule or plan. How would one give an account of the process of being guided by a rule? Is it like tracing a mental finger along a line on a mental map, which then in some way produces a correspondence between the rule or plan and actual behavior? Wittgenstein in the *Philosophical Investigations* argues that from the point of view of the person who guides his behavior by a rule there is no separate "experience" of being guided, apart from the awareness of the rule and awareness of one's own conduct. And there is another range of problems as well which have to do with the notion of awareness of a rule or principle. To be aware of a guiding rule must one have it constantly in mind while it is performing its guiding function? Surely when an experienced chess player moves a piece he does not rehearse to himself the rules of chess authorizing that move, and perhaps he does not even go over in his mind the principles of his strategy. Insofar as a particular move is concerned, he may just move, or he may consider in an explicit way some but not all parts of the total complex of rules and strategy determining the move. So also a trained mathematician doing a mathematical problem may just come to his conclusion without anything like a conscious awareness of the theorems or intervening steps which are the basis for his conclusion. This issue raises the question whether indeed there is a clear distinction between rational actions like playing a game, performing a ritual, doing a mathematical problem on one hand and (what I have called) instinctual actions like eating, swimming, or walking on the other. There is a question since in the rational as in the instinctual cases there need be nothing like conscious advertence to the ordering principle during the performance of the action (or pursuit of the end). And thus there is a question whether the asserted reflexive quality of the ordering in rational ends, which allows a deeper level of philosophical analysis of those ends qua ends, is indeed present.

The question might be resolved in the following way. One might describe a rational action or end as one in which the ordering principles, though not explicitly in mind at the time of the pursuit or performance, might be brought to mind, articulated, and would then be recognized by the actor as the principles which have indeed guided his performance. But this resolution seems too vague and ambiguous to do the job. In what sense can one have been guided by a rule one did not have in mind and never stated until after the performance? This problem has been explored in depth in the recent linguistics research of Noam Chomsky and others who have been associated with Chomsky's approach. The use of language may in most cases be seen as an action which is instrumental to the attainment of some extrinsic end, and thus does not fit under the conception of rational end or action defined in the preceding section. Nevertheless the question of the nature and status of the structures underlying linguistic performance are analogous to those I raise here about the rules and principles underlying rational ends and actions.

It is Chomsky's position that linguistic competence can best be accounted for in terms of certain common, general linguistic structures which organize and underlie all human linguistic behavior. In his view the complexity of any particular language is such that it is implausible to assume that a language user acquires the competence to speak and understand it — and particularly to understand and to form a potentially infinite set of novel but correct statements — in the first few years of life simply by a process of trial and error. The infinity of correct statements is understandable only because they are generated by a finite, indeed quite limited set of general principles. Nor is it plausible, Chomsky argues, to assume that these general, structural principles are inferred by the young child from the data of the language use he encounters and attempts in his early years. Rather Chomsky argues that these structures are in the human mind from the start, and that the encounter with language only actualizes these latent structures. Moreover, these structures are common to all men, since they underlie all languages. For Chomsky the task for linguistics, which has only made rudimentary findings, so far, is to discover these innate structures and to show how different instances of linguistic performance are generated by them.

For our purposes Chomsky's hypothesis is interesting as providing one possible model of a relation between rules or principles and performance. Can a Chomskian language user be said to follow the rules of language in the reflexive way that I posit a person follows a principle in a rational end or action, when the speaker is usually unable to articulate them, and Chomsky himself believes that the articulation of these structures is a task for laborious and imaginative research?

The answer depends not on the explicitness of the principles, but on what happens when the principles are made explicit, or what good it does to make them explicit. In the case of a rational end or action — as I have defined those terms — if it is shown that the performance does not correspond to the principle, the performance will be amended to conform because what is desired, the very thing that is sought, is a performance according to that principle. That is not to say that I envisage a kind of game the object of which is to conform to rules — though such a game might of course exist. I am not asserting that the end one pursues is to conform to principle, but rather that one pursues and attains one's end only in conformity with the principle; the performance ordered by the principle is the thing desired. So to have a clearer idea of the ordering principle is not to be in a better position to attain some end which is clearly in view. It is instead to understand better what it is one wants. When the principle is articulated, the performance is corrected, not because it has been shown that the actor's technique was faulty, but because the actor understands better what it is that he wants.

Thus one need not have in mind an explicit formula in order to act on a rational principle. Indeed, clear articulations of rational principles may be hard to come by. The criterion I propose for identifying a rational principle (and then a rational end or action) is the attitude a person takes up when he is presented with and recognizes a statement of the principle. If he recognizes the principle as the principle of his end, and not just an external, theoretical account of his behavior, then the principle is a rational principle. Two examples of such a recognition are the recognition of the general theorems underlying a mathematical proof by a person who accepts the conclusions of the proof, and the recognition of the general conceptions of courage, or wisdom, or justice which Socrates elicits from his interlocutors, who previously held and acted upon intuitive and fragmentary attitudes and beliefs about these entities. Indeed the procedure of formulating rational principles might be taken as similar to the method of Socrates.

In a sense the whole conception of rational principles and ends and the philosophical justification I give for analyzing them is circular. I assert that there is a procedure for analyzing ends which illuminates the end or value, qua end or value, for a person holding it. Here I go on to identify rational ends as those ends the principles of which inform those ends in that to understand the principle is to understand better what it is to have that end. But I do not believe this circularity is vicious. Rather what is offered is a particular conception of ends and values. There is nothing vacuous about the account of that conception; there is nothing vacuous about a conception of ends as informed by principles in a certain way. The difficulty — circularity, if you will — comes in only on the question of whether this conception corresponds to any part of our own experience of ends and values. If it corresponds, then it opens the way for an analysis of those values of the peculiarly illuminating sort I hope to undertake. But the definition or statement of the conception does not guarantee or even provide evidence for the proposition that any significant ends correspond to that conception. In the last analysis this is a question the reader must resolve for himself.

The essential criterion of a rational principle is the attitude to the principle of a person who understands it and whose end it underlies. This leaves unresolved the status of that principle for a person who does not have it in mind at the time he acts, or for a person who has not yet had it fully articulated for him, or for a person who is incapable of grasping the principle of an action he is able to perform satisfactorily. In all these cases, and to an increasing degree, the principle is what I shall call inchoate or implicit. The term implicit is better suited to cases of an awareness which is not present at the time of action, while inchoate principles are those which a person has not yet and perhaps is unable to formulate. I would like to posit that inchoate principles are still principles for persons pursuing ends scored by those principles if two conditions are met. First, the actual behavior, attitudes, and beliefs of those persons are generally consistent with those principles. Second, those persons have a disposition to acknowledge the principles and to amend their behavior, attitudes, and beliefs to coincide with the principles once an inconsistency is made manifest. A difficulty is presented in the case of persons who are unable to grasp an abstract statement of a principle. Examples are persons who have an intuitive grasp of mathematical procedures, of the principles of harmonics in music, of poetry, or of chess, but cannot grasp any statement of those principles. Nevertheless, I would include these cases in the conception I am developing, for theirs may be only an inability to grasp certain formulations of the principles, not the principles themselves. For instance the process of understanding and conformance might be exhibited by them if the principles were brought to their minds by examples or analogies.

This brings out the important point that it is the *principle* which underlies, informs, and orders the end or action, not some particular formulation of it. And for any principle there might be a large number of alternative formulations, none of which is the principle — just as an actual musical score is not the piece of music, it is not even the idea of the piece of music, or just as some particular text setting down the principles of association of a society or nation does not itself constitute those principles, but is only one possible formulation of them.* So that different people may be capable of understanding the same principles under different formulations.

I leave unanswered the question how inchoate or implicit principles guide and order conduct, attitudes, and beliefs. There is also unanswered, however, the question how even explicit principles and rules guide behavior. That in the latter case they can and do seems clear, and I pass from that only to the proposition that in the former case they do as well.

Finally, to anticipate subsequent discussions, implicit principles are important particularly in relation to acts of justice, friendship, love, and trust. For each such act is scored by principles at several levels of generality and abstraction. Acts of friendship, for instance, entail conceptions of mutual right and entitlement, which it is an

---

* One is tempted to say that the United States Constitution is not the constitution but only a statement of the constitution.

aspect of friendship freely to relinquish. And these notions of right and entitlement derive from more general principles of fairness and justice, which in turn are related to a still more general principle, which I call the principle of morality. Generally this structure of principles is largely — if not entirely — implicit, and often it will be inchoate as well. But once the notion is accepted that these rational principles of ends and actions may order and order reflexively those ends and actions while yet being implicit or inchoate, the way is open for an elucidation of such complex structures of principles and ends.

Chapter III
Rational Ends and
Their Principles

The central notions I have put forward thus far are that a man may have a large number of ends (and therefore values), which it is not necessary or even plausible to represent as means toward some single end; that among these are ends that consist of a multiplicity of elements ordered in certain ways — that is, that to attain a particular end is to perform a series of actions, or to experience a congeries of sensations or emotions, or to hold certain beliefs or attitudes, or some combinations of these — and finally that among these complex ends is a subclass, which I have labeled rational ends. Rational ends (and rational actions, when the attainment of the end requires the performance of certain actions) are those ends to which may be ascribed a principle of ordering, which explicitly, implicitly, or inchoately is a principle the person holds or accepts as his own. I have not sought to prove that rational ends exist, and the examples I have given may perhaps be brought under different analyses. Rather, I have introduced and illustrated an account of certain ends and actions which I believe is a possible account of the subject. Nor shall I seek in this and succeeding chapters to prove that this is a correct account, and I hope that the reader will bear that in mind and thus justify my omission of tiresome qualifications and comments. Rather I shall proceed to elaborate and illustrate this account. In the end I hope that I shall carry conviction despite the lack of either logical or empirical proof, on the basis of the fullness and coherence of the elaboration and on the basis of the potency of the theory to illuminate the problems and experiences with which it deals.

The Rationality of Rational Ends

In introducing the concept of rational end in the prior chapter I was concerned particularly to consider the way in which the principle of such an end ordered the elements in it, and the sense in which this principle of a rational end is an element of that end and thus a principle of the person whose end it is. I have left entirely vague the structure of such rational principles. And incidentally I have not given a sufficient justification for choosing the term "rational" to denote this class of principles and ends.

In referring to this rational element in rational action I use the terms reason, rule, principle, and argument. From time to time I invoke a musical metaphor and use the term score. Suggestive as these terms might be, since the concept they designate is crucial to this study a fuller exposition is in order. In rational ends and actions the elements of the end or action are ordered by reference to a plan or principle. Will any scheme of ordering at all count as a rational principle? Is no more necessary than that there be a number of elements whose order in time or space is prescribed? Intuitively this seems too permissive, if we are to look to rational principles as the underlying form of significant human ends. One wants to be able to do more than just present and describe a particular ordering. If the end is a significant one — that is, if persons expend significant life resources in its pursuit — one wishes to give an account of that ordering: why it has the form it has, its rationale. In calling these principles rational principles I had in mind that analysis might indeed push beyond a simple description of the principles, and that the principles are rational in a deeper sense than that they ordered the elements of a complex end in a reflexive way.

Now in logic and mathematics an ordering is simply any rule that arranges a number of elements in a prescribed way. And the questions arise what more can ever be said about a particular ordering than to describe it; and in what sense can it be said of an ordering that it is or is not rational? The formal answer to these questions is that a rule for ordering elements may perhaps be derived from a more general rule of which this rule is a specific instance. Indeed in a formal sense the process of accounting for a particular instance is generally that of finding some more general rule or principle of which it is an instance. What else can the process of accounting for the principle consist of than referring that principle to some more general concept?

Let us consider two examples. There is the ordering or plan which has the form: "place rear wheel on axle," "insert cotter pin," "spread prongs in cotter pin," and so forth. Then there is a rule of this sort: "place the right foot forward one step," "count two beats," "bring the left foot up to the right." The first ordering may be understood or rationalized by reference to the purpose of, say, assembling a tricycle. The particular form of the ordering is determined by this purpose. Although it would be difficult to formalize this relation precisely, the broad outlines are clear. Every effort is determined by what will lead to the production of an external object, presumably as efficiently as possible. It will be recalled that this kind of action and end does not fit into the category of rational ends, as I have defined them. If the point of the activity is to have a tricycle, then the end is external to the activity and the activity is entirely instrumental to the end. Indeed it is this relation of instrumentality which is expressed in the way the end determines the ordering of the activity. (If the end is conceived differently, for instance as a game or puzzle or some feat of skill, then the activity of making the tricycle might well fit into the category of rational ends.) The dance example, by contrast, illustrates the different relation possible between an end and elements in the plan, for it cannot be said that the steps, rhythms, and pauses are instrumental to the dance; they are the dance, and the choreography determining these elements is the principle or argument of that dance.* As defined, a rational end is of this latter

* There is the following complexity: an activity may be instrumental to an external end, while that end itself is a rational end. Thus this end orders one activity instrumentally and the other activity in the way I have defined as rational. For example, one may tune his violin in order to play a sonata. The tuning is instrumental while the sonata itself orders its elements rationally.

sort, consisting of a number of elements ordered in accordance with a reflexive principle. At issue now is the question of what determines the principle of such an end, what corresponds to the coherence provided in an instrumental activity by the external end which determines the form of that activity.

The most general notion of coherence is that of logical consistency. There is a difficulty in applying this notion of coherence as consistency in the case of rational ends like a dance. A dance is an entity which cannot be conceived apart from its constituting gestures. It is unsatisfactory to say that the coherence of the plan consists in its aptness to the product, since the plan is the product. It thus seems that it is the dance itself — that is, the end itself — which must be coherent, which must be consistent. In a sense the end must be consistent with itself. But what are the criteria of that consistency? The answer is a complex one, with several different levels: I shall start with a rather desultory sketch based on some examples.

Consider the performance of a dance or a piece of music, the solution of a mathematical problem, the playing of a game. In each case there is a plan which determines the particular ordering of elements of this end. But in each case there are other principles as well that control more actions and ends than this particular one and others identical to it. The dance may be one of a more general type; a piece of music may be an instance of a particular form (sonata) in a particular convention (twelve-tone). A game will be dictated by the individual players' strategies, but it will be constrained as well by the rules of the game being played. And in a mathematical proof, in addition to the definitions and axioms of the particular problem there will be the general conceptions of what constitutes a valid proof. Nor is this point confined to obviously rule-governed activities like games. For there are more general principles still which control these ends. There are canons of grace which determine what constitutes a good dance. In the case of games there are notions such as difficulty, equal opportunities for winning, a certain possibility for a crescendo and maintenance of suspense, the relevance or irrelevance — depending on the kind of game — of chance. In music too and poetry there are determinants of what is a successful composition. I do not mean to suggest that these higher level principles are explicit in the way that the rules of chess are, or even in the way that the form of the sonnet or sonata is explicit. On the contrary, the general principles of aesthetics, or of a particular art form, and even the aesthetics of games, are perhaps as deeply buried in our experience and modes of acting as are Chomsky's deep structures of language. My thesis is, however, that such deeper and more general principles do exist, and that the coherence of the more specific principles and plans of particular rational ends is a function of their consistency with these deeper, more general principles.

Before proceeding to formalize these notions, I should like to make them intuitively more plausible. Consider again the case of a mathematical proof. The elements of this rational end are the actual steps in the proof, and the rational principle is the plan which determines what those steps are and their order. Now what is it that determines the steps in a proof? Obviously there is the problem that is set: given certain premises, show that a certain conclusion follows. But what of the process of proof? The premises themselves do not generate and constrain the form of the proof. There are, then, certain general conceptions of valid proofs of that sort, and more generally still principles of what constitutes valid reasoning in any case. Each more general kind of principle applies to a wider range of ends (always assuming the total proof as a single rational end). This does not in the least suggest that these more general principles are any the less intimately involved in determining the particular end. What is often the case, however, is that the more general principles remain implicit or inchoate, and sometimes can only be explicitly formulated with great difficulty. In the aesthetic examples I have adduced the general principles of a good poem or a good dance are still more elusive. Moreover, I do not wish to suggest that some unique set of these principles exists in that realm. There may be several alternative sets, and it may be the function of creative genius to make additions to these general controlling conceptions. Further, these principles are probably harder to articulate explicitly, so that they may remain inchoate and intuitive for even the most skillful practitioners of these arts. Yet I assert that the very sense we have of the comprehensibility of works of art, our ability to recognize skill and inventiveness, bear witness to the existence of such general organizing principles, which introduce order into diversity, and allow us to relate the unfamiliar to the familiar.

In the next chapters I shall discuss one such system of principles, having to do with moral actions in respect to other persons. For the moment I shall just mention that an action like the making of restitution is governed by principles at several levels of generality. The particular restitution will be determined first by the circumstances of the case: the kind and value of the property to be restored, the situation in which it was acquired. Beyond this are more general principles which define the concept of unjust acquisition, adequate restitution, appropriate gestures of respect, apology, and recognition that should accompany the physical retransfer. Again these more general principles may be implicit or inchoate in a given case, yet they underlie particular acts of restitution not only in the sense that they provide a theory to describe behavior, but because they are the actor's implicit or inchoate principles in a reflexive sense.

What these observations are intended to indicate is the sense in which rational ends and actions and their principles may be said to be rational. They are rational in two senses: first, the principle of ordering of their elements is a reflexive one; and second, these principles exhibit a coherence by reason of their consistency with higher order, more general principles, which are therefore as much implicated in the ordering of the particular end as the more specific plan or ordering. These more general, higher order principles are, however, usually implicit and inchoate. The actor whose end is ordered by such a principle rarely has an explicit formulation of it in mind as he pursues his end. However, if these principles are indeed the actor's principles, then the articulation — the making explicit — of these more general principles should invoke from the actor a sense of recognition of what he had in mind all along, a sense of deeper understanding of his own ends and values. It is by exhibiting the relation between particular ends and these more general principles that the rationality of the ends is shown, and at the same time this is the process which brings to view the most significant part of what is hidden to persons who have such ends. Thus the articulation of the *system* of principles underlying our rational ends is the main task for a rational analysis of ends as such.

It is that task which will be undertaken in the balance of this book, after certain further general clarifications have been attempted.

I do not wish to overstate the extent to which these concepts of rationality and coherence are applicable even to rational ends. For in all such ends, and in the system of these ends, the elements which are not susceptible to an analysis in terms of consistency with more general principles are as important as those which are susceptible to such an analysis. I shall call such elements material elements. Consider again the example of a formal proof. The canons of logical consistency supply the formal, what I have called the rational, element in the ordering. But what of the primitive terms in the proof, the definitions and premises? These, by hypothesis, are not derived from more general principles. They are given; they are a starting point. Roughly and loosely, the problem one wants to solve — where solution means consistency with general formal principles — is not set by general principles. It is the material element. This is perhaps clearer in the cases of music, poetry, art, and games. In each of these there are various levels of material elements, of givens. In painting they may be the facts of color, shape, two dimensionality. In dance the material elements are the human body and its capabilities; they may also be a more limited and structured repertoire of gestures and movements drawn and stylized from the gestures and movements of everyday life. So in music these givens may be as general as the capacity of the ear to distinguish sounds and to sense rhythm in any arrangement of sounds over time, or the more limited and structured repertoires of sounds and rhythms which are the repertoire of familiar givens out of which a particular musician or musical tradition will construct its music.

It is out of these material elements, underived from general principles, that rational actions and ends are constructed according to rational plans. But even the most general of rational principles is a given, a material element. For the more general the principle the less likely it is that analysis will show it to be generated by some other, still more general principle, until at some point our most general principles must also be accepted as given. And finally even the notion of coherence must in the end be seen as a given. Coherence and consistency are notions of unification in simplicity of a diversity of elements. But ultimately this very notion and the way it operates are given. The importance of this coherence cannot be derived (coherently) from more general principles. It is a starting point. And so it is with the most general principles of certain systems of ends, like the bases of grace and elegance in dance, of fun in games and, as we shall see, of morality in actions and ends affecting other people. These most general principles are all starting points from which whole systems of more particular principles derive. These more particular principles then order elements some of which themselves are given, material. And nowhere more than in art has this duality of the formal and material been more fully brought to the surface. Indeed, there has been a constant dialectic between the formal and the material, the rational and the arbitrary, with the artist seeking to overcome and incorporate the material limits of his work into his formal structures.* But art is not the only area where this dialectic takes place. The general topic is that of all rational actions and ends, and in subsequent chapters we shall see it illustrated in regard to moral ends and actions.

It should be said that what, from the aspect of rational action, is a given or material element from other points of view, the psychological or biographical for instance, is not at all given or arbitrary. The rhythms which are introduced "arbitrarily" into a piece of music as axioms for its structure may be traced to significant sources, just as the notion of rhythm itself — which also is in this sense a given — may be traced to exceedingly primitive and pervasive facts about ourselves, such as the regularity of our heartbeat or breathing. So also such basic notions as unity in diversity or the satisfying trajectory from quiet through tension to quiet again may have biological roots. One might wish to maintain, of course, that it is the sources of each of these given elements that are the keys to rational action, since these represent biological or psychological determinants of what will give pleasure in specified circumstances. Thereby all instances of rational action would be assimilated to the model — illustrated by the case of the tricycle — according to which the plan of an action is generated by an end external to that action, which external end determines the choice and ordering of elements in the action. I shall not seek to refute this suggestion. It

---

* Consider the tendency in modernist painting to take certain assumed constraints on painting, like the framing edges or two dimensionality, and turn them into structural principles generating the substance of the work.

is sufficient to note that behind the thesis that, for instance, the imposition of coherence can be accounted for as an attempt to obtain some satisfaction of the "need for order," there may lurk simply a particularized version of the hedonistic hypothesis, by which all activity is aimed at producing some single, separately identifiable end called pleasure. If not, the concepts of "need" or "satisfaction" become quite mysterious or perhaps congruent with my thesis, since they may denote no more than a disposition to engage in rational actions of various sorts.

Kinds of Rational Ends; Rational Ends and Rational Actions Distinguished

The discussion of rational ends so far has relied on examples such as games, a dance, music, an act of restitution, the execution of a logical proof. All of these examples share two important features: (1) they involve a number of gestures or operations (2) ordered in time. It is important now to break out of any limitations these features may seem to impose on the concept of a rational end. I have defined a rational end as an end which is constituted by a number of elements, ordered according to a plan, where the understanding and acceptance of that plan or principle are themselves constituting elements of that end. This definition is broad enough to include elements that are neither actions nor gestures; nor does it necessarily speak only of an ordering of elements over time. Where the elements, or some of them, are overt gestures or items of behavior I have used the term rational action. In this section I shall fill out the concept of rational end to the limits of the definition, and thus show that rational actions are but an important — perhaps the most important — kind of rational end.

Consider the examples of looking with appreciation at a picture or understanding a logical proof. Both take place in time and take time, but they are not defined by a temporally extended series of gestures or thoughts. Yet taking in a picture or a proof both entail the understanding of just the kind of coherent relation between parts that was explored in regard to serially extended actions. Thus appreciation of a picture consists — in part at least — of grasping the relation of its various elements to each other as they form a structured whole. That relation will express principles of coherence, some of which transcend the particular painting, others of which are defined by it, and the act (or if one prefers event) of understanding must be structured by an understanding of those principles. Whether coherence is achieved (or appreciated) in respect to elements extended in time — as in a game, or dance, or a piece of music — or extended in space is less of a difference than the similarity of the factor of coherence. This is even more striking in respect to the understanding of a logical or mathematical relation, proof, or argument, for there the elements are extended neither in time nor in space. Examples based on understanding are drastic, since we can imagine understanding as being instantaneous, timeless. Such examples illustrate the general point, that the rational coherence of an end need not exist simply in terms of the elements of a temporally extended series of gestures. The end itself is an example of a rational end just because it is derived from and against a context of more or less complex arguments or principles.

Now we may wish to speak of an *act* of understanding or an act of appreciation, in which case these acts would be rational acts and rational ends. To speak of them as actions seems strained. But whether or not one wishes to consider understanding and appreciation as acts or actions, it is important to see (1) that these may be ends in themselves, and (2) that they entail the understanding and acceptance — explicit or inchoate — of principles, whose function it is to order a multiplicity of elements in a particular way. Nor do I wish to insist that such "acts" of appreciation or understanding are instantaneous in fact. I suppose that they rarely if ever are. I am arguing only that temporal seriality is not an essential feature of such ends, as it is of a piece of music, of a dance, or (if rational principles are to some degree involved, as I believe they are*) of eating a fine meal or making love.

Finally, there is a kind of rational end which stands midway between temporally extended rational ends and those that are not necessarily extended in time. An act of respect is an example. This

* Briefly, my suggestion is that in these cases persons do not act just instinctually. There are significant elements of attitude and belief which are not only important elements in some instances of such acts, but which direct to a certain extent the form and ordering of the behavior in the reflexive way characteristic of rational action. It is simply that the proportion of the action which is "given" is far greater. There is a fuller discussion of some aspects of this in Chapter Five.

may consist of nothing more than a slight bow and a smile. But it is an act of respect only if it is derived from an understanding of the relative status of the two persons, and that can be a very complex matter indeed. The coherence and unification of complexities in this simple act depend on the correct application of complex principles to a complexly structured and defined set of circumstances. (After all the solution to a complex problem may be a very simple equation.) Nor is it correct to say that an act of respect is just a move in a game of showing respect, like "pawn to king's four" is a move in a game of chess. Rather, it is itself a one-move game. To be sure, there are certain dispositional entailments to a correct statement that one has shown (or felt) respect, as there are to knowledge and understanding, but one can show respect once or understand briefly and then forget.

An act of restoration is, in its reference to principles of fairness and so on, like an act of respect in its reference to ideas of relative status. But it may be greatly more complex, involving an ordered series of very many gestures. This may be true as well, in appropriate circumstances, of acts of respect. And so the distinction I make between rational actions, which show a complexity in the relation of their temporally extended elements, and rational ends, which are just contextually complex, is neither a sharp nor a basic one. It is not as important to my argument as the distinction between rational ends and instrumental actions, or the distinction between rational and instinctual actions.

Particular Ends and General Principles

As a final point of clarification, I wish to insist on the integrity of particular ends. The particular end is the unit of value, even where it is scored by principles which are general enough to point well beyond that particular end, principles that might also score other ends of a different sort, and might even imply that such other ends will be pursued in appropriate circumstances.

In the case of composing, performing, or listening (with appreciation and understanding) to a piece of music there are several levels of principles, starting with the score for the particular piece, ascending through principles of harmonics, rhythm, and the like, and perhaps culminating in some very general notions of what constitutes coherence in music. Not one of these is necessarily tied to the particular end — or instance of the end. Even the most particular principle will govern every performance or every case of listening to the particular piece of music; while the more general principles will apply as well to other pieces of music. Nevertheless, the end still is the particular piece heard or played on the particular occasion. Everything else is an abstraction from it. The significant entity is the particular end, even though it is scored by principles that are absolutely essential to its being what it is, principles that are potentially also the principles of an infinite number of identical, similar, or quite different entities. In laying the stress on these principles, and in choosing these principles as the elements of an end in terms of which the end may most significantly be analyzed, I should not want to suggest that it is these principles which one pursues, or to suggest that we pursue these ends for the sake of these principles, or that the entity that has significance for us is anything other than the end itself. On the contrary, I believe it is our ends that define us at every moment of our lives, indeed that we are our ends. The systems of principles are significant only in that it is these principles that make our ends what they are. But apart from their embodiment in particular ends, the principles are abstractions.

This may seem quite unexceptionable in the case of games and their principles of fun, in the case of a sonata and its principles of musical form, in the case of a dance and the canons of grace, or even in the case of the act of love and the principles of love (if such there be). In all these cases I think it is intuitively acceptable that the particular instance is the end itself, which is the focus of pursuit and, in its attainment, the focus of satisfaction. But I have adduced other examples too, such as acts of respect and restoration of unjustly acquired property. As to these the primacy of the particular act seems more problematical. Yet I would insist on the correctness of the application, and further I believe that it is just in applying this analysis to such problematical cases that something is learned about them.

Consider the example of the act of respect. That act is comprehensible only in a complex context of beliefs and attitudes, which together are the constituting principles of the act as an act of respect. But is an act of respect — which may be a complex ceremony, or a slight nod — an end in itself? Surely it points beyond itself in a way that a game does not. It is not just that the principles of respect can be applied in a variety of different situations, for so can the rules of a game. Nor is it just that some of the more general principles which stand behind respect — like a recognition of virtue or value — are implicated in different kinds of acts, as for instance in acts of kindness or generosity. For the general principles of fun may be implicated in an infinite variety of different games. The point is rather that a person who truly shows respect may be expected also to perform other acts that are associated with an act of respect through the underlying principles. It would be odd indeed if one honestly showed respect with a bow one minute, and the next picked the man's pocket. A person who shows respect, just because of the principles involved, may be expected to act in certain ways in a wide variety of situations. This leads one to question whether it is the act of respect which is the end. Perhaps it is some more extended series of actions that is the end, or perhaps the end is some emotion or attitude, to which the act is conducive but which is external to it. So also with the act of restoring unjustly acquired property.

I cannot prove that such small scale acts are indeed ends in themselves. Nor shall I at this point elaborate the analysis of such ends. Here I want only to bolster the assertion with some arguments, in order to fill out the concepts of rational ends and rational principles. If these acts are not ends in themselves, then what end is being pursued in such cases? Is it a certain relation to the other person, or a certain feeling or emotion? But if those are the ends, what do they consist of, and when can one be said to have attained them? I prefer to look at a relationship as consisting of ends which a person is disposed to pursue. It seems truer to say that a person stands in a relation of respect to another when it is his end — an end which he pursues and from whose attainment he draws satisfaction — to show respect to that person, to act respectfully. I find it ultimately puzzling, by contrast, to say that the end is to stand in some general way in that relation. If this is interpreted to mean that the end is acting in a respectful way *because* one stands in a certain relationship, I would not disagree. For this seems to me to be just the point I wish to make: that the end is the particular act of respect (or restitution), and this is an end requiring the acceptance of certain principles.

Now it is true that the acceptance of such principles, as manifested in a particular act, implies a disposition to perform other acts on other occasions. A person who restores wrongfully acquired property accepts certain principles of justice and fair dealing, and that implies that he will honor his promises, not cheat or deceive, and so on. But the disposition is not the end. Instead it is a disposition to pursue certain ends. A way of putting this is that the rational principle of an end may constitute a man's reason for pursuing that end, but his *disposition* to pursue it cannot be *his* reason. Yet there remains the puzzle why should some principles (like respect or fair dealing) imply dispositions and others (like the principles of games) do not. The puzzle is in part resolved if one appreciates that what implies the disposition is not the principle but the acceptance of it by a person in respect to a concrete end in which he invests life resources. Once this is seen, it is just a matter of degree: acting on the principle of respect or fair dealing implies a disposition to do so on further occasions, while acting on the principle of fun on one occasion carries lesser implications of a disposition to play on other occasions as well. Is it stranger to think of a person doing justice only once in his life, than it is to think of a person playing a game only once, or thinking logically only once, or appreciating only one painting on one occasion?

The connections between ends and attitudes, emotions, relations, and beliefs will be worked out more fully in analysis of the concepts of respect, friendship, love, and trust. For the time being, I have tried only to develop the concept of rational end, and to distinguish it from the general principles of such ends, from systems of ends, and from the disposition to pursue systems of ends.

Chapter IV
The Principle
of Morality

Certain ends are constituted by the principles which score them or give them coherence. For instance, the principles which determine a good game of chance may lend coherence to a number of different games, and the rules of a particular game in turn govern many individual matches. But these relations are complex: the more remote the principle the less explicit is the agent's reference to it. For quite remote and general principles many agents may lack altogether the sophistication needed for their articulation. Nevertheless by analyzing our beliefs and preferences — aided perhaps by the probing of an inquirer — we can be brought to articulate these principles as principles which we have always held, and where such analysis reveals inconsistency or incoherence the articulated revision is reflected in the more specific and concrete behavior and ends which are scored by these principles.

In this chapter the analysis focuses on what I shall call the principle of morality, which is the term I shall use here for a particular principle of the more remote and general sort. In the terminology of this discussion a moral end is an end which is constituted by the principle of morality. A moral action is an action scored by this principle. It is a concept which refers to a very general principle —

like the concept of a good game of skill — in that it cannot be instantiated in specific ends or actions without the elaboration of intervening principles and arguments which derive from the entailments of the principle of morality in conjunction with other material premises. Thus fidelity, for instance, is a more particular
principle derived from both the principle of morality and more
particular principles having to do with promises, mutual expectations, and the like. And a particular act of fidelity, say the keeping
of a burdensome undertaking, which would be an instance of a rational action, would involve the application of this general principle
of fidelity to the circumstances of a particular case, and these circumstances, too, might impose their own rational structure.

Morality, moral principles, principles of justice and fidelity, and
the other principles related to morality have usually been viewed
as constraints upon actions and the pursuits of ends. In this account
I shall present them rather as rational principles giving certain
actions and ends their rational structure. In other words I look at
a just act or an act of fidelity to one's trust not simply as instances
in which impediments are placed and accepted in the way of
pursuing other ends. Rather, such acts are viewed as performed for
their own sake, and thus such acts are properly viewed as ends in
themselves. These acts are performed in accordance with certain
complex reflexive, rational principles — the principles of morality
and of justice or of fidelity — and therefore they are instances of rational actions and rational ends.

Much of what is said in these chapters about morality and its
derivatives is not at all new. It is squarely in the tradition of Kantian moral philosophy. What is less familiar is the focus on the
individual act as an end in itself, an end whose structure is determined by the complex of moral principles. In this way a quite
definite sense is given to the notion that moral acts are done for
their goodness alone.

The Principle of Morality Introduced

*First, the domain in which the concept of morality (as I now
define it) applies is the domain of all ends and actions which impinge in any significant way on other persons.* (I shall on occasion
use the term transaction to denote an action having impingements

41

on other persons.) This aspect of my concept both includes and excludes aspects of what is often comprehended in the concept of morality. The concept perhaps is wider, in that it includes acts, ends, and relations of love and friendship and other situations in which obligations do not fully specify the content of the situation. It is narrower than some conceptions because it excludes acts and ends which have no significant impingements on others, but on the agent alone. Such totally "private" acts and ends are not, however, necessarily of lesser significance than those comprehended under the concept of morality; nor are they by reason of their privacy less susceptible to the kind of rational analysis I undertake in this essay as a whole.

Second, the principle which specifies the concept of morality is an expression of the concepts of equality, of impartiality, and of regard for all persons as ends in themselves. More precisely, morality requires that an action involving persons other than the agent be compatible with a principle which has the following formal properties. (*1*) *The interests, preferences, or desires of the agent have no special status or higher priority just because they belong to the agent; that is, an agent may not prefer his own interests as such.* (*2*) *The interests of no named party may be preferred simply because he is that named party.* Thus morality requires that justifications not rest in principle on first person references or on references to proper names. (*3*) *The interest of no party may be preferred simply because either that interest or the party having it is preferred by the agent or a named individual.* This is a perhaps obvious corollary to the first two propositions. (*4*) *The interest of no party to an action may be preferred except by reference to a principle which each party to the action does, or would, or should (if they know their own interest) recognize as according equal weight to his interests in the long run.* Thus, there will be situations where in conformity with morality persons may prefer their own or their families' interests, but these are situations in which all parties would or should agree that their own interests would best be served by everyone preferring his own or his family's interests.

There is, of course, an obvious problem lurking in the phrase "each party does, or would, or should recognize as according equal weight to his interests in the long run." If all parties do or, if asked, may be expected to agree that a principle is properly impartial, there is little problem, but what does it mean to say they *should* agree? If this were itself a moral standard, the criteria would be viciously circular. Although I am not prepared to give a full account of when parties should accord this recognition to a principle, I would propose that any account have the following additional formal property. (5) *It may be asserted that a person should acknowledge that his interests are recognized by a principle only if the interests, which he does or should acknowledge as his own, are interests which in some sense it is plausible to say he himself has.* This leaves open the question whether we are taking an extreme libertarian position where only those interests are taken into account which the person actually asserts for himself; or a Platonic position by which a person is asserted to have certain "real" interests, whether he acknowledges them or not; or intermediate positions which impose various rationality requirements on assertions of interest.

Finally, there is a rather technical issue raised by the notions of equality and impartiality. Propositions 1–4 have been put in terms of impermissible bases for preferring the interests of any person. This leaves open the following question as to the basis for an inequality. There are two choices open: one has the characteristic that A is preferred to B, and B is preferred to C; and the other would treat A, B, and C equally. Is it a sufficient justification for the choice of the first in spite of its inequalities, that the *average* level of the satisfaction of interest is higher in the first than it would be in the second, even though C is worse off in the first choice than in the second? In other words, is the availability of a higher average level of well-being a justification for making a particular person worse off than he would be if all were treated equally; may the interest of an individual be sacrificed for this conception of the general good?

To meet this issue, I posit a further formal requirement of the concept of morality, which goes beyond propositions 1–4. (6) *The principle of an end or action is consistent with morality only if that principle gives equal weight to the interests of each person affected by an action, except as departures from equality improve — overall and in the long run — the position of the least preferred person, in relation to what it would be in a position of absolute equality.*

43

This proposition derives from John Rawls's second principle of justice which states that "inequalities are arbitrary unless it is reasonable to expect that they will work out for everyone's advantage." * It is obviously related also to Kant's universal principle of right: "Every action is just [right] that in itself or in its maxim is such that the freedom of the will of each can co-exist together with the freedom of everyone in accordance with a universal law";† and to the third formulation of the categorical imperatives: "Act so that you treat humanity, whether in your own person or in that of another, always as an end and never as a means only." The present formulation differs from that of Rawls in that it, like Kant's, applies to particular actions. It is more general than Kant's principle of right because there is no commitment to the proposition that the sole significant interest in respect to which equality must be maintained is the interest in freedom.

Although the full ramifications of this concept of morality are elaborate, and some of its features must be argued for in detail before they seem plausible, I shall at this stage of the argument only make the connection with the preceding discussion of rational action and rational ends. Morality is a principle or set of principles characterized, let us say briefly, by the notions of impartiality and equality. It is a principle which is of a higher order of generality than certain other moral principles, say fidelity or trust, which in turn are of a higher order of generality than some systems of conduct built on or exemplifying trust or fidelity. Finally, particular actions are structured by such rational systems from the lowest order of abstraction to the higher.

The concept of rational ends and rational actions that I have developed is entirely formal, and an infinite array of principles may be put forward to fulfill the defined constitutive role in a rational end. Morality — as I have specified it in this chapter — is just one such principle, and nothing has been said to show that it is a particularly significant one. I shall now try to show not only the significance of the concept of morality as defined, but also that it is a satisfactory formalization of a concept which corresponds to or lies behind a whole set of concepts of generally agreed significance and potency.

* John Rawls, "Justice as Fairness," *Philosophical Review*, 67 (1958): 164.
† *Metaphysical Elements of Justice* (Ladd trans., 1965), p. 35.

The Principle of Morality as the Most General Principle Applicable to Relations with Other Persons

In this and the succeeding section I shall argue for the proposition that the principle of morality is the most general principle applicable to ends and actions having significant impingements on other persons. This argument will not be a logical proof. In this section I shall argue: (a) our dealings and relations with others often and significantly are ends we pursue for their own sakes and they are rational ends, so that what I call transactions make up an important subclass of the class of rational ends and actions; (b) therefore there must be a rational principle or set of rational principles for these rational ends, and among such possible principles are those which have the characteristic of incorporating into one's own rational ends the rational principles and ends of the other party to the transaction; (c) such ends thus are those in which the other party to the transaction is not used merely as a means to the accomplishment of one's own ends (there are adduced reasons why principles expressive of this reciprocity are of significance); and finally (d) the principle of morality is that principle which best expresses this kind of reciprocity. In the next section I shall argue why the principle of morality should be considered not merely a significant principle for transactions but, on certain assumptions, the controlling general principle of dealings with others.

Transactions as rational ends and actions. If no rational principles whatever applied to transactions — that is, if transactions could never be counted as rational ends in themselves — then it would follow of course that the principle of morality would never apply in our dealings with other persons. The reason is that the principle of morality is a general rational principle scoring a whole family of possible particular rational ends.

Let us begin by considering this preliminary question. Do relations with others ever involve ends in themselves, or are such dealings always instrumental to the attainment of goals which are separately identifiable from the relations with others and which are only means to their attainment? If one adopted a severely unitary form of hedonism — a single distinct entity like "pleasure" is the sole basis for all value and the end of all striving — then obviously transactions would be excluded (along with everything else except "pleasure") from the category of ultimate ends. I have developed at length the arguments against this kind of unitary theory. The more plausible view recognizes a plurality of ends.

To the general statement of this pluralistic view I would now add that one's relations with others are the ground for a significant number of ends. Conversations, competitions, amusements, love, kindness, sex, domination, submission, all of these and many others are the forms of ends we attain in relations with other persons. And as to some or all of them it would be artificial to say that these ends are not ends in themselves, but means only to the attainment of some single end (or perhaps some small numbers of ends). In our relations with others, then, we find the occasions for a large number and for most of our significant ends and values. If it is true, as I shall later argue, that our ends define us, then the most significant thing about a man is the ends he chooses to and can attain, and then also we can see the sense in saying that man is a social animal: among his ultimate ends, those involving others occupy a prominent place.

But are these ends rational ends — ever, often, always? I think we may establish quite easily that ends involving others are primarily rational ends. When an end requires a certain kind of recognition of an outside object involved in that end, there is already present in implicit or inchoate form a rational principle. Does that mean that a dog chewing a bone or a sea anemone closing upon a speck of plankton performs a rational action and attains a rational end? Certainly not — but it may mean that for men even such "instinctual" activities as sex should be viewed as rational in the special sense I have defined. For the sea anemone and the dog the recognition of its object is not a rational recognition, because the process of rational analysis — of bringing to the surface the features of the object of the action — will not in any way illuminate or alter either the agent's conception of his end or his actions in respect to it. But with human ends involving other persons this rational recognition will frequently be present. Nor is this recognition purely instrumental. If a person is assembling a tricycle, then an understanding of the nature of his tools or of the parts he is operating on may of course be helpful, but it is not a better understanding of his *end*. He does not care how the tricycle gets assembled, so long as it does — unless, of course, he is assembling the tricycle as a puzzle. But where the end essentially involves another person as part of its very structure, then to understand the other person, to recognize what sort of "thing" the other person is, will entail a better understanding of the end itself.

Now let us consider a bizarre example: a cannibal who wishes to prepare and consume a very special dish of human flesh. Does this example bear out the point I have been making? I think it does. Assuming that cannibalism has no ritual significance for our agent (that makes a more complex case) but only a culinary significance, if the cannibal is a true epicure he will be as potentially interested in the nature of his ingredients as Escoffier might have been in the coagulent properties of egg yolk in *sauce béarnaise*. Or to take a less bizarre example, a person who is doing anatomical sketches will have an interest in and manifest a recognition of the lines and form of the human body that I would call rational. The reason that cases of eating, drinking, and sex might be considered borderline cases is that it has been often asserted for all of them that the agent may be utterly unconcerned and unilluminated by a further understanding of his objects. He is simply driven instinctually to their pursuit, and reason is relevant only instrumentally, that is, only in telling him how to "get" his objects. I do not wish to argue that there are no such instinctual ends for men, or that ends involving other persons are necessarily never wholly instinctual. Perhaps acts in the realm of sex, aggression, or maternal care are sometimes wholly instinctual in the sense that recognition is merely the sensory apprehension of an object meeting some instinctually imprinted archetype. I only say that I doubt very much that such an instinctual analysis is *ever* wholly appropriate to ends involving others — "enemy" is a concept made up of significant conventional and rational elements, as is "appropriate sex object" or "object of maternal affection." But whether such ends are ever wholly instinctual or not, at least as regards persons of any maturity and civilization it is far more plausible to build on the assumption that most, if not all, of their ends involving others are rational ends.*

---

* Once again, I decline to offer a proof for this proposition that transactions involve rational principles, just as I declined in previous chapters to offer a

The rational principles of transactions: recognition and reciprocity. I have stated that transactions will involve significantly the kinds of recognition of their objects — that is, other persons — that is characteristic of rational principles and ends. Can anything more be said about the content of the rational principles for transactions? The examples I have just adduced are cannibalism, sex, figure drawing, and acts of aggression. In previous chapters, I have used examples such as acts of restoration and respect, and competitive or cooperative games. What are the principles of recognition, the rational principles, in these cases?

We can begin to specify by asking in each case what is the significance for the end being pursued that it requires a human object. In the case of (nonritual) cannibalism the significance resides in whatever special qualities of taste or texture there may be in human flesh, and this suggests that if some other kind of flesh had similar (or superior) qualities, then a human being would no longer be necessary to that end. Similarly in the case of the anatomical sketch, if what is desired is a rendering of strong musculature perhaps a human subject is also quite adventitious to the end. Contrast to such cases that of ritual cannibalism or — what may be surprisingly analogous — the case of an artist who is interested not in bodies and musculature as such, but in the human body. The ritual cannibal draws significance from his act just because it is human flesh. Transactions, then, may involve a recognition of various aspects of their objects — their taste (in the most bizarre example), their appearance — but the major significant recognition is of the humanity of the object. And so also in acts of kindness, hostility, love, sex, or play.* What does it mean to recognize the humanity of the object of one's end?

In general, to recognize the humanity of one's object is to recognize whatever is distinctive about a human object compared to other possible objects. One might wish to include features such as shape and size (I will now leave taste behind for good and all,

---

proof for the existence of rational ends and principles in general. I have said only so much as is necessary to give a sense of what I mean by these notions, leaving it to the reader to decide for himself whether they illuminate the experience to which they apply.

* Playing a game against a computer may be fun, but it is not the same as playing against a human opponent, unless one believes he is playing with whoever built and programmed the computer.

while adding the availability of the person's tissues and organs for study and transplantation), but the most important characteristic is the other's capacity for behavior and performances of his own. This capacity ranges from elementary reactions like jumping when burned or frightened to complex intellectual performances like performing a difficult theoretical task, joining in a musical improvisation, or cooperating in the governance of a polity. The most distinctive and unique human qualities and capacities for our purposes is the general capacity — exhibited in an infinity of particular acts and capacities — to pursue rational ends, to follow rational principles, and to engage in rational actions. Thus for instance, to join other players in a musical improvisation is not only to perform a difficult intellectual task, nor indeed is it only to perform that task as an end in itself — a rational end: it is to pursue a rational end which has as a part of its constituting rational principle the rational actions of others, and those rational actions and ends of the others have as part of their rational principles the same or analogous recognitions of the rational principle of the agent. These rational ends and actions I shall therefore call reciprocal: reciprocal ends, actions, and principles.

Before indicating why reciprocal ends and principles are so important, I shall contrast them to cases that are close to reciprocity, but yet are not truly reciprocal. Consider the case of intelligent compliance with a complex demand exacted under threat of extreme and immediate violence. The threatener certainly assumes the existence of significant human capacities: The capacity to understand and comply with the demand and the capacity to understand and respond to the threat. But this transaction does not exhibit what I have just defined as reciprocity because, although the threatener attains an end of his own, the only end of the victim's that is attained is the avoidance of the threatened consequence. Furthermore, the end of the threatener is not usually necessarily one that involves the participation of a threatened human agent, unless exercising dominance over another human agent is itself all or part of the threatener's ultimate end. Except for that special case, both the threat and its victim are mere instruments, standing outside the conception of whatever end the threatener seeks to attain: for example, having the victim assemble a tricycle for him. A bribe would exhibit similar characteristics, contrasting it to the case of reciprocal pursuit of ends. In such cases, then, there are two reasons why there is no reciprocal rational action and end: (1) the agent does not use another person as a necessary constituting element of his (the agent's) end, but only as an instrument for attaining a separately identifiable end, and (2) the action of the other party to the transaction is not a necessary constituting element of that other party's end. Let us now consider cases in which reciprocity is lacking in one, but not both, of these respects.

A most interesting case of near reciprocity is what I shall call the case of perversion: the actor uses another person to attain his end, and it is a necessary constituting element of that end that another person be used (that is, the other person is not just a contingent instrumentality), but it is also a necessary element of the actor's rational principle that the other person thereby *not* attain an end of his own. Cases in which it is an essential part of the actor's rational end to exert power over another person or to inflict pain illustrate such a perverse rational principle. The principle (1) recognizes the other as an essential part of the end, (2) recognizes as an essential part of the plan that the other is capable of pursuing rational ends of his own, and (3) makes it an essential part of the plan to interfere with those ends.* I would add that in its most developed form this kind of perversion requires (4) that the victim know that it is the actor's end that his (the victim's) end be frustrated. (As truly reciprocal ends have the quality of two mirrors endlessly reflecting each other, these perverse cases may be called cases of the sinister mirror.)

The less sinister departure from perfect reciprocity is the one where the actor uses the other as a mere instrument of his end, but in so doing is indifferent whether the other person attains an end of his own. Such cases are far less dramatic. I need a task performed, and I can get it done cheapest and best if I pay you. The reason you accept my pay is that it allows you to do something which is an end of your own. I wish to have my watch repaired, and pay you to do it. You love repairing watches, and only by being paid can you afford to spend your time that way. But I do not care *why*

* Intermediate cases of cruelty and perversion are those in which it is of the essence of the actor's end to inflict pain on a nonhuman agent, one that does not have the capacity to pursue rational ends. Similarly, it can be part of an actor's rational end out of some sort of kindness to allow a nonrational creature to attain his nonrational end.

you choose to repair my watch, and would let someone else who hated the work or let a machine do it if it could be done cheaper or better. If the departure from reciprocity in the perverse case is repellent it is because of the acknowledgment of the victim's human capacities; in this case any repellent quality derives from indifference to those same capacities.

I have now introduced and elucidated to some extent certain forms of principles that may obtain in respect to dealings with other persons. Principles involving what I call reciprocity are among those — they are candidates, they are possible principles of ends and actions. Moreover, I believe that we may assume even at this stage of the argument that some degree of reciprocity is an important aspect of some significant human ends and relations. What needs to be considered now is whether recognition of others and reciprocity have any special significance among all the possible principles in dealings with others, and what that significance is. My argument is that the capacity to entertain rational ends and principles is of peculiar significance, and that for that reason the principle of reciprocity has a peculiar significance.

I have stated frequently in this essay that our ends define us. This is not a point I shall try to prove. It seems to me implicit in the concept of an end that it is our ends that move us and express our values. The concepts of striving, preference, satisfaction, and value all are related to and depend on the concept of end. Nothing is more important to a person's understanding of himself than an understanding of his own ends. Indeed, it is an analytic truth in this system that a man's ends are the locus of significance for him. Now we come to a person's understanding and recognition of *other* persons. By the concept of reciprocity a person recognizes another person from the same perspective as he sees himself, and from the same perspective as that other person sees himself — that is, in terms of that other person's ends. If for any two persons, A and B, the most important aspect of A for A is A's ends, and of B for B is B's ends, then by the principle of reciprocity the most important aspect of B for A is B's ends, and vice versa. Thus each person recognizes as most important in others just what he recognizes as most important in himself, and just what they recognize as most important in themselves.

Now beyond ends as such, I have specified further the category of rational ends. I must now make out the claim that there is a special significance to viewing oneself and others in terms of *rational* ends. Once again, I shall not attempt anything like a proof. The claim shall rest on three arguments. First, most human ends can be, and are more plausibly, conceived of as having a rational element. This argument is made in the preceding chapters. Second, human ends involving others are particularly likely to have a rational element, this being the element of recognizing the nature and capacities of those other persons. Finally, there is an argument that is considered in Chapter Three and in Chapter Six: the general capacity to entertain rational ends and principles corresponds to a tendency for order and simplicity to be created out of the multiplicity of elements of desire, observation, and need a person encounters. Together these three arguments sufficiently support the hypothesis that persons most appropriately regard themselves as entities having not only ends, but rational ends; and not only as having rational ends, but as having rational ends in respect to their dealings with other persons.

Reciprocity, therefore, is significant because when pursuing ends involving other persons, it is only by scoring those ends by principles consistent with — or expressive of — reciprocity that a human agent recognizes another in the terms that the agent recognizes himself and in the terms that that other person also recognizes.

Reciprocity and the principle of morality. It remains to demonstrate that the principle I have called the principle of morality is the principle expressing the notion of reciprocity.

Reciprocity is the recognition of the other participants in a transaction as entities having ends and rational ends. That recognition is not just a formality, a brief concession preceding the working out of the elements of the end itself. The recognition of this quality — I shall call it human personality, or personality — must be part of the structure of the end itself. The recognition of personality must, therefore, be part of the ordering principle of the end. We are seeking now a principle of ordering of rational actions and ends that expresses this recognition. Such a principle will be a very general one, since it must express this reciprocity in all conceivable forms of transactions. For this same reason such a principle will not constitute a complete ordering of any particular end or action. A concrete end will be scored by much more detailed and particularized principles. All that is required is that such a detailed, particular principle conform to the general form of the general, partial ordering expressive of reciprocity and recognition of personality.

The principle of morality as detailed above is the *general* principle expressive of the *general* recognition of human personality (defined as the characteristic of having rational ends) in any dealing with other persons. To summarize, the principle of morality accomplishes this recognition by requiring that the most general principle of transactions place all persons in a position of parity. In this way the equality of all persons at the most general level is the starting point for any more particular principle. Why does this equality or impartiality of the principle of morality express recognition of personality? My thesis is: all persons are alike in respect to the characteristic that they conceive of themselves as entities having ends and rational ends; and any essential preference between persons entails a violation of reciprocity in the direction of using the other person as an instrument.

Consider the case where the principle of morality is not met because the actor assumes in his rational principle that his (the actor's) interests or ends are to be given preference for the reason that they are *his* interests. Let us call this the egoist principle. Clearly such a principle entails the assumption that all other persons stand in the relation of instruments to the actor's ends, since in the particular end the other person is not realizing his (the other person's) ends, while the actor realizes his own end. Consider, then, a more plausible general principle for transactions: that the actor may prefer his own ends or the ends of some other person not because of the identity of the person whose ends are preferred, but because of the nature of the end — that is, whoever's end it is, that end is entitled to preference because it is an end of some particular sort. But a principle permitting a preference of this sort also violates reciprocity since it allows the person whose ends are disfavored by the principle to be used as an instrument (in the above sense) for the favored ends.

Finally, as a third alternative to the principle of morality, consider the principle by which a person's ends could be preferred if by so doing the ends of a larger number of persons or a larger number of ends would be attained. This (let us call it utilitarian) principle also violates reciprocity, since it allows the disfavored person to be used as the instrument for the attainment of the "greater good" — as measured in terms of the number of persons benefited or the number of ends attained.

There may be other principles besides these for transactions, but if these are the chief alternatives — as I believe they are — then the principle of morality is the only principle that completely expresses reciprocity, and it does so by requiring that the interest of no party to a transaction may be preferred except by reference to a principle which each party could recognize as according equal weight to his interests in the long run.

Now the principle of morality is sufficiently general and abstract that it allows for the derivation of more particular principles in terms of which in a particular case the ends of all persons will not appear to be given equal weight. Some of these derivative principles will be considered below. To anticipate that discussion, consider the case of a father who takes his son fishing one Sunday, and thus misses the opportunity to take some one else's boy on such an expedition. It may appear that such a transaction is not in accordance with the principle of morality, since it prefers a designated person. But if the more particular principle of that transaction refers to the relation of any person with his own child, and if — as I believe may be the case — such a more particular principle regarding the relations of parent to child can be shown to be consistent with the principle of morality, then what appears to be a breach of reciprocity is in reality not. Or take the even clearer case of a person who restores a stolen umbrella to its rightful owner during a thundershower. The actor in that case appears to be treating the owner differently from the way he is treating other persons in need of the umbrella — should he not at least hold a lottery? But if we see his action as scored by a more particular principle about returning unjustly acquired property, the claims of the others that they are being unequally treated may be defeated. For the more particular principle again may be derivable from or compatible with the general principle of morality. Or finally consider the case by which a person discharges his obligations out of fidelity to an office or an undertaking. If as a judge he finds for one party as against another, he acts in accordance with morality, for morality requires fidelity to one's office, and the facts of the dispute require a particular decision in fidelity to that office.

Personality and respect. Two terms I have introduced in the foregoing argument must be defined formally: personality and respect. Personality is the aspect of a human person which is made up of his capacity to entertain rational principles, actions, and ends, of his actual disposition to do so, and of the particular dispositions to entertain particular principles, actions, and ends. In short, a man's personality is a function of his rational ends and principles — both potential and actual. Respect is the disposition to entertain rational principles in accordance with the principle of morality — that is, rational principles which treat other persons implicated in them as ends rather than means. These two terms, and particularly the term respect, are drawn from Kantian moral philosophy, and the fact that they fit so well into this analysis shows how close to Kant these arguments are.

Why Should We Be Moral?

The question why should we be moral is used to raise an issue which was avoided in the preceding discussion of the principle of morality. In that discussion no more was done than: (1) to introduce morality as a general rational principle applicable to any end and action involving other persons; and (2) to show how, via the concepts of reciprocity, personality, and respect, the principle of morality is a concept of peculiar significance for actions and ends involving others. But the usual conception of morality accords to it the status of a categorical principle. It is not just one principle among many, nor just a peculiarly significant principle. How does the analysis I have been developing allow us to show that morality is not only a possible and even a plausible and appealing general principle for transactions, but the mandatory general principle with which any more particular principles and ends must be consistent?

It would seem that the tack I have been taking will make it particularly hard to accord such a status to morality. The focus of this essay has been on particular acts and ends (although I have shown that particular ends are scored by principles, some of which can apply to whole families of other ends). Thus by showing that moral ends — that is, actions and ends scored by and consistent with the principle of morality — are ends persons have on particular occasions, the particularity of morality, its concreteness, is brought to light. That is a gain. The cost is that there seems to be nothing to require that a person always act morally, or at least that his ends always be consistent with the principle of morality. I have shown how morality can be an end in itself and on a particular occasion; but why exclude from the repertoire of human ends particular acts scored by inconsistent principles like the egoist principle, the utilitarian principle, or the perverse principle? These questions are hard to answer. They are hard questions not only because of this essay's focus on particular concrete ends, but also because of the evident fact that with rare exceptions even the most moral of men sometimes act on principles inconsistent with morality. So if I come up with an argument for the priority of the principle of morality, I will be putting forth a norm that departs from the almost universal, observed behavior of men. On the other hand, the belief that if there is a principle of morality it does have priority is almost as universal as the behavior that violates this conviction. In spite of these difficulties, I shall attempt to account for the priority of morality in terms of the focus and concepts of this essay.

The man who is not moral. What if a man chose never to score his ends by the principle of morality? He would never choose ends exhibiting reciprocity with others. But so what? There is no categorical answer to this question. One can only point to the system of particular ends that are controlled by morality and reciprocity, and ask, "Do you or do you not want to be a man who excludes from his repertoire of ends all of that?" The challenge is a serious one, for as I have and will argue, we *are* our ends, and so in asking that question, one asks, "What kind of man do you choose to be?"

What, then, are the ends from which such a man would be excluded? In general, they are all actions and ends in which a person treats another as an entity, the realization of whose ends is in principle of equal importance to the realization of his own ends. Such a man would be excluded from all ends recognizing the personality of others, from all ends exhibiting respect for another person. In particular, he would not perform acts of justice, of generosity, of trust, of faithfulness, of love, or of friendship. This is a strong assertion. I shall support it in respect to justice in the next section, and in respect to love, trust, and friendship in the next chapter. My thesis is that all of these, justice, generosity, trust, faithfulness, love, and friendship, are concepts that relate to particular rational ends, and that the principles of each of them are concrete derivatives — with the addition of various additional premises — from the most general principle of morality. To put this point differently, all of these have in common the feature that they depend on respect for the personality of the other person involved. Moreover, to pursue these ends is to stand in a certain relation to the other persons implicated in them — relations of love, trust, and so on. And finally, to stand in such relations is a necessary condition of experiencing certain emotions, for example, guilt, resentment, love, trust. These matters are all gone into in detail in the next chapter. For present purposes it is important only to assert that feeling love, friendship, or guilt depends on standing in relations of love, friendship, or justice to others, and it is a necessary condition for such relations that one be disposed to entertain ends exhibiting respect for other persons. He who cannot respect others (in the technical sense I use here) cannot love, trust, feel guilt or resentment.

My answer, therefore, to the question, "Why should a man *ever* be moral?" is that a moral person, by virtue of having certain ends, stands in certain relationships to others and feels certain emotions. He is a certain kind of man. And the consequences of never being moral are that one is another, quite different sort of person. Then the question is, does one want to be excluded from these ends, relations, and emotions. This is all I shall say now about why men act on the principle of morality.

Must we always be moral? So it seems there may be good reason to accept moral ends not only as possible ends but as ends which a man would on some occasions choose to attain. But this is not enough. The concept of morality that we usually have is categorical — one must *always* act consistently with it. It is not like a game that is such fun that most men would choose to play it from time to time.

The chief reason that morality as a rational principle makes a claim to absolute priority over other principles derives from the content of the principle itself. Unlike some other rational principles applicable to some other rational ends, it is universal in its very statement. It states that other persons are to be recognized in a certain way, so that every action involving dealings with others is either in accordance with the principle or in violation of it. Indeed, it is universal in the sense that even if an end does not involve others at all, the very failure to involve others may either be in accordance with or in violation of the principle of morality. A person who sits at home and does a mathematical problem may be entitled to ignore others in this way or not, depending on the circumstances; and that is a question to be resolved by reference to the principle of morality and some one or more of its derivative principles — that is, sometimes it is my moral right, as it is the moral right of everyone, to ignore others, and sometimes it is not. Thus the principle itself applies in some way universally, if only by way of permission to ignore others.

Granted the principle is universal, why must a man universally comply with it? Might not a man at one time act in a way that implies acceptance of morality and another time not act in that way? Of course, a man is physically able to do this, and all men do. What does this mean? It means that at the time he acts morally he acknowledges the principle of morality, and he acknowledges its universality. For it is of the essence of the principle that if its universality is not acknowledged, the principle itself is not acknowledged. Consider the case of a person who restores unjustly acquired property. For this to be an act of restitution — an act in accordance with the principle of morality and, more specifically, justice — it is not sufficient for the actor just to transfer physically the property. He must also acknowledge some principle about restitution. What can that principle be? Can it be that one restores unjustly acquired property: (a) if one no longer needs it, (b) if one feels like it, (c) once in a while, (d) if it was acquired during a full moon? Obviously, none of these will do, and the reason they will not is because they lack the appropriate universality; *not* because they admit of exceptions. So also a person who shows respect to another not only bows, or smiles, or tips his hat, but he acknowledges something about that other person and his own relations to him. What is it that he acknowledges? That he will tip his hat when the spirit moves him, that if he has pleasant thoughts about the other person when he encounters him, he will express them? None of these will do, again, because the very concept of showing respect is a universal one. And in general, the actions and ends deriving from morality require the acknowledgment at least of some principles whose very statement is universal. One simply does not recognize the personality of another unless on the occasion where it is recognized it is recognized as being universally owed respect. For a man to love another person he must at least once recognize that other person as a person deserving reciprocity — he must recognize that person's humanity. But that recognition is a recognition that the other person is owed reciprocity, owed recognition as a person generally, universally.

If so much is accepted, there is still left unanswered the following question: what of the person who on one occasion acts morally — fully, truly, sincerely respects another, recognizes his personality — and does so with a full acknowledgment of the universality of those concepts, but on another occasion acts in a way inconsistent with these principles and acknowledgments? It must be clear that such inconsistency not only is possible but is exemplified to some extent in almost everybody's behavior. Does this then mean that common understanding is mistaken in according to morality a universal and categorical status? Not at all. What follows only is that persons are not perfectly — perhaps not even approximately — consistent in their principles. To recognize morality is to acknowledge its universality, but such an acknowledgment does not compel one to act accordingly thereafter. First, a person can always change his mind, and conclude that he prefers or accepts a different universal principle from the one he accepted before. Second, one can accept a principle and simply fail to act on it — this is the problem of *akrasia*, weakness of will. Both these reasons for violating the principle of morality once one has acknowledged it are related to familiar and difficult philosophical problems. For the purposes of this argument it is not necessary to solve them here.

Take the case of the person who accepts the principle of morality and then changes his mind, choosing instead the perverse principle. The point still holds that we are what our ends are — we are just, loving, trusting persons if our ends are scored by those principles. So the man who changes his principle is a man who himself has radically changed, become a new kind of person. Whereas he once was capable of entering into relations of love and trust, capable of feeling love, guilt, and resentment, he is no longer. A somewhat more complicated version of this is the case where a person does not just make a great change, does not just suffer a conversion, but instead shifts back and forth without coming to rest. If such vacillations are extreme enough, one does not know what to say about him — what his ends are, what his values are, whether he is a person capable of friendship; indeed, one does not know who he is at all.

The second reason, weakness of will, can be treated analogously. Our conception of ourselves and others as trusting and trustworthy or loving (or what have you) persons allows for certain lapses and shortcomings, but after a point such lapses make it unclear whether a person is moral but extraordinarily weak-willed, or whether in fact he really does not subscribe to morality at all. In either case he can no longer enter into reciprocal relations of love, trust, or friendship.

Finally, I should like to anticipate very briefly what shall be discussed at length in Chapter Six: consistency as an end or general principle in itself. My thesis is that one significant human disposition is to seek consistency as an end in itself. And this disposition to order our particular ends into consistent wholes — a kind of highest order rational principle and end — would entail a consistent working out of the various principles one adopted for his significant ends. This would provide an additional ground for acting in a way that recognized over time the priority and categorical character of the principle of morality. To fail to do so would be to introduce significant inconsistency over time in the general ensemble of ends one pursued and principles one accepted.

And so to the question why should we be moral, I would answer that no obligation to be moral can be adduced. One either is or is not moral, with all the ensuing consequences for the individual and his relations. But if one is moral, then categorical obligations relevant to all one's ends arise. Obligation and its categorical quality arise out of the concept of morality; they do not precede it. If one asks "why should I be moral," the answer is "you are under no obligation to be moral, but if you are moral, these and these are your obligations."

Justice and the Obligations of Fairness. The Rawlsian System

A whole family of principles derives from the most general principle of morality: the principles of justice, which refer to the structure of institutions and practices, and the principles of fairness, which relate to the obligations of individuals involved in more or less formal institutions and in practices such as promising. This family of principles is important because it illustrates a part of the process of particularization of the general principle of morality. Without such particularization that most general principle can never apply to particular ends and actions. These do not represent the complete system of principles derivable from morality. There are more specific principles regarding natural obligations, such as those arising out of family relationships, and principles about injuries to others apart from institutional contexts. Analysis of the principles of justice and fairness should indicate, however, how the working out of such principles might go.

The principles and arguments I present here are drawn directly and explicitly from the work of John Rawls. I should say that I will not at all times stay with Rawls's precise terminology, in part because that terminology is in process of development and in part because some simplification (and perhaps distortion) is necessary in a brief account of his often very complex argument.

Justice and the original position. Rawls defines justice as that concept that applies to the design of institutions and practices insofar as they assign to persons and classes of persons benefits and burdens, offices, privileges, liabilities, and the like. He puts forward, as specifying this concept, his two principles of justice: "first, each person participating in a practice, or affected by it, has an equal right to the most extensive liberty compatible with a like liberty for all; and second, inequalities are arbitrary unless it is reasonable to expect that they will work out for everyone's advantage, and provided the positions and offices to which they attach, or from which they may be gained, are open to all. These principles express justice as a complex of three ideas: liberty, equality, and reward for services contributing to the common good." *

The first principle requires maximum equal liberty. This means that equal liberty is not sufficient if everyone could have more liberty. The second principle, that departures from equality are permissible if they work out to everyone's advantage, has been specified by Rawls as follows: a departure from equality of distribution (and I shall say in a moment what goods are being distributed) is permissible only if the result of such an inequality is to make the worst-off person better off than he would be in a situation of pure equality. The first principle of equal maximum liberty applies primarily to the rights of citizenship, political rights, civil liberties, and religious liberties, and entails guarantees of the suffrage, due process of law, freedom of speech and thought, and freedom of religion. The second principle applies primarily to what Rawls calls distributive shares, or the distribution of economic and related benefits and burdens in society. It should be noted that Rawls believes that the two principles of justice, applying as they do to the design of institutions, refer in the first instance to the liberties and the social and economic position of classes and categories as they are defined by the institution. Rawls views his two principles of justice as superconstitutional, in the sense that these are the most general criteria against which constitutions are to be judged. If the constitution meets these criteria, then it is a just constitution, and the laws, social arrangements, and particular actions taken in accordance with such a just constitution will also be just, at least prima facie.

The argument for these two principles as the most general principles for judging institutions is based on notions of reciprocity, fairness, and ultimately on the notion of the equal dignity of all persons. In this it shows its derivation from Kantian moral philosophy in particular and the contractarian tradition in general. Rawls comes to the two principles from these general notions by means of what he calls an analytical construction. This is a kind of simulation in which persons with defined characteristics and in a defined situation choose the principles in terms of which the justness of their institutions will be judged; or, put differently, they

* In "Justice as Fairness."

choose the criteria by which claims and complaints against concrete institutions will be judged. The defining characteristics of the persons and of the situation in this heuristic model are not intended to correspond to any realistic situation, but rather each feature expresses some significant aspects of the general notions from which justice derives.

The analytical construction is that of an "original position," a hypothetical state of nature, in which persons choose the principles of their institutions. The defining features of these persons are: (1) they are rational, in the sense that they can recognize their own interests, that their interests can be coherently ordered, and that if need be they can postpone immediate gratification for the sake of their long run interests as they conceive them; (2) they are self-interested in the very broad sense that whatever their interests, tastes, preferences, and values may be — whether they be for sensual gratification, acts of charity, contemplation, or whatever — they wish to maximize those interests; (3) they are capable of understanding and adhering to moral principles, which for these purposes Rawls defines as principles which constrain the pursuit of self-interest.

The situation in which these abstract persons are placed is one in which (1) they know the general facts about human nature and human society, and that on leaving the original position they will take up some role or other in human society; but (2) they know nothing — not their sex, nor generation, nor country, nor intelligence, nor state of health, nor tastes, nor religion, nor values — about themselves as concrete individuals nor about their concrete situation; they do know, however, that they will have tastes, interests, values, and a concrete situation. (3) Behind this veil of ignorance they must choose finally and irrevocably the moral principles in terms of which to judge the concrete institutions in which they will find themselves in real life. These principles are moral in the sense that once having chosen them the abstract persons must abide by them, and they can expect others to abide by them, even when it is not in the best interests of the person abiding by them to do so. (4) Rawls specifies that the principles must be chosen unanimously and without opportunity for coalition. This last seems unnecessary because all participants in this simulation are defined in the same way and have the same knowledge — for instance, they do not even know whether in real life they will or will not be risk averse — and there is therefore no reason for any one of them to choose differently. Nor is there any reason for them to form coalitions, since they cannot tell when such a coalition will be in their own best interests.

Now each of these features of the original position is expressive of some general notion that stands behind this system of moral principles. First, the ignorance of the participants about their own interests and circumstances assures that their choice will have the quality of impartiality and equality. As Rawls puts it, they will choose principles as if their enemies would assign them places. (If you want a fair division of a pie between two persons, let one person divide the pie, and the other choose the first piece.) This also gives a sense to the notion that social arrangements must be such that no one is an instrument for serving the interests of another, unless at least his interests are also thereby served. This expression of the Kantian notion of not using another as a means only is a consequence of the original position, since a participant being rational, self-interested, and ignorant of his particular characteristics and circumstances cannot discover a principle which would allow him to use another as a means alone, and he would also want a principle that would protect him against being so used.

The definition of these persons as self-interested — that is, disposed to pursue their interests and values whatever they might be — is an expression of these notions: that all persons have an equal dignity, no matter what their values and interests; that our interests or ends define us, so that to compromise our interests in some essential way is to compromise our essence as persons; and third, that the principles of justice do not express a complete ordering of values and interests, but only a partial ordering dealing with the resolution of conflicts between different persons whose interests may be in conflict. In regard to this third point, the notion is that some ethical, aesthetic, or other principle may resolve conflicts between and establish a complete ordering among all ends and interests, perhaps even ruling some out altogether. It is not the job of compulsory social institutions to do this, but only to establish some order among persons when their ends conflict. Furthermore this third point expresses the notion that complete orderings for an individual person, if they are to have value, must be freely chosen.

But freedom cannot be so complete *between* persons, at least where the liberty of one conflicts with that of another. Finally, we can see also how the ignorance and self-interestedness of the participants is a way of guaranteeing that the principles they choose will have the character of Kant's principle of right: that all actions must be compatible with a maxim by which a like freedom is accorded to all.

The features of the original position that the principles chosen are chosen by moral persons as moral principles, and once and for all, express a number of important aspects of justice. First, that justice is a moral principle — that it will sometimes operate as a constraint on the pursuit of self-interest, or that it is an end in itself, and not just a way of getting to other ends. Second, that the principle is chosen once and for all expresses the notion that justice, being a moral principle, is universal and categorical, and cannot be avoided just because it may become inconvenient.

To return to the two principles of justice, it is Rawls's thesis that persons in the original position would choose, as the criteria for institutions and practices, the two principles of justice, because these are the principles which would offer to each the best protection of all his interests, whatever they may turn out to be. And if the analytical construction does indeed yield the two principles, Rawls, in the contractarian tradition, has found a way to give a determinate sense to notions such as equal dignity, the essential liberty of man, and the like.

Rawls's principle of right; its relation to Kant. Rawls uses the analytical construction not only to generate principles for judging long-term social arrangements. He uses it as well to develop the principles for *individual* obligation within such arrangements, and to generate the principles of beneficence and of natural obligation. Thus we might say that the original position and analytical construction is the most general schema for obligations of one person to another. Rawls does not put forward the analytical construction as itself being a principle, but in one sense it clearly is the most general principle of the class of obligations, for it stands behind all such more particular principles and generates them, with the addition of further premises. The analytical construction, viewed as a most general principle, is expressive of certain general notions such as liberty, equality, the right of all men to be treated as ends in themselves, and moral nature as defined by freedom and rationality.

The close affinity of Rawls's system to Kant's general ethical system and to his philosophy of right in particular should be evident. I shall not attempt to make the connection in any detail. I would point out that the specification of the features of the original position gives expression to the main features of Kant's account, which unfortunately in Kant's writing are never presented in such a way that one can be sure how they might be made to apply to particular situations. First, there is Kant's notion that morality is freely chosen, never imposed — the principles of justice and other principles of obligation are freely chosen in the original position. Second, there is Kant's notion that a moral being is essentially a free and rational being. This idea causes trouble for Kant, because he never quite shows how man's substantive ends gather moral significance; unless one finds a place for these substantive ends the system is in danger of circularity or vacuity, as Hegel was the first to point out. Rawls meets this point by according substantive interests to the persons in the original position and by positing that they are self-interested, while at the same time depriving them of knowledge of what their substantive interests are. This leaves them as purposive beings (that is, beings with substantive ends) who are free, rational and capable of understanding, and disposed to follow moral principles. Finally, Rawls's whole complex scheme, beginning with the analytical construction, passing through the two general principles of justice, and ending in the principles governing individual obligations, gives sense to the rather vague Kantian notion that morality or right consists in the compatibility of the maxim of a particular act with a universal law having a particular characteristic: namely, that it is a law which free and rational beings would choose.

Individual obligations. As I have stated, the principles of justice apply to institutions, not to individual obligation. An institution may comport with justice and thus be immune to complaint on that score, but still further principles are needed to account for the moral obligation of particular persons to fulfill the roles and obligations defined for them by the institution. For example, a society's constitution and laws may comport with justice, but what is the basis of the citizen's moral obligation to obey those laws? Now to pose this question is not to deny the moral character of just laws — they still have some moral force, even if no individual obligation followed. Thus a just society may enforce its laws against individuals, and the justice of the laws gives the society a moral title to do so and deprives individuals of any justified complaint against the laws. But society's moral right to coerce compliance with just laws does not entail a moral obligation on the part of individuals to obey these just laws.

The question thus arises what is the individual's moral obligation in institutional settings. Rawls considers three plausible alternatives: (1) that the individual has no moral obligation; (2) that the individual has an obligation to obey the rules and practices of any just institution; (3) that the individual has an obligation to obey the rules of a just institution if he has or intends to accept benefits under that institution — this is the principle of fairness, of doing your part if you have benefited from others doing their part. Rawls tests these three candidates by the analytical construction.

The first fails because the benefits to all under a just society would be significantly less if the citizens were morally free to disobey its laws, so that obedience could only be assured by threats and coercion. The cost of the enforcement mechanism as well as the cost of a lower level of compliance under such a system could be saved, and the saving distributed to all, if compliance could be assured in the main by each citizen's self-enforcement via his sense of moral obligation. Thus it appears that morality — by running counter to self-interest in particular cases — is in the long run interest of all. But being a moral obligation it is binding even where in a particular case it runs counter to self-interest. On this argument Rawls concludes that in respect to individual obligation some moral principle is preferable, and that the analytical construction leads to the acceptance of some moral constraints by individuals. It remains to discover what that moral obligation is.

The second candidate — full obligation to any just institution — is also rejected because it entails an excessive restriction on liberty. This can be seen by comparing it to the third principle, the principle of fair play or of fairness. By this principle there is a moral obligation to a just institution but *only* if the individual accepts or intends to accept benefits from the sacrifices of others who accept the moral constraints of the institution. With this third alternative available, Rawls argues, there would be no reason for rational, self-interested individuals to accept the greater constraint on liberty implicit in the second principle. For the third principle promises the benefits of the second but leaves open an option of refusing the burdens if one is willing to forgo the benefits. There is, however, another way one could come to this same conclusion. Under both the second and the third alternatives the obligation only attaches to just institutions, and it might be argued that it is a corollary of the first principle of justice that the rules of a just institution not apply to unwilling participants who have not accepted benefits under the institution.*

Utility and self-interest. A striking feature of Rawls's account is the contrast he draws between his principles — of right, justice, and fairness — and the utilitarian principle or any principle of self-interest.

The contrast to self-interest has already been adverted to. Perhaps the notion of self-interest should be more clearly specified, especially in the context of my essay, which defines morality as a substantive end. Rawls appears to conceive of self-interest as those substantive ends of a person which do not derive from moral considerations. His argument is that, though we accept right, justice, and fair play in the context of other substantive pursuits, we accept these principles as constraints on the other pursuits. Thus, though the most advantageous principles to adopt in the original position are justice and fairness, it does not at all follow that in particular situations in the actual world, the most advantageous thing to do is to adhere to those principles. On the contrary, if these moral principles were coextensive with simple advantage in concrete cases, they would be superfluous. Nor is there any reason to believe that principles generated in the deliberately contrived model of the original position — contrived to express important values — are the same as would be generated by self-interest in concrete, actual cases. It may be in my interest to have, for instance, an institution of property, on the assumption that I can only have what all would agree to in the original position, but surely the best

---

* It should be added that the principle of fairness applies not only to social institutions like states and organizations, but to promises, and indeed to any just practice from which a person accepts or intends to accept benefits.

for my narrow advantage would be if everyone else were bound to honor just institutions, to respect property, to keep his promises, and so on, and only I was not. In this crucial sense justice, fairness, and morality in general — though they take self-interest into account — are obvious constraints upon self-interest.

A much more difficult and philosophically controversial issue concerns the contrast between the Rawlsian system of principles and various forms of utilitarianism. Rawls is very explicit in pointing out how both the principles of justice and of individual obligation can lead to different results from what utilitarianism prescribes as a rule for institutions or individuals. The principles of justice do not allow departures from equality to be justified simply on the ground that they lead to a higher sum of utility or a higher average utility. Only if the increased utility can be shown to benefit the worst-off person or class can the departure be justified. Thus Rawls concludes that a caste or slavery system can never be justified on the ground that it is more efficient — that is, leads to a higher level of utility. And this accords with the moral premise that no person is to be used as the mere instrument of any other person. If inequalities are justified by reason alone that the sum of utilities or average level of utility is thereby raised, then the less well-off in such a scheme are the uncompensated instruments of the greater well-being of the better-off. Rawls's principle of distributive justice precludes such a situation. In respect to the contrast between his scheme and utilitarianism, a passage from an unpublished paper of Rawls's summarizes his views well:

> The striking feature of the principle of utility is that it doesn't matter, except indirectly, how this sum of satisfactions is distributed among individuals any more than it matters, except indirectly, how one man distributes his satisfactions over time . . .
>
> There is, however, no reason to suppose that the principles which should regulate a group of men are simply the extension of the principle of rational choice for one man. To the contrary: if we assume that the correct principle for any thing must rest in part on the nature of that thing, and if we regard the plurality of distinct persons as an essential feature of associations (as the spuriousness of all organic theories of society con-

firms), we should not expect the principle of social choice to be utilitarian. Yet classical utilitarianism by means of the conception of the impartial sympathetic spectator conflates all persons into one, the many systems of individual desire into one system of ends; for by identifying in turn with the interests in conflict the impartial spectator treats all desires as if they were his own. Since this construction gives no place to the separateness of individuals but dissolves them into one, it must surely lead to an erroneous theory of right. Furthermore, if we believe (as we seem to) that, as a matter of principle, each member of society has an inviolability founded on justice which even the welfare of everyone else cannot override, and that a loss of freedom for some is not made right by a greater sum of satisfactions enjoyed by many, we shall have to look for another account of justice. The principle of utility cannot explain the fact that in a just society the liberties of equal citizenship are taken for granted and the rights secured by justice are not subject to political bargaining or to the calculus of social interests. Hence, on reflection, the notion of maximizing the good is not a plausible conception of right, nor does our reasoning in regard to fundamental liberties appear to conform to it.*

In respect to individual obligation and utility an analogous point holds. Rawls's principle of fairness requires not only that an individual forgo personal advantage in fidelity to his obligations to a just

* There has been considerable debate on this point: Why would the persons in the original position not choose, instead of the principles of justice — and particularly the corollary of making the worst-off best off — simply the principle of the highest average utility? The reason that is given for their doing so is that since they do not know their positions, the highest average utility assures them of the best chance of occupying the most satisfying position, while Rawls's principle may mean that considerable advantages may have to be forgone. Rawls answers this objection by arguing that to gamble in this way would be irrational in the absence of any knowledge about one's actual situation, that such a gamble would be inconsistent with obligations to one's children or a religion one might possibly have, and that the resulting institutions would be subject to peculiar strains and instabilities. I would add the point that it misconceives the analytical construction to argue as if the persons in the original position had the kind of continuity of identity and experience with the actual persons who are governed by the rules there chosen that would be necessary to console them in the real world for the unfortunate outcome of a lottery that never actually took place.

institution or practice, but also that he fulfill his obligations where to break them would lead to a greater sum of utility. This is the classical problem of keeping a promise when utility would be increased if I broke it, or obeying a just law — say a tax law — when cheating would lead to a higher level of utility; and it is not assumed that the beneficiary would always necessarily be the obligation-breaker himself. The usual objection to a utilitarian conception of obligation, "But what if everybody did the same?" is recognized to be inadequate. For in those factual circumstances where one person's acting on the utilitarian rule will not cause others to breach their obligations — as where the violation can be kept secret — the argument that this violation in other circumstances might lead others to do the same, thus undermining the institution, seems beside the point. Rawls, by recurring to the conception of fairness chosen as a public rule in the analytic construction, expresses the independent value that no person should be required to make sacrifices to an institution on a principle that will not also be binding on others, for otherwise such a person is again used as an instrument to produce the benefit for others. Indeed, he's been had. Nor can it be argued that the utilitarian principle of obligation would itself ever be chosen or promulgated as a public principle of obligation. For, as Kant pointed out, as a public principle of obligation utilitarianism would make all institutions and practices unstable.* Thus Rawls's principle of individual obligation meets the utilitarian objection not by showing that utility is indeed served by disregarding utility — this is an argument that rests on a fallacy — but by bringing in a value apart from utility that is served by fidelity to the obligations of institutions and practices.

The relation of Rawls's system to the concepts of this essay. The point of this elaborate presentation of Rawl's system of concepts is that I wish to incorporate them by reference, as it were, into the system of this essay. Specifically, I wish to incorporate the principles of justice and fairness as rational principles available to score rational ends and actions. They are less general than the principle of morality, but are derivable from that principle. They are, however, still too general to score rational ends directly. Fur-

* For Kant and Rawls it is an important criterion of the morality of a principle that it can be publicly promulgated. This is related to the notion of respect for the rationality of moral agents.

ther principles and material premises are needed to control concrete ends and actions. Thus the principles of justice apply to institutions, and institutions, as I shall argue in Part Two, are themselves systems of principles and rules. Justice applies to institutions, a particular just institution has a further system of rules — from very general ones like a constitution, to very particular ones like a particular contract drawn according to the civil law — and finally a concrete end will be scored by all of these together with the principles and material premises arising out of the circumstances of the concrete situation in which an agent pursues a particular end.

The principle of morality, it will be recalled, is the most general principle applicable to those rational actions and ends that impinge on other persons. It is put forward as that principle in terms of which a person can recognize in his dealings with other persons the personality of those other persons. It is that principle in terms of which an actor may assure that the principle of his rational end incorporates or is compatible with the rational ends of those with whom he interacts. Or, to state the point differently, it is that principle in terms of which an actor treats other persons as ends and never as means alone. It should be obvious that my principle of morality is equivalent to Rawls's principle of right, at least as I have understood it and presented it here. Rawls's principle of right is expressed in terms of the analytical construction. The determinants of the analytical construction are each expressive of a number of related values: liberty, equality, impartiality, morality as a constraint on self-interest, and respect for others as ends. And these are precisely the same conceptions which my principle of morality is intended to express. Both are related to Kant's categorical imperative and his "universal principle of justice." Thus I intend my principle of morality to be substantially equivalent to Rawls's principle of right.

There is another equivalence between these two principles which I would call an equivalence of function. Neither Rawls's principle of right nor my principle of morality is meant to apply directly; rather both are intended to generate further more particular principles. In the scheme of this work, the principle of morality is the most general principle for transactions. From it are derived more specific principles, until finally we arrive at the rational principle for a particular end or action.

I have contrasted Rawls's principles to both self-interest and to utility. That contrast has a peculiar significance for this essay. A person acting out of morality, or out of justice, or out of fairness acts on a rational principle which is not completely equivalent to the principle he would adopt if he were seeking to further any other interests, either of his own (self-interest) or of others (maximizing the sum of utility). In the case of such rational actions and ends the actor does of course also pursue certain interests of his own or of other persons. There is no such thing as an act or end which is simply just, simply moral, simply fair; rather, these other interests are pursued subject to the constraints of morality and justice. But to pursue one's own ends or the ends of others morally and justly is not the same as simply pursuing them. The principle of morality and its derivatives constrain or shape the form and ordering of those other substantive pursuits. A person who returns stolen property serves the ends of another, but he does not do so simply to serve the ends of the other nor even to maximize the sum of utilities. Rather he does it in accordance with the principles of morality and fairness. Of course, those principles would not require that act if it was not an act that also served somebody's interests — one need not return the sword of a man who has gone mad. Thus the fact that these principles lead to particular concrete ends and actions, that have an ordering and content different from that entailed by other interests, gives a precise and palpable sense to the proposition that there are ends and actions which may be described as moral ends and actions. And also this conclusion provides an interpretation for Kant's claim that an act is good only if it is done for the sake of morality or duty.

Finally, by incorporating Rawls's principles into this account to serve as rational principles at our intermediate level of generality we can see better how rational principles not only are constitutive of particular ends but also imply an ordering of ends. For each of Rawls's principles applies to an infinity of situations, and does so categorically — that is, whenever a situation of a particular sort is present, then the principles apply and demand that an end of a particular sort be chosen. Justice is a constraint applicable to any institution or practice; fairness is a constraint in any situation of mutual aid, forbearance, and expectation. Thus the orderings implied by these principles can be quite dense and exigent, though they are far from being complete — there is still a lot of room for diverse ends and actions within the framework they establish. I have shown that it is implicit in the principle of morality that if a person accepts the principle of morality for one action this commits him in a special sense to accepting the ordering of all his other ends. The same arguments hold true for the orderings implicit in justice and fairness — if a man would be a just man or a fair man, who does a just or a fair act, he must accept those principles not just as principles for this end or act but as principles for the ordering of all his ends and actions.

In the next chapter I shall take these principles to a further stage of particularity and show how they are implicated in the concepts of love, friendship, and trust; in emotions and relations of love and trust; in particular rational actions and ends expressive of those relations and emotions; and in the ordering of ends and relations implicit in love, friendship, and trust.

Chapter V
Love, Friendship, and Trust

Moral Feelings

In "The Sense of Justice" Rawls discusses how the principles of justice and fair play are related to what he calls moral feelings (such as guilt, shame, remorse, indignation, resentment) and what he calls natural attitudes (such as friendship, trust, love). And he discusses the relation of these moral feelings and natural attitudes to each other. According to this account moral feelings have the following three essential characteristics. First, they imply a disposition to engage in certain conduct, say, to make apology or offer restitution, to resolve to improve, or to pronounce blame, for the reason that such conduct is appropriate to the occasion, given a specified moral principle. Second, moral feelings imply the acceptance of moral principles. Guilt implies the acceptance of the principles of justice and fair play; shame implies a principle of excellence. In this way we can speak of the appropriate conduct being engaged in because of or out of an acceptance of a moral principle. Third, Rawls states that moral feelings "have necessary correlations with certain natural attitudes such as love, affection, and mutual trust and were a liability to have these feelings completely absent there would be an absence also of these natural attitudes."

The first two characteristics of moral feelings — let us call them their dispositional and their principled aspects — show that they bear a direct relation to the concept of rational ends which it has been the purpose of this inquiry to develop. What Rawls discusses from the perspective of this concept of justice and its ramifications I propose we view from the perspective of the concept of rational ends. Now the moral feelings which Rawls associates with justice, primarily guilt but also resentment and indignation, seem to be — in their dispositional and principled aspects — dispositions to accept and pursue certain rational ends, that is, justice and fair play. Rawls insists that the bodily and kinesthetic sensations (sinking feelings, palpitations, chills) are not necessary aspects of moral feelings, so the moral feeling must be the disposition to perform those rational actions which the rational end requires under the particular circumstances. Since the end is a rational end and the action a rational action, the subject of this disposition must understand both the rational principle and how it entails a concrete action in the specified circumstances.

Rawls asserts only that the liability to moral feelings (or at least those associated with the concept of justice and fair play) in the appropriate circumstances is necessary if one is to entertain certain natural attitudes: love, trust, loyalty, friendship. Thus the absence of these moral feelings entails an absence of love, trust, and friendship, and the presence of love, trust, and friendship entails the presence of the moral feelings. One who loves must be susceptible to feelings of guilt, and one who is insensible to guilt is insensible to love as well. What Rawls leaves open is the converse entailment: natural attitudes as entailed by moral feelings. Rawls is not prepared to maintain that one who is sensible to guilt and all the other feelings associated with a sense of justice is for that reason susceptible to love, friendship, and trust. I should like to show how these relationships and the concepts of emotions such as love, trust, and friendship may be elucidated if they are viewed from the perspective of rational actions and rational ends.

In the previous chapter the principle of morality was proposed as the remote rational principle of a whole family of ends, actions, and emotions. Its relation to the principles of justice and fair play, and therefore to moral feelings such as guilt and indignation, has already been developed. But these concepts — justice, fair play, guilt — are all rather juridical and cold concepts. They seem to express limitations on activity rather than occasions for positive expressions, although it would be commonly agreed that justice is a cardinal virtue, and acts of justice sometimes heroic. Love, trust, and friendship are more spontaneous, warm. Rawls calls them natural attitudes and defines them in part as dispositions "to experience and manifest . . . [certain] primary emotions" such as anger, joy, and fear in appropriate circumstances. Yet love, trust, and friendship, for all this, also depend on the principle of morality.

Love

With love more even than trust or friendship there can be no thought of counting on an accepted core of meaning in developing the concept. What I say about love therefore cannot be taken as expressing some core of meaning common to much of what has been thought and said on the subject. I shall here try to develop a conception of love which is consistent with at least one important tradition. According to this conception it is a necessary condition of love that the lover love his beloved for the sake of the beloved and not for the sake of something that the beloved can do for him. Thus if a person values another only because that other is useful to him, or even the source of pleasure by reason of appearance or manner, then the emotion and relation cannot count as love. For if a person's sole reason for valuing another is what that other can do for the person, then the object of the emotion (whatever that emotion is) is viewed as an instrument alone, a means only to the valuing person's end. He uses his object, for it is *only* in terms of the object's usefulness — in the broadest sense — to him that he values the object. What is lacking in this attitude is an appreciation of the other person as a personality, a recognition of the other person as an entity valuable in itself and quite apart from any advantage or pleasure to the valuing agent.

In the conception of love I put forward the lover must see in his object a source of value independent of his own ends and preferences. In short, the lover must love the beloved for the beloved's own sake. Now the principle of morality provides a meaning for the notion of respecting or valuing the personality of others as opposed to valuing some attribute pleasing to us. By virtue of the impartiality of the principle of morality an agent can give and another feel the assurance that the recognition he receives belongs properly to him and not to some attribute or product which the agent may find pleasing or useful. But surely love is not so impartial, and implies a valuing of the beloved not just as a bearer of human personality — which is what justice requires — but as a specific individual. Furthermore, respect and fair play can be demanded, they are entitlements. This is not true of love. From this I think we can see that although love is related to the principle of morality and the notion of respect for personality, the relation is a complex one. We might ask particularly how to account for the free and spontaneous aspect of love.

A solution lies in attributing (as Rawls does) to the principle of morality and the associated notion of respect a necessary but not a sufficient role in the structure of love. A person can be said to feel love or to act lovingly only if he first accepts and respects the personality of the beloved. Love, then, presupposes that the lover accept the beloved as an independent personality with a claim to his respect and to fair treatment from his beloved. Thus lover and beloved confront each other as persons. Love can exist only on the basis of the mutual recognition of personality which respect and morality express. The further element which makes the attitude one of love — the free and spontaneous element — has to do with freely and readily abandoning the entitlements accorded by the notion of respect and personality in favor of the interests of the beloved. This generosity and freedom are essential to love, but it is my point that generosity and freedom depend on the lover acknowledging the principles by which his own moral claims and entitlements, and those of other persons, are securely established. Only if he is secure in the sense of moral possession of these is he in a position to be generous and free, relinquishing what is his own. For one cannot give away what is not his own. But the very principles which accord to him his moral personality, entail the recognition of the moral entitlements and personality of others. Respect and self-respect are thus precisely correlated, and both are logical prerequisites of love.

I cannot and I do not pretend to present even in outline a com-

plete analysis of the concept (or concepts) of love. My primary purpose is to establish the relation between that concept and what
I have called the principle of morality. But if the argument I make
on that point is to be convincing then I must show how it might be
seen as part of a complete and intuitively acceptable concept of
love. So far I have called attention only to the aspect of love which
is the free resignation of claims and entitlements in favor of the
beloved person. But this is too narrow and incomplete a conception.
It is not clear how such a principle distinguishes love from friendship, which involves, in Aristotle's phrase, wishing another good
for his own sake. Further, though the principle I have put forward
gives a determinate sense to the freedom of love it is too abstract
and leaves out of account the spontaneity of love. Finally, this principle seems excessively self-effacing, taking as its model perhaps
parental love for a small infant, or some romantic picture of un-
reciprocated love, where the lover sacrifices himself for a beloved
who may perhaps not even be aware of his existence.

Taking the last point first, I would agree that an important and
perhaps the central conception of love between persons involves
a notion of reciprocity, and that the self-effacing model represents
an aberrant or developmental or at any rate special case. This central conception of reciprocity must be formalized not in terms of a
free renunciation of entitlements to pursue one's own interests in
order to take up the beloved's interests as one's own, but rather
in terms of mutual sharing of interests. The dialectics of this conception seem to me, nevertheless, to show its dependence on the
concept of morality. The two lovers surely make no claims on each
other, yet what they do or give must be given in mutual recognition of the firm base of each other's personality. This interest which
the lovers pursue, having abandoned self-interest, is not simply the
reciprocal pursuit of the other's self-interest in place of one's own.
That would be an absurdity. (One might call it the absurdity of
pervasive altruism.) There is rather a creation of love, a middle
term, which is a new pattern or system of interests which both share
and both value, in part at least just because it is shared. This system of shared interests which the lovers create has as one of its
defining principles that the contribution of each is free and spontaneous. In this way reciprocal love represents a kind of resolution
of the paradoxes of self-interest and altruism. If this is an impor-

tant principle of reciprocal love, one might see why sexual love is both such an apt and such a fragile symbol and expression of mutual love. And incidentally one can at last see why I have tended to include sex in the category of rational ends.

As to the element of spontaneity, there is almost more difficulty. That the love relation should be a joyful one is obviously important and expresses the fact that love is not a logical exercise. But even joy is not an easy concept. I do not imagine I have exhausted it when I have pointed to the elements of readiness and absorption. Nevertheless something recognizable as the intuitive conception of love begins to emerge when we compound with the conception of mutual sharing the notions of a readiness on the part of the lovers to work, play, and do things together, that is, to engage in activities that are informed by the above principles, and to do so with an intensity about the engagement. In short, to the lover the mutual sharing of interest in love is very important, and this is shown by the place it occupies in the economy of his life. These ideas, at least, are wholly compatible with the conception of love as an emotion and a disposition having a rather elaborate rational structure — albeit the sense and grasp of this structure may be implicit and inchoate. And the very principles which give the concept its structure help explain the element of spontaneity, in that they hold that the gift of love must be bestowed freely and, as it were, arbitrarily, without entitlement. There is one conception of love with which this account is necessarily incompatible: that which holds that love in principle is devoid of a rational element.

Friendship

The foregoing should go some of the way in avoiding the objection that the conception of love I put forward fails to allow a distinction between love and friendship. For it seems to me that love and friendship are close in many respects, and that the important differences have to do with the degree of intensity and significance of the relation, and with the appropriate modes of expression. These differences may be acknowledged without denying that both love and friendship have a similar connection with the principle of morality. And that similarity is all that I care to propose concerning friendship.

Trust

Of the three concepts love, friendship, and trust, the easiest to relate to the concept of morality appears to be trust. Moreover, it is a more evidently rational, a more cognitive disposition than love or friendship. Is it not simply the recognition of a disposition in another and reliance upon it? To put that question is to reveal the complexity of the concept of trust. To be sure we have expressions such as "trust him to do that" where "that" may be a vile deed which we know to be in character for that person, or perhaps "that" may be having a fit of sneezing during a grand evening at the opera when he is a person given to sneezing in close proximity to perfumed ladies. But these usages are ironical and the central meaning of trust has to do not with *any* expectation at all pursuant to any disposition whatever.

The concept of trust does involves reliance on a disposition of another person, and it would seem to be an acceptable further specification of that concept to limit it to reliance on the disposition of another to act on the principle of morality, that is, to act justly and fairly when the occasion demands. But I suggest that even this fails to capture the essential structure of the concept of trust, for it suggests that a well-founded prediction that another will act on the principle of morality constitutes trust. What this misses is the reciprocal element in the concept, which requires that the one who trusts as well as the one who is trusted be disposed to act justly and fairly. Consider what justice and fairness require in respect to one who is *not* prepared to act justly or fairly to us. Justice and fairness require that a person forbear to pursue his own interests fully on the assumption that another will also do so and thus a scheme of cooperation will be established. They do not require that one forbear to pursue his interests *as if* the other would do so too, when there is good reason to believe that the other in fact will not do so. Thus fairness does not require that one abide by what appears to be a mutually cooperative scheme when one learns that in fact he is a victim of exploitation. To be sure morality requires a certain posture of respect and forbearance even toward the thoroughly untrustworthy individual, but it is enough to see that this is different from and less than what is required toward a normally trustworthy person.

In this regard trust exhibits the same reciprocity which characterizes the notion of respect and the principle of morality to which trust is related. Thus, if A trusts B, then he must expect of B that B trust him. But even this further requirement leaves the concept of trust at too cognitive a level, and fails to express fully its quality of reciprocity. For the above account would not distinguish between the case (1) where A relies on B's disposition to behave fairly toward A, which involves as we have seen a belief by A that B believes A is similarly disposed, *even if A in fact is not so disposed and is exploiting B,* and the case (2) which is the same as case 1 except that A is not only believed to be trustworthy, but actually is. The issue might be put thus: Can a thoroughly untrustworthy person adopt the attitude of trust or feel trust toward another? I deny that he can, and I would make the concept of trust sufficiently stringent to exclude an exploitative attitude or a mere neutral prediction. This can be done if the relation of trust to rational ends is brought in. To trust another is, in part, to have certain dispositions. These are dispositions to adopt ends scored by the principle of morality, to engage in actions involving others in which both may exhibit their mutual respect and their acceptance of the principle of morality. Thus trust, like love and friendship, is a creative attitude. Trust implies a disposition to engage in activities and adopt ends that are in part defined by the mutual acceptance of respect and morality. Moreover, trust like love and friendship is free, in the sense that ends and activities exhibiting morality are not in every case required by it. One can — as it were — invite another to participate in such an activity or not, without offending morality, and the other in some circumstances at least is free to accept or decline the invitation.

Trust is similar to love and friendship, then, in that it implies a disposition to adopt ends exhibiting respect for others and acceptance of the principle of morality. It is creative, leading to the free adoption of ends. Trust differs from love and friendship in that it is a colder, less spontaneous feeling or attitude. Trust is less intrusive than love or friendship. And trust is more functional.

Persons build relations on trust in part because this is useful in the accomplishment of other ends. But this is a subtle and crucial point. A cooperative endeavor built on trust may well be an effective way of attaining the ends of that endeavor, but it must be appreciated that the desire for those ends alone cannot sustain or account for the relation of trust. As was pointed out in the previous chapter, morality and moral relations are never completely coextensive with self-interest or utility. If a participant in a trust relationship were solely interested in maximizing some set of interests and ends of his own, he would on occasion have sufficient reason to violate the moral relation, which here is the relation of trust. But it is the essence of moral relations and of trust relations that self-interest is not a sufficient reason for breaching them. Thus a person in a cooperative, trust relation pursues certain interests outside of the relation — as do lovers and friends — but he accepts the terms of the relation as a constraint on those pursuits. Now in the account I have presented, these constraints are not simply negative elements. They express positive values, concrete ends, and those values and ends have an independent status.

To be moral is also an end in itself. (As Kant puts it, morality is a good.) That is why we accept the constraints of morality, indeed it is the only reason why we should. And applying this generality to the case of trust we see that trust relations involve the pursuit of other ends, supported by and subject to the constraints of trust. This means that in those relations trust is an end in itself. It is an end which would be empty, purely formal, devoid of substantive content, but once that content is supplied by other ends, trust and its forms becomes an end in itself. So the affirmation of human personality implicit in trust is not only a means to other ends; through those other ends, it is itself an end of independent significance. Thus even if we could achieve our other ends as well or better apart from trust relationships, we would have reason to pursue them in the context of trust. In trust the functional relation may loom larger, and the relation be limited to certain pursuits, but their analysis shows the affinity between trust and love or friendship. Trust can be limited to the particular matter at hand, and does not imply a disposition to seek more and more mutually shared ends. Thus, one can trust persons for whom one has neither love nor liking, although friendship and love imply, at least in the standard cases, trust as well.

Love, Friendship, Trust, and the Ordering of Ends

It will be recalled that Rawls has stated that "the absence of certain moral feelings [for example, guilt, a sense of justice] implies the absence of certain natural attitudes [for example, love, trust, friendship]; or, alternatively, that the presence of certain natural attitudes implies a liability to certain moral feelings." Rawls declines to draw the converse implication that, say, a sense of justice implies a liability to feel love, trust, or friendship. The foregoing account supports Rawls's conclusions. For I have argued that love, friendship, and trust imply morality as a necessary condition. It shows why morality is only a necessary not a sufficient condition for these feelings, why the converse implication does not work. Love, friendship, and trust — in varying degrees — go beyond morality. The principle of morality is formal, it places limitations on what may be done, and in accepting those limitations for their own sake a person exhibits respect for others. Thus, acting on the principle of morality is both necessary and sufficient for respect. But love, friendship, and trust are more positive dispositions. They imply seeking out and creating occasions where ends may be pursued exhibiting acceptance of the principle of morality in various complex ways. In short, trust, friendship, and love, go beyond morality, to exhibit the elements of respect and reciprocity in ever more substantial and pervasive ways. While these three concepts imply morality, morality does not imply them. It is at least not logically incoherent to imagine a person who accepts the principle of morality but neither loves, trusts, nor feels friendship, although such a person would be a very cold and odd person indeed.

The discussion must now return to the concepts of rational ends and rational actions. The principle of morality was introduced as one particularly potent and pervasive rational principle. In the discussion of the concepts of justice and fair play it was shown how these rational concepts mediate the abstract principle of morality and finally determine concrete ends and concrete actions. Thus morality, justice, and fair play all provide examples of rational ends and rational actions whose performance constitute those ends.

Love, friendship, and trust provide further examples of how ends in themselves are structured by rational principles. Each of these implies a disposition to adopt certain ends and pursue certain activities. These — as in the case of justice and fair play — are rational ends and activities, first because of their common dependence on the formal principle of morality, but also because of their specific concretization of that principle in the various forms of reciprocity which structure and exemplify each of these dispositions. This formal, rational element I have sought to bring out in the dialectics of love and trust.

Love, friendship, and trust differ from morality, fair play, and justice in that terms like love primarily designate a disposition to adopt certain ends and to perform actions constitutive of those ends. They do not directly designate those ends and actions, whereas justice, morality, and fair play more nearly do. An act of love, of trust, or of friendship is more of a philosophical construct — though a perfectly valid one — than is an act of justice, a just act or an unfair act. But this should not detract at all from the argument that love and trust ultimately refer to rational ends. In justice or fair play the direct focus on a concrete act is more appropriate because these are more juridical concepts, and an action involving others either accords with or violates them. Love, on the other hand, can rarely be identified and rarely appears in respect to a single discrete action. Where there is love, it tends to spread, to pervade, to assume dominance in the long-term pattern of ends pursued. Nevertheless it is the end and the principle constituting it which is love.

Finally, I should like to make explicit what has been implicit in this chapter: how love, friendship, and trust not only constitute ends in themselves but entail an ordering of ends. These relations depend on the principle of morality — there cannot be such relations without an acknowledgment of that more general principle. And these more concrete entailments, as I argued in Chapter Four, provide a reason for being moral: unless one is moral one cannot pursue those ends, stand in such relationships, or feel such emotions. And to acknowledge morality is already to accept an ordering of one's ends, for morality is a universal and categorical principle.

But as I have argued in this chapter these relationships imply further orderings. Trust, while less universal than morality, has implications beyond one particular end — a person who is in a relation of trust may be constrained in a whole range of actions over a considerable period of time. Love is even more exigent, for to love another is not just to pursue a particular end at a particular time. It is to assign a certain significance to that relation. It means that in the whole pattern of one's ends, those implicated in the love relation will stand very high, perhaps have first priority. One does not love unless he devotes considerable life resources — time, energy, even risk of death as I argue in Part Three — to that relation. And this significance of love can only be exhibited by a willingness to order one's total repertoire of ends in certain ways, and to assign certain priorities. It is striking that such an ordering — the ordering of love — is a disposition which is exhibited not only over time as one views the choices and patterns of man's life, but in a particular case when he chooses to pursue this rather than that end. Friendship is a similar but less exigent case.

Chapter VI
The System of Ends:
The Concept of the Life Plan

In this chapter I shall first discuss several categories of ends other than moral ends, that seem to me to be of a similar order of significance. I do not intend to consider the complete repertoire of available human ends, but I do hope thereby to give a fuller sense of the diversity and number of ends in that repertoire. I shall then go on to consider the problem of establishing an ordering among ends.

At various points in the preceding discussion I have adverted to or assumed the existence of other ends (indeed other rational ends) than those necessarily related to the principle of morality. I am less prepared to generalize about these other ends. They are a vast, heterogeneous array, and no very perspicuous system of relationships can be demonstrated. Nevertheless certain very rough categories may be suggested, and a modicum of structure discerned in at least some of these categories. These very rough categories of ends I shall call knowledge, art, instinct, and survival. It is apparent at once that this is indeed a mixed bag.

Knowledge and art, although difficult in detail, clearly enough refer to the ends of knowing and of creating or appreciating beautiful objects. Instinct is a much more dubious category, including appetites and drives such as hunger, thirst, sex, protection of the young. Survival is an even more dubious category, and a hard one to distinguish from the instinctual. In it I include all the ends we pursue not from an immediate instinct, but from a more or less rational understanding that their pursuit is necessary to our survival and growth — thus I would include eating when one is not hungry, medical care, training in skills.

Knowledge as a Rational End

The philosophical tradition recognizing knowledge as an end is more venerable than the recognition of the ends associated with morality. For all that, it is a less popular subject of analysis as an end than it once was. Indeed, the advance of certain psychological theories has made the very notion of knowledge as an end seem problematic. For instance, there is the psychoanalytic account of scientific curiosity as possibly being rooted in infantile sexual curiosity, or as perhaps being a hypostasis of the need — located in the activity of the ego — of a person to assert himself by attaining a sense of mastery over his environment. On this view scientific curiosity about processes, which realistically there is no chance of controlling, yields a sense of control which comes from an understanding of those processes. Thus there is something magical about the very springs of scientific activity.

Whatever the validity of such psychological theories of how persons come to have certain ends — here the attainment of understanding — it seems to me that it would be a mistake to deny on that basis the autonomous character of this end. It is not as if this theory allowed us to say with confidence that the mature scientist now passionately engaged in testing the validity of the general theory of relativity could be satisfied in some very different way designed also to give "a sense of mastery over the environment." Whatever the original source of the passion, it seems very implausible to treat this end as anything other than an independent end, which has split off from what may have been its origins. It seems far sounder to assume that the knowledge he seeks he may at least sometimes seek simply for its own sake.

In contrast to morality (with its associated concepts) knowledge may appear very much like a game. As a rational end it has the logical structure necessary for coherence, but it appears to lack the urgency and weight of morality, which is the general principle of all our relations with other persons. For rational structure without significant content is almost a definition of at least some games. But knowledge is not a game, and in grasping why it is not, a point about rational ends should come clearer. The form of the various moral ends, their rational coherence, places them in the category of rational ends, but it is the substance this form organizes that gives them their significance. So in the case of knowledge we must seek to identify the corresponding substance. Knowledge has as its substance all reality as it may be conceived to be external to the agent. In moral ends the point of the encounter is a certain form of interaction between agent and object — as in acts of justice or love. The end of knowledge, by contrast, requires the agent to abstract from his own characteristics as much as possible, so he sees his object just as it is. The agent may be forced to become aware of his relation to the object known, but the end in view requires this awareness only so as to allow a more complete abstraction of self from the activity. (Of course, knowledge can make the self an object of knowledge, in which case the self must seek to abstract itself as agent from the end which is the self as object.)

Thus knowledge is a more inclusive end than morality, since the range of objects which can plausibly be involved in moral ends is restricted. It is restricted to other moral agents. Indeed knowledge appears as a more basic end than morality in the sense that if the issue arises, morality cannot shrink from knowledge. It is a part of love, friendship, or trust to want to know its object. It is, to be sure, a commonplace that love is blind. But this is a mistake, at least as regards the concept of love — and the associated concepts — developed in the previous chapter. According to these, the object is valued for its own sake, and this entails a conception of the object as it is, that is, the argument entails knowledge of the object. To see in a beloved object only what one wants to see is related to valuing it only in the light of one's own interests and not for its own sake. On the other hand, knowledge does not require love. Indeed, it is part of the notion of knowledge that the conception of the object be abstracted as much as possible from the knower.

Moreover, the end of knowledge and the capacity and disposition to pursue that end are as significant to a person's conception of himself as are the ends associated with morality. Indeed, here it might be said that knowledge is more basic. In knowing ourselves to have an interest and a capacity to attain knowledge we take a position in respect to all possible objects including ourselves. We distinguish between things as they are and what we want of them, and are prepared to conceive of and pursue our ends under the constraint that objects enter into our ends as they are. The stance is so basic, indeed, that it is hard to say more about it than that it is a sense of reality, of reality as ineluctable and not subject to our wants, and that it is a sense of ourselves as a part of reality. Indeed it is only this stance that makes possible the concept of reality. Whether or not this point can be formulated further, the foregoing should suffice to indicate why the rational end I call knowledge, which is the attainment of a fuller appreciation of external reality as such, is a significant end.

Art

Aesthetic activity and appreciation seem to fit the conception of a rational end more readily and intuitively than any of the examples discussed.* That this is an activity pursued for its own sake and constituted by its structure is relatively obvious, and correspondingly the assertion that *really* some independently identifiable end is being pursued in this activity to which art stands in the relation of means to end seems most arbitrary or doctrinaire. Indeed there is the danger that the case for art as an end in itself is so strong that it seems inapplicable in other instances. Art is a paradigm of the rational end. But the conception of rational end applies as well, I have tried to show, in cases of knowledge and morality. That there is this common structural element in knowledge and art is a point that is often made in various ways, particularly where the art is relatively formal and the knowledge sought relatively abstract and theoretical.

I find it difficult in the case of art to say anything which is both general and perspicuous about the kinds of formal structure specific to art or about the kinds of material which these structures organize. Knowledge is a set of ends directed to reality as such, and morality a set of ends directed to other moral persons as such.

* See also the discussion of aesthetic ends in Chapter Three.

What is the corresponding general relation of artistic ends to the objects of the activities in which these ends are pursued? My inability to answer this question generally does not suggest to me that there are no distinctions to be made between art and other ends. Thus, though art may, perhaps, be related to play, as a class of rational ends art is more significant and substantial. What is this significance and substance? I would suggest very tentatively that art unlike play imposes its particular category of coherence on significant substance, even the substance of other rational ends. Art may take as its substance love, friendship, and the violation of these, or our perception and knowledge of external reality. But it is also true that artistic forms are significant as such, as artistic forms.

Instinctual Ends

It is the most familiar of commonplaces that men have certain instinctual drives — hunger, sex, aggression, maternal love — and that one of the basic categories of ends is the satisfaction of these instinctual drives. How are these to be located in the general conception of ends I have been developing? Certainly my emphasis on the rational should not be taken as denying their existence or peculiarly insistent quality. But there are very great problems about the concept of drive, desire, instinct, satisfaction, and the like. And neither philosophers nor psychologists have reached anything like agreement about them. I have so far avoided these controversies by considering ends that men do in fact pursue, the structure and relations of those ends, and the systematic implications of having or not having one or another class of ends. Without denying the seriousness of the ancient controversies, I propose to continue in that vein.

Eating, sex, and maternal love all refer to acts and ends pursued on particular, concrete occasions. Whatever else can be said about these instinctual drives, it seems correct to assert that these drives can be viewed as a disposition to pursue the relevant ends in the appropriate circumstances and to feel the relevant emotions and feelings. Moreover, as I have argued in Chapter Three, it is hard to conceive of many significant instances of ends and actions involving these instincts that do not also involve significant rational elements. Finally, to the extent that the pursuit of these ends impinges on others — and it always will in a remote or direct way — they must be consistent with the principle of morality and its derivatives. What, then, can be said of these ends as ends? Are they ends at all?

I suggest that there is no need to be intimidated by this class of ends — if it is a class — just because it has received considerable attention from scientists and because some theorists would somehow reduce all human behavior to the satisfaction of the desires associated with it. There is, to be sure, the notion by which desire is associated with an end, on the analogy of some sort of physical force impelling behavior. But if, as I have proposed, desires are viewed as dispositions to pursue certain ends in appropriate circumstances, the contrast to the various rational ends I have been discussing disappears. For morality, love, trust, fairness, art, knowledge, and play are ends which are related to dispositions to pursue those ends as much as are sex or eating. Moreover dispositions to pursue ends such as love or fairness or knowledge are significant, for what dispositions one has and lacks are crucial to what sort of being one is, what sort of person, and whether a person at all. I can think of no reason to conceive of the instinctual dispositions otherwise. A person who is or is not disposed to pursue sexual ends, to display parental affection, indeed to eat or drink, is or is not a particular kind of being. It is our ends — including our instinctual ends — that define us.

What then of the desire, the need? To the agent, who is defined by the ends he pursues, palpable desire, I think, appears as several things. It recalls to him an end that he has, but it recalls it to him as an end — that is, it does not simply recall to him the *fact* that he entertains in the repertoire of his ends such and such an end. It is also a necessary prelude to the fulfillment of that end, for without desire the activity is not pursued as an end in itself but as a means to some other end. Finally, desire is part of the end itself. The end is constituted by an orchestration of gestures, sensations, and perceptions extended in time, and palpable desire is an early constituent of the totality. To desire an end is in part what is meant by having that end. Once again there seems to be no reason here to conceive of instinctual desires and the ends associated with them differently from the desire to play, to hear music or write poetry, to show kindness or love, or to restore un-justly acquired property.

Is no distinction to be made, then, between the rational ends I have been discussing and these instinctual ends? Since my focus in this essay is on ends and values as they appear to a person having those ends and values, the familiar distinctions in terms of greater or lesser similarities to lower animals, in terms of the ontogeny of these dispositions, in terms of the neurophysiology of these dispositions (are the drive centers cortical or peripheral), are quite ir-relevant. The distinctions that are important from my point of view have to do with the prominence of the rational element, and their relative givenness.

Instinctual ends involve less of a rational element than do ends like morality, art, play, or knowledge. Although instinctual ends are complex, ordered wholes, as I have argued, yet the ordering is one the understanding of which has less effect on our under-standing of the end as an end, on what it is about the value that makes it valuable. A statement of the ordering, of the principle, is less a statement of a principle we subscribe to than it is a de-scription of what we do. As a statement or a principle it is external to us — although the ordering and the end itself are our own. I have not been absolute about this because many of the instinctual ends — sex, food, maternal love — have a considerable rational element in them, for instance, as regards the choice and perception of their objects. More important, these instinctual ends are them-selves constrained and incorporated in various ways by the rational ends I have been discussing — for example, sex or maternal love in "rational" love.

This explains what I mean by the relative givenness of these ends and dispositions. They are given because in our experience of our selves as purposive beings, the instinctual ends appear more nearly imposed on us by our nature than do our rational ends, which we feel more closely to have chosen. This may provide an interpretation of Kant's argument that these ends represent the order of heteronomy, while rational ends are autonomous values. But I am dubious about considering this aspect of our nature as less our own than rational dispositions.

What is most interesting about instinctual ends from the point of view of this essay is the way in which they are incorporated into and ordered as elements of rational ends by the rational principles of those ends. Thus maternal love can become the occasion for the relation of rational love. Sex can become a means of expressing love or friendship, it can be the kind of shared, mutually created end which is the substance of love. An instinctual end like sex is given, and much of what will count as sex is given, but the rational end of love defines the occasions, objects, and mode of pursuit of that end. In the same general way art and play as rational ends may incorporate instinctual ends — eating, the pleasure of combat, smell and touch, and again sex.

Survival

There comes now a residual category of ends which I refer to as the general category of survival. The concept is unsatisfactory, but some provision in the conceptual system of ends is necessary for the phenomena I shall identify. There are a vast number of activities — for example, eating again but under different circumstances, flight from danger, provisions of shelter, relief from pains and ills of various sorts. These cannot be said to be pursued for their own sake as can the rational and instinctive activities already discussed. Where activities are pursued with a more or less conscious purpose in mind — wood is collected and a fire made in order to provide warmth — they are again quite unproblematical. But what of activities — like flight from danger or eating without pleasure — where the end, survival or security, need not be consciously adverted to, and may indeed never present itself at all to the agent? Of these activities — unlike instinctive ends — it would be true that the agent would prefer that the occasion for them would never arise. Perhaps the correspondence between an instinctive end like sexual activity and a survival activity like flight is this. In both cases there is an end which is postulated by the agent. In the former that end is the activity itself; in the latter the end is not constituted by any activity, but rather is a state which calls forth activity only to bring it about or to maintain it. The end in both cases, however, is quite instinctive in the sense that it is not constituted by a rational principle. It is only because in the case of behavior like flight the end is instinctive while the activities that bring it about may be more or less deliberate and "plotted" that these activities appear to be ends in themselves. I suspect that it is by using these survival cases as a paradigm for the relation of act to end that one might come to believe that all activity is instrumental to some separately identifiable end state like "well-being" or survival.

I believe that survival may also appear as an element, as raw material, to be ordered in other, more complex, rational ends. First, survival is importantly constrained by morality — we seek survival for ourselves and others subject to the constraints of morality. Also we desire the survival of those to whom we stand in relations of love, and we may decrease the chances of our own survival for the sake of those we love. More striking, the whole attitude we take toward survival — for what we shall live, for what we shall die or take the risk of dying, and when — is determined by the overall coherence and ordering we impose on our various ends. This subject, how our rational life plan effects our decisions as to survival, as to life and death, is the subject of Part Three of this essay.

Relations and Priorities among Ends

In economic theory and modern decision theory the problem of ordering is solved by the technique of maximization. A person's preferences and priorities among his ends are ascertained and an ordinal or cardinal ranking is thereby established. This ranking is obtained either by observation of behavior or by direct inquiry, and weights are assigned by such methods as determining preferences among lottery tickets carrying various ends as more or less probable outcomes. Then, assuming only transitivity and a few other weak rationality criteria, a complete set of priorities is thought to ensue for any circumstance, on the assumption that the actor desires to maximize the sum of his utilities so weighted.

I should emphasize that I have absolutely no quarrel with this technique so far as it goes, but I also believe that it does not go far enough. I am not concerned with the notion that rational men may be thought to assign weights to their preferences and then seek to maximize their sum.* What I wish to do is to discover why

---

* Robert Nozick points out that "it may always be possible to produce a gimmicky real-valued function such that its maximization mirrors one's moral views [whatever they may be] in a particular area." "Moral Complications and Moral Structures," *Natural Law Forum,* 12 (1968): 3.

a person, having certain ends and values, will assign them certain weights, and why and how those assignments of weight will differ in particular circumstances. Now on these points utility theory and decision theory have nothing to say, for it takes values, ends, tastes, or preferences, and the weights assigned to them, as given, and works out the consequences of those given items. In this essay I have been seeking to unpack the internal structure of those ends and values and thus to show if possible why a particular value requires that it be assigned a certain weight. Thus, a person bound by a serious obligation of fidelity may choose ("prefer") to discharge that obligation in the face of considerable hardships and temptation. Utility theory would record only the weight he attaches to that end relative to the benefits he must forgo and the costs he must incur. (Utility theory may conclude that he assigns it absolute weight.) This is sound and valid, but it does not ask why he assigns that weight to obligation. The account of the value of fairness and of its relation to other ends should elucidate that further question.

Orderings and priorities among ends have been generated by the discussion in the previous chapters in two ways. First, certain ends entail priorities over other inconsistent ends. Thus justice entails a priority over ends related to or ordered by a principle of utility maximizing, and fairness and friendship entail priorities of various often complex sorts over other ends related to what might be called self-interest. In short, justice or love means that a person will order his priorities in certain ways. A person who has no time or resources to devote to his beloved simply does not love; a man who always prefers his own advantage to that of others is not a just or fair man.

Second, certain ends incorporate other ends within themselves, and thus express themselves as orderings of these other ends. Love again is an excellent example, for love not only pushes competing ends into a position of lesser priority, but also takes up certain ends and lends to them a special significance and priority. Art and knowledge also take up other ends and interests as their subject matter. Anything at all may be the subject of a dispassionate inquiry or a literary account or artistic rendering. But the relationships that may exist are more complex than this too. One may, for instance, seek a better understanding of another out of love for that other person, and not in order to render some loving service, but just because knowledge of the beloved is desirable to the lover as a lover. So also with art the relationship between art and some other end involved in it may be complex. It would seem particularly in regard to instinctual ends, sensuous pleasures, there may be an imposition of rational structure which is art, and in those cases sensuous pleasure is more than simply the subject of art, as it may be simply the dispassionate subject of knowledge.

In general, then, the significant rational ends and systems of ends have very considerable implications for the way a person orders his priorities among his ends. To have those ends just is to have a certain order and priority among one's ends; it just is to have a certain kind of life plan. But there is a different point that emerges from this as well. It will be recalled from the discussion in Chapter Three that one of the important aspects of rational ends was their very rationality, the very order and coherence they imposed on the disparate materials that they ordered. I suggested there that among the ends or dispositions men might have is this very disposition to order, rationality, coherence. In this way it is a value of justice, of love, and very definitely of art that it does order the chaotic and disparate materials of our existence into coherent wholes.

The question I would ask finally is whether the order implicit in the ends I have discussed is a complete order, whether it completely determines the structure of our lives. I think that these ends do not. Morality and the moral relations certainly pervade all our lives and particular ends, but one can be thoroughly moral and yet order one's life in a vast number of different ways; moreover, one can love without thereby also determining all of one's existence. And art is limited to particular artistic acts and appreciation. There is still a great deal that is left indeterminate, unstructured. I would like to suggest now a notion that takes up all our ends — morality, love, knowledge, and the rest — and seeks or tends to organize them all into a single, coherent whole, into a rational life plan.

The Concept of the Life Plan

Morality, love, and friendship imply an ordering of ends. But it is only a partial ordering, and the question arises whether beyond these incomplete structures any more complete ordering of ends exists. There is reason to believe that such further ordering is present. Consider the conception of human personality that would emerge if there were no ordering of ends, if our behavior and preferences as to art and knowledge, instinct and survival, were totally random. This randomness would go deep, since whom we loved, whom we befriended, and what moral obligations we undertook would also be an entirely random matter. Nor would this randomness take the form of a random choice of an ordering in which objects of love, concern for art, or for knowledge, or for objects of instinct would be contained and ordered. I am proposing for consideration the stronger case where, subject only to the constraints of morality and moral relations, there is no pattern or consistency whatever in the ends we pursue. Our interest in art or knowledge, the kinds of things that please us, even the objects of our love would change frequently and unpredictably. This is what it would mean to entertain rational ends, but to have no ordering (apart from that implicit in morality and the moral relations) of those ends themselves. This is what it would mean if the arrangement of our ends over time were entirely random.

It seems clear that such a picture is incompatible with both our experience of ourselves and of others, and with the notions of rationality I have been developing. Persons are comprehensible both to themselves and others, but a creature whose ends and values varied randomly would not be comprehensible. We can only understand that in which we can discern some pattern or order. A randomly varying person is one who could make no plans, who could neither develop skills and depth nor take advantage of them if he did. Similarly, others could not make plans in respect to such a person. Indeed, I would say that our concept of ourselves and others as persons with a continuing, coherent identity over time depends in part on our exhibiting some order and consistency in our values and ends. Josiah Royce makes the same point when he writes that "a person, an individual self, may be defined as a human life lived according to a plan." *

The point goes deeper. Even the pursuit of particular ends assumes some order and consistency. Intellectual and aesthetic performances in particular cases depend on a background of developed

* *The Philosophy of Loyalty* (1908), p. 168.

skills and interest. So also love and affection for another person assume that we can know and count on that other person to be a certain sort of person, and that means that we can know what counts and will count as significant ends for such a person over fairly protracted periods of time. For these reasons it seems clear that persons must and do exhibit some order, some consistency in their ensemble of ends, that their ends as a whole comprise a system. I shall call this order the life plan.

The ordering of the life plan could be of two sorts. It could be a pattern discerned by an outside observer seeking to arrive at a predictive theory about another's preferences and behavior; a person could also observe himself and perhaps arrive at a predictive theory about his values and choices in the future. But the pattern could be of a different sort, the sort that I have described as ordering the elements within a particular end. The life plan could be a rational principle, a score which the person knows, understands, and follows as a plan or principle of his own. In other words the life plan might be a general rational principle for ordering ends, just as there are particular rational principles for particular ends. There are two considerations that lead me to suggest that the life plan is of the latter sort, and that the coherence it provides is what I have been calling rational coherence.

First, the life plan must order a set of complex and disparate rational ends. The very complexity of ends, such as those involved in relations of love and trust or those involved in artistic creation, means that if those ends are to be realized there must be elaborate and conscious planning at least of an instrumental sort. This deliberate planning presupposes not only stability but some compatibility of the ends provided for. This stability and compatibility imply a system of ends of which the person must be aware, if he is to plan in terms of it. So that finally we come to ask whether having accepted the existence of particular rational ends and of a conscious deliberate plan to realize those ends, it is plausible at the same time to consider the ordering and priority of those ends as something which the person does not understand and experience as his own. Just as the rational principles of ends are one's own, and not mere predictive entities, just so their relative importance, their relative urgency, and hence their ordering and priorities are experienced as one's own.

This does not mean that the life plan and the coherence it provides are necessarily freely chosen, that we choose and make up our life plans, as it were, ad lib. It may well be that the major structures — or some of them — of our priorities are biologically or psychologically determined, but this may also be the case with the whole system of moral principles, principles of games, logic, and art. I have never argued that the test for the rationality of a principle is its ontogeny. The test rather is the way we regard the principle once it is brought to consciousness. Now I do wish to suggest that there may be considerable ad lib creativeness in respect to life plans, and that to the extent that we can be said to choose a life plan we can be said also to choose ourselves, to choose who we are. But the rationality of the life plan does not depend on the existence of such a freedom of choice.

The foregoing leads to the second reason for supposing the life plan is a rational plan, a most general rational principle. The capacity to impose rational order on ends is necessary to morality, to knowledge, to art. In general these rational ends suggest a disposition for order as such, a disposition to transform contingent, arbitrary matter into rationally ordered systems. The suggestion in this section is that this formal capacity, which is exhibited in various discrete rational ends and in systems of ends, also appears as a disposition to impose order and system for its own sake. This general disposition is exhibited in respect to the life plan, the ordering of ends. The disposition to impose this highest-order rationality is neither moral nor theoretic (that is, related to the end of knowledge), and indeed it bears closest resemblance to the aesthetic, for it is in aesthetic ends that order is imposed on disparate materials for the sake of order itself. And thus it might be said that man has a disposition to make of his whole life an artistic creation.

The picture that emerges is of man as a rational animal, in the sense that his world and instincts are pervaded by a tendency to system, to rational coherence. There is a tendency to order the whole repertoire of ends a man pursues, to make inclusive coherent wholes. This is the drive for coherence, and if any unitary end can plausibly be suggested, it is not some end like pleasure, but coherence, in which all material elements are made part of a single, unified system.

I do not go so far as to assert that all our ends, desires, and emotions do in fact make up one single, perfect, and coherent system. We are aware that they do not, that there is a large element of conflict and discontinuity in our lives. A person whose system of ends formed a completely coherent system, whose every end was part of one single end, whose every action was a gesture in a single unified action, might be as strange to us, I suppose, as a person whose actions and tastes were largely lacking in coherence. I suppose we would say of the first sort of person that he lacked life, spontaneity. On the other hand, a person whose ends and principles lacked a coherence even beyond that of morality would also present a flawed and puzzling aspect. A person who did love, who was faithful to all his obligations, and yet exhibited no further coherence and pattern in his ends and dispositions would be a vacillating and elusive being. We could not feel we knew him as we know real persons. And the fact that he exhibited the other traits of personality and lived up to our moral expectations of him would make such a person not less but more puzzling. That is because, his having so much of human comprehensibility about him, we would be puzzled that he fell apart at the center, as it were.

There is, finally, the question of the form of the life plan. Can an account, even as general a one as that offered for morality, love, trust, knowledge, or art, be offered for the structure of life plans? It is possible, of course that no general propositions obtain in respect to life plans, that each person's life plan has a different structure and coherence. The fact that people are at once similar and not identical suggests that some general forms or sets of general forms might be discerned.

I have proposed general forms for a number of significant rational ends and principles, principles such as morality and love, which have considerable implications for the shape of the life plan containing them. In Chapter Ten I propose some general propositions about the form of the life plan as it orders ends relative to questions of life and death. Perhaps these might be developed into a comprehensive theory of the form of life plans. I am content in this essay, however, to propose the existence of life plans and to sketch their rational structure only in respect to that one crucial issue.

Part Two
Rational Ends and
Social Structures

Chapter VII
The Concept
of Society

The system of rational ends provides an analysis for the proposition that man is a social animal, that a social context is natural to man. This proposition has often been urged against attempts to build a concept of society and of a man's relation to it out of simpler elements which make no necessary reference to social existence. The account of man's social nature based on the system of rational ends is a simple one. In affirming that man has a social nature philosophers are seen from this perspective as reacting to a conception of society as purely instrumental, as a means to ends which are identifiable and significant apart from social forms. Thus the assertion of the essentially instrumental nature of society is related either to some variety or hedonism, or to a view that the ends men pursue are not essentially social. On the crudest level these theses are quite implausible. Only the most doctrinaire reductionism would deny basic status to the sexual, maternal, and perhaps the herd instincts. But the arguments elaborated in Part One of this essay carry us a great deal further. They lay the foundation for a theory of society according to which large parts of the social system are necessarily ends in themselves, and the whole system potentially a system of ends and thus itself a comprehensive end. If such a theory can be formulated then a meaning has indeed been given to the notion that man is naturally a social animal, that society not only is a means to the satisfaction of ends but social forms themselves constitute and define many of men's most significant ends. It is a virtue of this analysis that it does not have certain implications disturbing for a conception of individual worth which have on occasion been drawn from the statement of man's natural sociability.

The task of moving from the concepts of Part One to an analysis of social structures is greatly facilitated because there is in Talcott Parsons' work *The Social System* a fully elaborated conceptual structure. This structure builds up a concept of social institutions from the basic units of individual ends and actions. The conceptual structure is both complete and general enough to allow me to take over some of its terminology for my purposes. A brief sketch of Parsons' account is necessary to show the context in which his concepts and terminology are embedded.*

A Sketch of Parsons' System

Parsons starts with three primitive orientations of an agent to his environment: the cognitive, cathectic, and evaluative. He then posits an environment in which other persons serve on occasion as the objects of one or another of these orientations. From this he elaborates a comprehensive theoretical framework for all possible forms of interaction between an agent ("ego") and other persons, and thus for all possible forms of social systems. By a cathectic orientation to an object Parsons means a relation in which the object is seen as a source of immediate, direct gratification. By a cognitive orientation he means the object is something to be known. Parsons' notion of evaluative orientation is considerably more obscure. It has to do with the integration of objects into cognitive and cathectic systems. Since Parsons' basic unit is that

---

* There is one caveat: Parsons' system is very much in process, and his position and concerns in *The Social System* are not in all respects those of his subsequent work. For the special purpose of providing a conceptual structure to bridge a theory of individual ends and a theory of social institutions, and for the purpose of providing a terminology, this is the work that I find most helpful. Nor do I believe that the very general exposition I give is in conflict with Parsons' later views.

of an action, the cathectic orientation is realized in an immediately gratificatory action, the cognitive in what I have called an act of knowledge, and the evaluative in what Parsons calls the "process of ordered selection" on either the cognitive or cathectic level. The process of ordered selection on the cognitive level gives rise to interpretation, to cognitive systems, and thus to knowledge as we know it. On the cathectic level it involves the possibility of system and ordering of desires, of postponement and harmonization of desires.

The elaboration of the structural framework for social systems then proceeds by calling attention to the fact that in the class of actions called social actions in which other persons are the objects, there will generally be an aspect of "interaction," that is, ego's action will presuppose an appropriate response from alter. The social system is elaborated out of the pattern of such interactions and the expectations on which they depend. The most basic step in Parsons' analysis of such patterns of interrelations is the identification of the individual's general position in the pattern of an interrelation (that is, his status) and the complementary identification of what the individual does in the particular pattern (that is, his role).

Parsons does not insist, as I understand him, that the location of a person in a status and the ascription to him of a role depend on an orientation which that person himself accepts — this may or may not be the case. It is only necessary that these concepts correspond to the functional positioning of that person in terms of *some* person's structure of orientations. Imagine the interactive system consisting of a dignified portly lady picking her way down a muddy street and a group of boys following behind her mimicking her gait. The boys assign a status and role to the lady which she is quite unaware of filling. She may believe that the boys are following her in order to be helpful if the need arises, and derive a sense of security from that. Thus from each point of view the interactive system and status and role in it are differently defined. One might contrast to this the system of musicians playing a string quartet where the system is known and shared by all. Finally Parsons points out that status and role are concepts relative to a particular scheme of interaction, so that in different contexts the same person will usually occupy a number of different relatively permanent positions (for example, head of household, worker) as well as any number of transitory ones (for instance, spectator at an entertainment, patient). These different roles may be more or less integrated in a total system, they may simply fail to intersect altogether, or they may conflict.

An important distinction is introduced in dealing with systems of any degree of complexity. This is the distinction between "affectivity," where the interaction is viewed in terms of more or less immediate gratification, and "affective-neutrality," where the interaction is instrumental to some ultimate end but has no cathectic orientation in itself. In his discussion of "expressive symbols," Parsons develops from the notion of affectivity an analysis of those actions which are part of a system and gather their meaning from the context of a system and which are primarily affective; that is, they have to do with immediate gratification. The symbol itself may be an object, a person (a "social object" in Parsons' terminology) or an action. Thus the playing of a piece of music or the perfume worn by a beautiful woman may both be expressive symbols: expressive because the orientation to each is directly cathectic, symbolic because the capacity of each to elicit an affective response depends on a context against which the symbol acquires its affective meaning.

An example of the dynamics of expressive systems would be a child's response to the caresses of its mother. At first the warmth and comfort satisfy primitive cathectic needs of the child. Later they come to be associated with a whole system of acts in which the mother expresses her love and willingness to care for the child. Finally, the same caresses, though maintaining some of their original cathectic context, become symbols — which are directly gratificatory — of and in this system of loving acts. Perhaps the paradigm of an expressive symbol is any sort of ritual: the ritual which symbolizes, for instance, solidarity with a group (or the expression of hatred for such a group, or whatever) is at the same time an expression and direct gratification of the need for such solidarity. It is, moreover, perfectly consistent with this analysis that one agent may have an orientation of affective-neutrality to an action system which for another is highly charged cathectically. An example of this would be the calculated staging of political rallies by propagandists to frighten enemies, or to create bonds of solidarity which can then be manipulated by leaders for their own purposes.

In putting forward these elements of combination in social systems, Parsons acknowledges that he has presented only a framework for the logically possible combinations. It is the job of empirical research to identify the actual combinations of these elements which existing societies represent. Empirical research must discover too the contents of the need-dispositions — that is, directions for cathectic orientation — persons actually exhibit. It must identify the external constraints, such as climate, resources, and even such uniformities as the fact of death, aging, and sexual reproduction, within which social systems operate. More or less general laws can then be framed and classification undertaken by the replacement with concrete data of the general conceptual terms of the framework scheme.*

Sociological and Normative Theory

I have undertaken this rather lengthy sketch of one sociological theory of social structures in order to compare it with a theory of society derived from the point of view of ends — and particularly rational ends — and to show how sociological theory may be compatible with this point of view. In this way an approach may be made to an account of the nature and value of social forms in general and of the social forms associated with law in particular.

The focus of this essay is broadly speaking ethical, that is, what are appropriate choices and values from the point of view of an agent who must choose, who adopts values. From this point of view, a sociological analysis has, first, obvious instrumental significance. Whatever uniformities sociology is able to discover may bear on the effectuation of purposes an agent has chosen. This would be true for instance if the elimination of poverty is an im-

---

* Parsons' illustration is the almost universal significance of kinship relations, which may on his scheme be related to certain empirical uniformities related to the biological facts of the human life cycle. This in turn opens up the question of the extent to which various need-dispositions related to kinship structures — for example, parental feelings, feelings of the child toward the parents — are innate and the extent to which they are the product of socializing forces which for various empirical reasons might be expected to be widely distributed in all cultures and societies.

portant value, which can only be attained through more efficient organization of the available labor force. A second more subtle relevance of sociological theory is that values may be clarified. An understanding of what efficient organization of the labor force requires might force the choosing agent to consider competing values that he otherwise might not have thought to be implicated. The third most drastic effect that certain sociological insights may have — those, for instance, dealing with "socialization," that is, the process by which values are instilled in individuals, maintained, or broken down — is to modify the agent's own value system by showing him its relativity and determinants. But such an effect is strictly speaking irrelevant, since a grasp of how one comes to hold certain values can undermine or bolster those values only in terms of some criterion that is itself a value criterion. Thus this most drastic effect is either an example of the second effect after all, or it must involve the abandonment of all values whatever, a situation that is hard to conceive for a functioning agent.

It should be noted, moreover, that Parsons' system is not purely descriptive for two reasons. First, the various terms used to denote value orientations — need-disposition, effect, gratification, cathexis — are not observational terms. Rather they correspond to the concept of end which has been put forward in Part One, and so far as one can tell have the same logical status as primitive terms in his system. This is not the place to argue whether an adequate account of human conduct could ever be constructed in purely observational terms, and without recourse to a term like end or its equivalents. It is sufficient to note that for the kinds of behavior exhibited in societies no adequate account has done so.

Second, Parsons' system assumes the rationality of his agents in two related respects. Having an end, they accept the necessity of the means. And where two ends conflict they experience a tension which bespeaks an appreciation of the incompatibility. A further aspect of rationality is less explicit but nonetheless seems present: that whatever value systems may obtain, they exist in tension and subject to strain if in some way they conflict with reality. The conflict with reality may be of two sorts. The acceptance of valid evidence may reveal a value conflict where none was felt before. (An example: can value systems referring to racial purity survive evidence of the irrelevance of racial differences to any other matter assumed to be of value?) Or the value system may itself simply impede the acquisition of more complete or more adequate conceptions of reality.

In what respect, then, does an account of the concept of society based on the concepts of Part One differ from a sociological account of the social system? To the extent that a sociological account proceeds from ends as primitive terms, and assumes rationality as well, the difference is one of degree, emphasis, and detail only. If there is a significant divergence, it arises from the differing perspective of ethical and sociological analysis, the former speaking directly to actors, the latter speaking about them, behind their backs as it were. Ethical or value-oriented inquiries, such as this one is meant to be, are basically Socratic in their perspective, that is, they are intended to express and clarify the ethical or value orientations of the speaker and his interlocutors, the readers. Sociological inquiries, by contrast, take an outsider's perspective, they are descriptive. But too much cannot be made of this distinction, at least in respect to an account such as Parsons', which is systematically teleological and makes certain rationality assumptions.

There is the further difference that in an ethical inquiry the argument is not neutral as to just any ends at all; it focuses on ends that are potentially or actually of significance to the parties to the discussion. By contrast sociological theory is free to go behind ends to give an account of them either in nonteleological terms or in the terms of ends which are utterly transformed in the processes of development, as Parsons — adopting a basically psychoanalytic orientation to personality — does. If, for instance, sexual curiosity (one kind of end) develops into scientific curiosity, and if scientific curiosity is an end which qua end retains no vestige of its genetic forebear (as may, perhaps, be doubted), then in ethical discourse with a person who has one or the other of these ends the fact of this potentiality for development can be relevant only in terms of some other more general or more basic end. Indeed, if it is possible to convince another that such a change of ends is bound to occur, the information must be seriously disturbing unless it can be integrated into a more pervasive system of ends that accounts for it. For descriptive or theoretical sociological theory such problems do not exist (except as the cases in which individuals encounter such disassociative information must be described and accounted for by the theoretical system).

Society as a System of Ends

As in the general analysis of ends in Part One, so in the more restricted context of a concept of society, the most significant distinction is between actions that are ends and those that are instrumental to ends. As applied to actions in a social context I shall adopt Parsons' terminology and speak of expressive and instrumental actions. Since the notion of an expressive action or end which is a simple uncompounded point, unextended in time and unmodulated in intensity, is very probably always an abstraction, in the social context particularly we need concern ourselves only with actions exhibiting various degrees and kinds of complexity. Again following the analysis of Part One, expressive actions — which will almost invariably be complex — will either form instinctive units or rational units, that is, rational social actions. In the general analysis the suggestion was made that the notion of purely instinctive end complexes was probably something of an abstraction, and that some element of what has been called rational structure is likely to be present. In the social context this suggestion gains considerable plausibility: expressive actions involving other persons depend on a context in which not only the presence and immediate perception of the other person is an essential feature, but also the perception of that other person *as* something or another. And this last lends what has been called a rational structure to such expressive social actions. Thus social ends — that is, ends essentially involving others — are primarily rational ends.

A choosing, valuing agent will have a number of rational, social ends, which are exhibited in rational, social actions. Moreover, to the extent that an expressive action is constituted by a rational principle that rational principle tends to include a significant reference of some sort to the specifically human aspect of the context: that the human object of the expressive action has a capacity for response and for rational response. For convenience and brevity I shall reserve the term expressive action for these paradigmatic instances: the action is a rational, social action (expressive of a rational, social end) which includes in its principle some significant reference to the capacity for expressive action on the part of its object.

For the choosing, valuing agent, then, the concept of society may be specified in terms of expressive actions of various sorts. If we analyze expressive actions still from the point of view of the choosing, valuing agent we may put forward the notion of an expressive relation, which is nothing but the abstraction of the "expressive" element in the principle of the rational action. Thus a man may engage in a joint enterprise with another. The action may (and possibly will) have an instrumental aspect, but let us posit that it is also an expressive action, expressive, say, of the end of friendship. The relation between the agents will then be a relation of friendship. In the same way there may be relations of love, hatred, exploitation, mutual degradation. The notion of relation designates the principle, the rational structure, of the social action and locates the significance of the other person in that principle. Thus one's relations to others are a function of the significance of those others in the ends one pursues.

But the concept of relation is most useful not in respect of a simple action but where there is rational integration of actions and ends into a system. Such systems may be generated by the constant expression of a single end in varying circumstances, or there may be a system of ends which are all related to a more general principle, as in the case of what has been called morality. In that case one may speak of moral relations. Finally a rational system of ends may be created to integrate, to lend coherence, to disparate ends or systems of ends.

The steps to an adequate concept of society are these: (1) the identification of ends one pursues; (2) the identification of those ends that implicate other persons; (3) the identification of the kinds of implication by the various forms of relation. Society, then, is the system or collection of relations that are entailed by the ends pursued by choosing, valuing persons.

From this perspective it is hard to see that it could even sensibly be suggested that society is only instrumental to human ends or goods, for that would require asserting that all — or all significant — relations are instrumental, which is a thesis lacking even a semblance of plausibility. To dispose of the instrumentalist so easily may seem too much like a mere definitional gambit, depending on a somewhat special definition of society at that. The more challenging thesis is this: There are expressive relations to be sure, and if I want to define these "into" my concept of society that is my right. The aspect of "society" (as I am using the term) that the instrumentalist is focusing on are the more public, the more extended and abstract relations, that the instrumentalist believes come to mind when the word society is used. He means institutions like property, the law, and bureaucracies, mechanisms like the market, systems of roles like professions or social class. Is it not, he would ask, considerably more plausible to see a society consisting of these as instrumental? So long as this argument is not trivialized by defining society as the system of instrumental relations, there is here a significant issue: Does the analysis of this essay lead to a different account of the balance of the instrumental and the expressive aspects in society, and does the recognition of a larger function for the expressive aspect lead to a different analysis of specific institutions?

A general and abstract answer depends on the prior analysis of moral ends and of the disposition to incorporate disparate ends into coherent structures. Morality is to a greater or lesser degree (moving along the spectrum from justice to love) an instrumental structure permitting the attainment of ends beyond itself. The constraints it imposes on the pursuit of external ends make for whatever instrumental efficacy morality has, but at the same time these constraints are expressive of principles which are ends in themselves. Moreover, as has been seen, it is only if the instrumental aspect of morality is subordinated to its expressive aspect that its instrumental efficacy obtains at all. And this predominance of the expressive in the system of morality is also exhibited by a disposition to build on the expressive content of morality more and more purely expressive structures, as in the case of friendship and love. Thus as society is constituted by instrumental relations under the constraints of justice, so these very relations will have an expressive aspect.

Finally, to the extent that there is an integrative disposition as such, and a corresponding end of rationality or coherence, then the rationalizing of social actions and ends will tend to become a higher-order end in itself, and the instrumental relations thus rationalized will tend to become expressive of this higher-order end.

But these general points can only be convincingly demonstrated in terms of concrete institutions and relations. It is to this demonstration that the next two chapters are devoted.

Chapter VIII
*Law as a Means
and as an End*

The Intrinsic Value of Law

I shall use the term law to cover a collection of social phenomena commonly connected with it: it is what lawyers advise clients about, legislators put into statute books, judges decide about, policemen and sheriffs enforce. Any more precise delimitation of the area of application of the term involves theoretical commitments which it would be better to avoid at the outset. According to this common-sense notion, law consists of rules and rulings. Without becoming technical, one can distinguish three different kinds of rules: rules which forbid or direct behavior, rules which provide facilities for making efficacious legal arrangements such as wills, contracts, and the like, and rules which create offices and give officials their powers. Included in this conception of law or at least closely associated with it are the procedures by which rules are enacted or legal determinations arrived at, the study and profession which identifies the experts in legal matters, and the documents and formulas in which the various rules are couched or effectively invoked.

There is little that appears to be of intrinsic value in any of these things. They all appear to be more or less serviceable tools for attaining various ends people might have. Even the rules themselves, both the ones which command or prohibit directly and the ones which derive from binding arrangements people enter into, seem valuable only insofar as they bring about conduct or states of affairs to be valued. Thus the rules, arrangements, and procedures in which these directing and prohibiting rules are made and manipulated seem even further removed from what people ultimately desire and value. And further removed still must seem the profession, study, and practices in which the techniques for law creation and manipulation are learned, transmitted, and practiced.

An example of a legal institution: marriage. Let us see how far this purely instrumental view of law survives the consideration of a concrete legal institution. The example I will use is the institution of marriage. As that institution exists in any system familiar to us, it is expressed and embodied in a complicated structure of legal rules. Very generally, persons are not considered and do not consider themselves married unless they have followed the formalities which are a prerequisite for their being legally married. Once married these persons are entwined in a network of rules which first of all support what is very likely to be their mutual intention. All sorts of property transactions — mainly of a day-to-day variety — decisions affecting their children, and dealings with government units proceed on the assumption that decisions made by one or the other person are made on the behalf of both. The institution also makes a negative impression, as it were, in that many relations which are recognized between husband and wife receive no protection or sanction outside of marriage or perhaps are the subject of actual prohibition. The law recognizes a right to privacy and confidentiality between spouses, a right of companionship and support which is compensable if interfered with, a right to defend the spouse against harm. Finally, the circumstance that the marriage relation can only be terminated with more or less difficulty and only with some form of official concurrence impinges on and is part of the definition of that relation between the parties.

Now the plain man is likely to be very suspicious of any suggestion based on all this that law or legal forms have any of the same intrinsic value as the personal and expressive relations in marriage.* After all, the law does no more than facilitate those relations and protect the occasions for them. But this objection reveals too crude a view of the matter, particularly in the distinction that would be drawn between the facilitation of a system of relations and those relations themselves. The legal institution provides a framework for relations — that is, a partially complete structure of relations — into which the persons may enter. The relations of persons outside that framework cannot be exactly or even substantially the same as they would be in it.

Consider the stability of the relation, and the commitment to it as a stable relation. Legal institutions make that commitment a different one from what it would be if marriage were a purely consensual arrangement which could be terminated at will. The formalization of the commitment takes some strain off the consensual basis of the stability, since legal pressures contribute to that stability. Just as important, the legal institution makes the original commitment a different one from what it would be in a purely consensual arrangement. The analogy might be made to the example of the gift. A gift cannot be given apart from a notion of property and apart from an institutional structure which recognizes the gift as a permanent, irrevocable transfer. The analogy points up the significance of the legal structure for the definition of the original commitment. And the element of commitment is one of the important aspects of the institution of marriage viewed as a structure of expressive (as well as instrumental) relations.

The expressive relations in the institution of marriage are determined by its legal framework in another way, that of the public quality of the relations. The quality of the relations between two persons will vary not only according to the overt actions implied by those relations but also according to the degree and nature of the notoriety of those actions. Assuming the actions and ends to be rational, the overt gestures must be read against the rational principles which determine them. Since rational principles refer to the context of the actions and ends, and since the knowledge and responses of third persons are potential features of that context, it follows that whether and which third persons know of the

---

* It will be recalled from the previous chapter that, following Parsons, an expressive relation is defined as a relation having intrinsic value, as for instance relations of love and friendship, or the relations in a game played for pleasure.

actions are important aspects of these principles, and therefore of the ends and relations that they structure.* This context of notoriety is important to an understanding of the marriage relation. Marriage is an institution which allows persons to enter into a system of relations with a specified form of notoriety, let us call it official notoriety. It is not just that the parties to the system of relations "do not care who knows about it," or even that they are "prepared to shout it from the rooftops," but they are using a form which gives any third person the *right* to know of the relation. It is part of an official record, and the parties invite anyone else to build expectations on the basis of that record. The official publicity of the relation produces a quite special context for them. It is the basis for expectations of a quite concrete order — for example, how credit shall be extended, who is responsible for certain children. It shields aspects of the relation from certain kinds of inquiry, that is, it defines an area of privacy, but oddly it does so by proclaiming to all the existence of intimacy which it is the essence of privacy to screen. People who marry, then, adopt a form for their relation that in various ways implicate a wide circle of other persons in that relation, and thus they make their relation and the ends it involves entirely different from what they would be without that form.

In respect to both these points, the aspect of commitment and the aspect of official notoriety, it might be argued that they do not show the expressive character of law — its intrinsic value — but only the expressive character, the intrinsic value, of various kinds of relations which legal forms make possible. The argument might go thus: the laws about marriage are no part of the values, the rational ends, and concrete human relations which may be shaped by legal forms. But this objection depends on an unacceptable notion of law. Certainly legal forms such as have been described do not constitute law by virtue simply of being formulated in a statute book. It is far more important that actual conduct adopt and conform to these legal forms. And when conduct does so conform, then the legal form is part of the rational principle, of the value constituting the end and action in that conduct. The legal forms in their abstract formulations are like words in a dictionary,

---

* This issue is explored in detail in the following chapter which analyzes the concept of privacy.

where they are only potentially expressive. It is only when the words in the dictionary are used that there is language. And it is only when legal forms shape actual relations and ends that their potentiality is actualized. There is no reason to reserve the term law for the abstract forms and to deny the presence of law in the instantiations of those forms.

Of course, the legal forms of the marriage relation are only partial determinants of the actual expressive relation. Concrete relations will vary enormously as other determinants, and especially concrete empirical determinants, are involved. It is this concreteness which makes the relations what they are, which makes them palpable, real, valued relations. But still the legal forms are significant determinants of these relations.

Finally, there is the argument that the forms I have been describing are primarily *social* forms, not legal forms, in that a system of expectations and understandings without any further apparatus might yield relations very like those I have described. This point might be supported by the circumstance that many of the important features of the institution of marriage might obtain in a limited group in a larger community, a limited group with its own customs and practices but no formal coercive mechanism. This only shows the problems and arbitrary distinctions in the common-sense limitation of the term law with which we began. Within such a limited group the institution of marriage, if it is to exist recognizably, must still be embodied in rules and systems of expectations: there must be forms to mark entry into and departure from the married state. Moreover, though there may be no sanctions involving the use of force, the adherence to or transgression of the rules and expectations of the system must have consequences. If, therefore, the expressive aspect of the institutional structure is acknowledged to be present, it would be arbitrary to deny this expressiveness simply because the institution of marriage is integrated into the legal system's larger, more comprehensive system of rules.

There are more general conclusions to be drawn from an examination of this specific institution. The discussion has shown how the law defines and creates part of the system which underlies expressive relations, and how certain expressive relations involve a structure of legal rules and relations. Ideally, the parties to a marriage integrate their rational ends into a system of relations. There is an integration of ends based on relations of love between man and woman and these two and their children. As we saw in the discussion of love in Chapter Five, these ends must be expressed in terms of the common pursuit of mutual interests. The interest will involve others more or less directly: directly when third persons are the objects of such interests (most typically children), less directly when the actions of the parties to the relation impinge upon others. Moreover, the relation will involve others in that they may be expected to support certain of the claims that the parties put forward, for instance the claim to authority over their children. Others are also involved by the circumstance that love depends on the concept of respect and of justice, and this concept can only be expressed between the lovers if there is a more general context of relations built on respect and justice surrounding them. Finally, a person will have ends and be involved in relations which have no necessary and close involvement with even as engrossing a relation as love; but the integrating disposition discussed at the end of Chapter Six bespeaks a tendency to bring all significant ends into a more or less harmonious system, into an integrated "way of life." Thus the institution of marriage can be seen as a system which integrates a number of more or less interdependent ends and relations. Since these relations are in large part expressive relations the system of such relations, the higher-order end, will in this way also be expressive. And the legal aspect of these relations will then also be part of this expressive system.

Law and justice. These conclusions about law can be applied to a wider range of legal phenomena by recalling the analysis in Part One of the concept of morality and its associated ends. We have seen how the constraints of justice express morality and respect for personality. We saw that the acceptance of these constraints is an independent end, and that the acceptance of the constraints of justice is constitutive of relations of respect and trust. But nothing is clearer than that for situations of any complexity and significance these constraints of justice are and must be concretized in systems of rules governing property rights, the enforcement of promises, the assurance of bodily security, and so on, in short, a body of legal rules. Moreover, realistically not everyone can be assumed to know what is just (generally, or as applied to a particular dispute), nor can everyone be assumed to adopt voluntarily the constraints of justice. Consequently, the application of legal rules must somehow be authoritatively determined, and compliance enforced, so that "those who would voluntarily obey shall not be sacrificed to those who would not." * Thus in most circumstances the constraints of justice are expressed in a legal system, that is, its system of rules, its procedures, and its means of enforcement.

The function of law in partially structuring the institution of marriage is not simply a special case of law as the concretization of the constraints of justice. The relation between law and the constraints of justice is complex and must be clarified if the notion of law as a system of expressive relations is to be understood. Justice, as we have seen, entails the acceptance of constraints in the pursuit of other ends. By analogy to this, a legal system expresses the principle of justice, but it may express as well other principles of rational social ends — such as love or friendship — which are pursued within the constraints of justice. And a legal institution like marriage may also express the general integrative disposition to systematize a variety of social ends into one end.

Nevertheless one feels that the function of concretizing the constraints of justice is the most characteristic function of law. The concept of law designates not just any system of social rules — rules of a game or the rules or directions for playing a symphony. Law is particularly concerned with creating the most general conditions and framework within which ends are pursued. This is of course a matter of degree, but there is an emphasis on such elemental concerns as regulating the use of force, and defining the basic area of personal liberty and security. Moreover, the concept of law is reserved for those rules which have a certain range of application, namely to the most general community, and this also points to the primordial, structural aspect of legal rules and regulations. And it is precisely the function of the concept of justice to define the basic, general structure of relations between persons showing mutual respect.

Though there is a close relation between law and the concept of justice, there is no simple one-to-one correspondence. Justice is always and in a significant sense a partially unspecified end, that is, its significance depends in part on the significance of the other

* H. L. A. Hart, *The Concept of Law*, p. 193.

ends on which it imposes constraints. Legal institutions define relations that are also partly unspecified, but — as the example of marriage illustrates — the partial specification determines more of the total system of ends and relations than does the concept of justice. Justice specifies this much: the basic position of respect of the parties vis-à-vis each other and third persons; from this may be derived the liberty to enter into any one of a theoretically infinite set of possible relations with others — of which marriage is just one — and a corresponding right to the recognition and protection of various interests arising out of such relations. The law goes beyond protecting the liberty of persons to enter into any arrangement, which is consistent with justice to third persons; it also provides some of the structure for these arrangements, as in the case of marriage. The law not only protects justice and the liberty justice entails, but provides certain facilities for the enjoyment or utilization of that liberty in certain ways. And thus law will involve the specification in concrete circumstances not only of the principles of justice but of other more particular rational ends.*

Rules of Law and Expressive Relations

Since legal relations, then, may be expressive relations, certain rational ends men pursue are partially defined by law. The fact

* It might still be objected that if law is a manipulation of sanctions, and if the ultimate sanction is the use of force, then after all law does remain at the level of justice, since justice defines the liberties and security of persons. But there is no reason to accept the premises. To be sure, the existence of a legal relation must make a difference, but that is true of any relation, and the difference need not be one as to the application of official force. Thus, for example, the aspect of notoriety of the institution of marriage does not concern the use of force. Even as to this example it might be argued that "ultimately" the rules are rules about the use of force: the authority of the state to keep and protect a record of the fact of the marriage, a redefinition of the rights of third persons who are thereby deemed to know of the relation, and so on. Such an argument is too farfetched to be plausible. It would be the equivalent of arguing that the state's organization of a patriotic ritual, say the funeral of a national figure, is *really* about the use of force: in preventing traffic from using the route of the procession, in permitting the disbursement of certain funds, in authorizing the punishment of soldiers marching in the procession for refusing to follow orders to march in slow march. Such a position seems absurd, and it would not be less so if ingenuity were able to discover some perhaps quite significant force aspect to every feature of every legal institution.

that legal relations and law are a sort of social relation and form parts of a social system helps to make this assertion acceptable. But law, as has often been remarked, is a term designating a rather heterogeneous assortment of entities: rules, systems, offices, decisions, procedures. How does our general conclusion that law contains expressive aspects work out when we confront law in this variety of forms? This is a question that can only be answered by considering a number of these aspects of law in detail.

Most characteristic of law is the aspect of rule. A rational action, it will be recalled, is constituted by a rational principle which lends coherence to the action it determines. A legal rule, then, may operate as the determining principle — or more precisely a portion of the determining principle — of a rational action. An example of a rational action which was referred to frequently in Part One was that of an act of restitution performed out of a sense of guilt and in response to the dictates of justice. It is plain that the whole system of such an act — what constitutes property, what constitutes its adequate restoration, when such property is unjustly acquired or retained — is or may be permeated by legal standards and norms. These standards and norms are embodied in rules. So also formal steps for entering into or terminating a marriage are embodied in rules. What, then, are legal rules, especially from the perspective of law as a determinant of rational actions? A simple-minded view of legal rules sees them only as sentences in certain books; a view not much less simple-minded sees them only as the commands of some person or persons, the sovereign. The perspective offered in this chapter would admit, of course, this aspect of law as formula, but it is essential to the concept of law that the formula be taken up as part of a rational action, that is become a part of a principle of action.

Moreover, where law is part of an expressive relation, of a rational end, the statement is not taken up into just any principle of action, it is taken up in a principled context which refers to the social and moral functions of the law. Thus a person who performs the rational action of paying his taxes because they are in justice owed to the community adopts the rule of the tax code regarding tax liabilities. But he performs the action on a principle which is larger and more complex than the rule in the tax code. The principle of his action, if he acts from a sense of moral obligation, includes an appreciation of the concept of justice and of the obligation of fairness as applied to a particular social and legal context. To be sure, the statement in the tax code may be seen as a rule in a complex game and its payment a move in that game, but if a significant number of persons viewed legal statements in this way they would lose their character as *legal* statements.*

Finally, legal rules which remain mere statements and do not enter into and determine actions, are only potentially law, only a possible legal system. A rule in a book or a rule recited as an abstract statement is of course far from being an expressive relation, or action, or end. So also are the rules of a game standing alone or the score of a symphony. Legal rules or the score of a symphony are abstractions, statements only, but they are the abstract statements of principles which can determine action, which can define and constitute ends in themselves. So we may concede that as mere statement legal rules are cold and remote from expressive relations, but expressive relations may be acted out, played out, according to the score which these statements provide.

Expressive Aspects of Criminal Procedure

Procedure is a part of law whose expressive aspect is easily overlooked. Consider a criminal trial. One who has followed me this far might be prepared to admit the existence of an expressive element in the criminal law. That element would be epitomized somewhat like this: (1) A crime is a violation of the obligations of justice and fairness to the extent that it undermines the general adherence to a body of rules imposing constraints on the conduct of all for the benefit of all and the more so when it infringes the particular rights of an individual. (A failure to pay a just tax is the first kind of unfairness, and theft is both the first and second.) (2) The principles of justice and fairness define not only primary obligations but speak also to the secondary set of circumstances where the primary obligation has been broken. (3) Restitution to an injured party is a minimal requirement. (4) Some form of pun-

---

* Game analogies have frequently been invoked in discussions of the philosophy of law. Such analogies have seemed both singularly appropriate and inappropriate. They are appropriate in that games and legal actions are both rational actions. They are inappropriate or only analogies, in that games belong to a quasi-aesthetic category of ends, and law to the moral category.

ishment or condemnation is at least prima facie indicated in order to help restore confidence on the part of a victim and society in general in the system of constraints voluntarily accepted which a deliberate criminal act disturbs. The various sacrifices of an orderly society are coordinated and justified in terms of like sacrifices by others. Deliberate violations not only constitute an unfair advantage but if generalized remove the grounds for obedience by others. Thus, a system of taxation which is generally complied with creates quite different obligations of fairness from one which is generally ignored. (5) Finally, the individual violator may wish to restore bonds of morality and trust with his fellows, and a formal acknowledgment of guilt seems a necessary aspect of this.

We may therefore identify five expressive aspects of the notions of crime and punishment: crime as a violation of morality, morality as speaking to the consequences of its own violation, restitution, punishment or condemnation, remorse or acknowledgment of guilt. What is the relation of the concrete steps and gestures of criminal procedure to this expressive complex?

Obviously it is the function of criminal procedure to determine the facts which are the predicate for condemnation and punishment. The often discussed puzzle about the utility of punishing an innocent man for the effect this may have on others — for example, deterrence or a sense of security — does not occur in the context of a just system. The deliberate punishment of an innocent man is inconsistent with the principle of morality, no matter what the net gain in utility, since it involves sacrificing the rights — as defined by the principle of morality and justice — of one man to increase the advantages of others. Indeed the willingness to forego such advantage as might accrue from such injustice is a manifestation of the moral feeling of respect for human personality. And in acting within a just legal system which foregoes such advantages one acts out of respect and thus performs a rational action, establishing expressive relations to the whole range of potential victims of such a violation of the principle of justice. Though the issue of deliberately condemning a known innocent is susceptible of straightforward resolution on the premises of a just system, it is after all a rather extreme and marginal issue. The pressing issues arise in cases where a person is in good faith accused of crime and denies his guilt.

Where there are genuine doubts we have first of all a more perplexing version of the issue raised by the "innocent man" puzzle: it is unjust to punish an innocent man knowing him to be innocent, but how certain must one be of guilt? It is only good sense to accept that one cannot resolve all doubt. If there is to be a system of criminal law at all some risk of condemning an innocent man must be deliberately incurred, and the question becomes one as to the acceptable level and form of such a risk. A formula for ascertaining the acceptable level of risk would be that of the reasonable man in the original position: what risk of being convicted of crime though innocent, would a reasonable man accept as tolerable at the outset, knowing that as the level of risk was reduced his protection against crime was also lessened. But this formula, while unobjectionable, simply conceals the issue whether the acceptable level is just the point where the marginal increment of risk equals the marginal increment in social defense, or whether the reasonable man would consider other factors. Before turning to that issue, it should be noted that even this economic view differs from the utilitarian calculus which might justify the deliberate conviction of an innocent man, since it is not an ad hoc calculation, but a general rule adopted openly as to the acceptable level of risk in any case that might come up.

A general rule openly proclaimed as to the acceptable level of risk would not I think simply seek to approximate the point of marginal equivalence of risk and protection. This is because criminal condemnation does not involve only a deprivation of advantage but also the element of moral guilt and an accusation of breach of trust. A man whose house is pulled down to stop the spread of a fire or who is chosen to fight for his country suffers a deprivation which is justified if the risk is fairly apportioned. Moreover, his sacrifice is an act expressive of his relation of trust and solidarity in justice with the rest of his community. But one condemned of crime is charged with a breach of trust by his fellows and the risk of being incorrectly charged seems different from the risk of being called on to make a sacrifice when it is one's turn to do so. The element of loss of respect makes the burden a peculiarly serious one. Thus the risk side of the equation should be heavily weighted, more so than the equivalent material deprivation in another context.

This having been said, it seems clear that a problem remains to which there is no happy solution, and a moral second best will have to do. The business of criminal condemnation is in principle a morally uneasy one, and a just system of criminal procedure should reflect that unease. This is in fact the case. The requirement that guilt be proved beyond a reasonable doubt is an attempt — surely not wholly successful — to come as close to certainty as the conditions of human knowledge allow. But there are a number of other features of criminal procedure that express the moral qualities and dilemmas of criminal condemnation. These are various advantages given the accused in preventing prejudice to himself even at the cost of excluding relevant damaging evidence. Perhaps one can count here too the varieties of the privilege against self-incrimination, which in one form or other in most legal systems allow the accused to refuse to cooperate in bringing forward evidence damaging to himself. It is often said that these procedural advantages are rather inadequate counterweights to the great advantages the prosecution has in gathering evidence and presenting its case. But it seems to me that they are better explained as manifestations of unease about the imperfect moral basis for morally condemning a man who denies his guilt.*

* The definition of the requisite level of certainty is but one aspect of the structural problem of criminal procedure. There is also the question who is to be certain of the guilt. In most civilized systems some separation is effected between those who investigate and formulate the charges and those who decide the issue of guilt. Similarly every civilized system gives the accused large opportunities to defend himself, and particularly assures him the assistance of a trained person to present his defense for him. These aspects of criminal procedure also are designed to give a general sense of security against the risk of false convictions, but not simply by defining the appropriate level of certainty of guilt. Rather these measures are directed to the psychology of the decider, even assuming his commitment to the standard of guilt beyond a reasonable doubt. It is recognized that where facts are obscure the process of resolving doubts is a delicate one which it is not always possible to control directly. Therefore the skepticism of the person who decides is sought to be assured by detaching him from the process of conducting the investigation and by demonstrating in dramatic form that the issue he must decide may have two sides. This purpose is carried out in the procedure for determining guilt and therefore in the definition of offices and functions in the process of encounter with a suspected criminal. Indeed it is this purpose that explains in part why society should deal with this problem by creating complex and interrelated structures of offices at all. The matter might have been left as the concern of whoever chose to take it up and execute punishment: the victim, his friends and relations, outraged members of the community, or executive officers who chose to take an interest.

These constraints should work to give the assurance against wrong convictions that a rational person would want before consenting to a system of criminal punishments. Our concern here, however, is to show how criminal procedure may itself be a system of expressive relations, and to show how its principles and rules define ends in themselves. The assurance provided by this whole elaborate structure is not, it should be recalled, measured by the situation of a particular accused person on a particular occasion — for viewed in that particularity the assurance may be and often is absurdly excessive or occasionally rather inadequate. The constraints accepted in dealing with an accused who on a particular occasion may appear to all as guilty far beyond even a reasonable doubt (for example, where he has formerly been acquitted and he subsequently admits his guilt and produces highly damning evidence, or there is highly probative evidence available which is legally inadmissible) are accepted because a just system requires that a system of constraints be accepted beforehand for all cases of a like class and then adhered to in particular cases. The acceptance of these constraints in a particular case is the most concrete demonstration of one's acceptance of the principles of justice — no direct considerations of utility conduce to the same result. The acceptance of the constraints, then, is the playing out of a particular action (or a system of actions) according to the principles of justice. The action is an end in itself.

The playing out of the criminal process according to a score provided by the principle of justice is an end in itself and is expressive of relation of trust and respect for the accused, for his victim, and for all potential participants in the criminal process. I do not wish to suggest that the details of a particular system of criminal procedure or a particular action within it can be strictly derived from a set of premises consisting of the principle of justice and the empirical circumstances in a concrete legal and social system. Even the relatively constant features of criminal procedure are hardly inevitable corollaries of the principle of justice. Does this mean that the particulars of a system are after all just instrumental, means to an end which is adherence to the principle of justice? I think not — at least no more than the words of a poem are a means to an end which is the structure and meaning of the poem. The words embody, make concrete and actual, the principles of the poem. So too the discrete actions in the criminal process make concrete the relations of trust and justice they express. To perform this function it is not necessary that they be the only actions which would do the job. The concrete entails also an element of the discretionary.

If we see this expressive and discretionary aspect of criminal procedure it may be possible to appreciate certain forms which while not inevitable seem elusively apt.

The adversary system working at its best, with good representation of the accused and no cynicism about the presumption of innocence, is an example of such a form. In the case where an accused denies his guilt there is of course the problem of resolving the dispute, and it is necessary to do so in a manner consistent with attitudes of trust and civic friendship before the fact is determined, while it is being determined, and after it has been determined — even if adversely. Ideally the adversary system seeks to do this. It puts the accuser and the accused on a systematically equal footing: that the accusation is brought by a more or less disinterested community representative against one who has every interest in denying his guilt is systematically ignored. The presumption of innocence has been criticized as unrealistic, and the image of a contest between two combatants has been thought irrational, but these criticisms are blind to the function of procedure as ritual, as an apt symbol of certain relations. Where a man denies his guilt he asserts not only that on the merits he has not broken trust with his fellows, but also that since he has not broken trust he deserves to be believed. This dilemma is the one discussed earlier. Criminal charges are very rarely self-verifying, so that what justice requires must itself be justly established.

When the accused is presented as an equal of the accuser his status as a member of the community is dramatically affirmed. Moreover there is dramatically affirmed the community's commitment to the principle of justice as superior to material advantage, for to forbear from disposing expeditiously of a person who is probably guilty and perhaps dangerous represents a real risk of material advantage. To be sure the safety of unquestionably innocent persons is risked, but it is the essence of the concept of trust that the person trusted have an interest in violating the trust and that the person who trusts accepts the risk that the trust be violated. In general it is a feature of morality that it involves risking the immorality of others, and that in a sense it is better to be just, to trust, to love, and be disappointed than to safeguard one's material interests without having entered into those relations. There is a positive value in having loved or trusted even if one has lost thereby.*

The point of this analysis is to show that, like certain specific substantive institutions, procedural institutions are not just means to an end. They are the concrete expressions of significant moral relations, and as such they have a value which is not adequately understood by analyzing them simply in terms of their consequences — unless, of course, the expression of the significant relation in the procedural action is taken as a kind of consequence. I have used the metaphor of drama, of dramatizing a principle. By this I do not mean to suggest that the adversary system is to be justified even in part because it makes in a dramatic, emphatic fashion a point which could be made otherwise as clearly but with less emphasis. The relations and principles which are dramatized in the adversary system are only actualized if they are relations in some action or the principles of some action. Their mere statement — dramatic or otherwise — is a statement of possible or potential relations and principles. Therefore in a sense every rational action is a dramatization of its principle; procedure, however, bears a particularly close affinity to drama and to ritual. An analysis very similar to this might be attempted for patriotic, religious, and other rituals, and — as Parsons' discussion of ritual very well shows

* The provision of the accused with counsel in every case is another dramatic gesture to be read in the context of what I have identified as the dilemma of criminal procedure and the principles of justice. It is by no means clear that justice alone requires the universal provision of counsel to accused persons. There are many cases where an unrepresented accused is perfectly capable of presenting his own defense, subject to the supervision of the court and the control of appellate tribunals. In such cases the provision of counsel must serve another function than that of assuring that a conviction occur only after a full hearing of the defense and on the proper standard of certainty. Consider a system where the judge not only decides whether a person who cannot hire a lawyer should be afforded one at public expense, but also whether a person who can afford a lawyer should be allowed to have one. Such a system might be based on the judgment that lawyers tend to protract and complicate proceedings and thus should not be allowed to participate "unnecessarily." Although a perfectly reasonable system and one that might well accord with justice, it would be a system that did not, as the adversary system does, dramatize the relation of moral equality between the accused and his accusers, and express a commitment to the principles constituting that relation. But this might perhaps be accomplished otherwise.

— the same mistakes of emphasis in explaining such rituals might thereby be uncovered and avoided. Indeed we might develop a general account of different kinds of rituals on these principles: religious, civic, purely aesthetic. In such an account legal procedure might well be classed as a moral ritual or a ritual of justice.

The Legal Profession

In tracing the aspect of law as a system of expressive relations some mention should be made of the legal profession. The previous examples — marriage and criminal procedure — have shown how substantive and procedural legal institutions have expressive aspects, define expressive relations. These relations may be viewed as well — following the Parsonian terminology — as systems of roles and statuses, such as that of husband, friend, citizen, accused. Further, one might speak of expressive roles. An expressive role is a role in an expressive relation, and an expressive relation is a relation between persons involved in an action which is an end in itself and which is constituted by a rational principle. My previous discussions may be taken as showing, then, that the roles of husband, accused, or citizen are in part expressive roles. I now wish to consider whether and how the various roles which are played by lawyers are also in part expressive roles.

Parsons proposes that a professional artistic performance is an example of an action system in which one group of participants, the audience, has an affective attitude to the action, and the other, the performers, possibly an attitude of affective neutrality. In my terms the relation is expressive for the audience but may be instrumental for the artists. As to the various professional roles of the lawyer, one might say that the lawyer as advocate, judge, adviser, or legislator is in the same position as the performing artist: his actions may be a way of earning a living, making a career, gaining prestige. One might say that the foregoing analysis of the expressive aspects of law applies only to the persons subject to substantive legal institutions or to the parties to a dispute, not to their lawyers.

Let us take the role of the lawyer defending an accused in criminal procedure. There is a large element of skill in the performance of this role, and therefore playing it successfully has the same satisfactions as the successful playing of a difficult and complicated game. This aspect of the lawyer's role is surely expressive. But such ends are not directly related to or symmetrical with the moral ends attributed to legal procedure in the preceding section. Such symmetry obtains, however, whenever the lawyer participates in the procedure in part at least out of a sense of justice. The most striking example of this is the defense lawyer who feels it is his duty to defend an unpopular accused. Often, this is not an enforceable duty, it is rather one that the lawyer takes up precisely because justice requires that he or someone like him defend the accused. In acceding to the accused's request that he act for him, the lawyer enters into precisely those relations of justice which it is the legal system's purpose to define. The lawyer, who accepts a client for the reason that a system of morality defines the role of accused and of his attorney, is making concrete and actual in his own relations to his client (and subsequently in his relations to the prosecutor, judge, and jury) a moral relation which is only potentially present in the abstract system of procedure defining the role he assumes.

A less striking and clear instance is that of the lawyer whose livelihood it is to take just this kind of case, and who therefore is not acting under any immediate moral constraint. A similar case is that of the judge who simply hears the cases that come before him. It is here that what Parsons calls affective neutrality would seem to characterize the lawyer's or the judge's role. But this is, I think, a mistake. First, the dramatic, self-sacrificing case is only a good test for showing on which principle the lawyer is acting, but it does not follow that one cannot act on this same principle when his other interests coincide with it. Second, any sharp differentiation in a particular case is bound to overlook the combinations and interpenetrations of principles in concrete life. It may seem that a lawyer in taking a particular case is acting in an entirely routine and businesslike way, but this ignores the whole complex of choices which put and maintain him in a position where acting on the principle of justice is *roughly* in line with his other interests.

One enters a profession which is systematically bound to certain aspects of a just system, and thenceforward one's advancement and prestige as a member of that profession will depend in part on how one fulfills its systematically defined goals. Thus a professional musician need play well not only because of his love of music but also because he has entered a profession which rewards playing well. In both cases — justice and music — the rewards will be accorded to those who best attain the expressive goals of the profession, — and in part at least the rewards themselves will be related to those goals. For instance, the reward may be simply recognition by respected colleagues or opportunities to undertake more challenging tasks. And again the character of a particular participant's motivation is tested by his willingness to attain these rewards without cheating, that is, within the system as defined. A concert pianist would not, I suppose, feel rewarded if the acclaim he won were procured by hiding a phonograph in his piano. So by entering into the legal profession and accepting its constraints a person accepts beforehand a system which should be defined partially by its commitment to the principle of justice. The pervasiveness of that professional commitment conceals the personal commitment to the principle of justice by a particular individual on a particular occasion. Thus, just as a criminal trial is a specific systematic concretization of the principle of justice, and the role of a judge or defense lawyer in the trial a necessary aspect of the justice of the whole, so the existence of the legal profession — with its structure of rewards and constraints — is another system which concretizes justice. At the point of convergence, which may be the activity of a defense lawyer at trial, these systems are actualized by a concrete rational action performed according to the principle of justice so mediated and specified.

There is one aspect of the lawyer's role that deserves special attention: his role as designer of institutions and procedures. The lawyer as designer does not work within institutions, but creates them for others by specifying the principle of justice for concrete circumstances. This is, of course, a matter of degree: in most such creative roles a lawyer works within the constraints of some higher-order process — for example, a legislative or committee process — just as in most performing roles there is room for considerable improvisation. In his role as creator of institutions and procedures a lawyer may adopt as the principle of his actions not just the principles of justice but other principles as well. If he is designing aspects of the institution of marriage, then the principle of love enters into his work. Working as a designer of structures also involves the disposition to create coherence and rationality among a multiplicity of ends — what might be called a higher-order aesthetics. Here the designer of social institutions is like a creative artist operating with and within the constraints of justice.

Law and Morals

The foregoing discussion of various aspects of legal institutions permits some larger conclusions relevant to the general subject of this essay.

First, there emerges an account of the relation of law to society, and of both to morals. There should be little doubt that law is nothing more than one — very widespread and important — form of social organization. The reason it has not been possible to come up with a definition setting forth the necessary and sufficient conditions for the application of the concept of law seems to me to be because such conditions do not exist. There are portions of the more inclusive concept of (explicit and implicit) social organization, which it is convenient and traditional to block off and call law, but it is a mistake to believe that this terminology of convenience coincides consistently with significant theoretical, logical, or even practical distinctions. On the practical level this is shown by the vagueness and purely traditional quality of the boundaries of competence of lawyers and legal scholars. On the theoretical level this is shown by the absurdity of affixing the term law to the ordinances of a village but not to the rules that govern the relations within a great university. Arguments can be made in terms of the monopoly of legitimate force, but they are evidently circular, and any attempt to break the circle requires the recognition of a variety of intersecting moral and social institutions which also "legitimate" the use of force. Similarly, theories based on the hierarchical structure of law, deriving from the ultimate authority of a sovereign, must either be formalized to the point where nothing corresponds to them or must be abandoned as simply false.

The account I have given in this chapter makes no claims whatever to identify law otherwise than nominalistically. I have suggested how specific institutions and types of institutions traditionally associated with the term law are related to and interpenetrated by other social institutions. The picture is that of several theoretically abstracted aspects of a single system of actions and relations.

Second, the foregoing account shows how social relations and social actions are — in all their sociability — ends in themselves, expressive, ultimately valued, and valuable. It shows how the various and differing forms of social relations and actions are not just the means to but the very expressions of values and ends that to be real must find some expression. This is shown by examples drawn from legal institutions. Legal institutions are after all a kind of social institution, legal relations and actions a kind of social relation and action. But have I not claimed too much? If the law is pervaded by expressive elements, if the law is not simply an instrument but also an end in itself, of what social institution cannot the same showing be made? Perhaps none. Economics would present an interesting test.

Third, this examination of specific social institutions illustrates a mode for evaluating and developing institutions that is appropriate to their nature as systems of expressive relations, as ends. The mode which I illustrate here (and of which the analysis of morality, justice, love and art in Part One are also examples) is not simply to aggregate values but to use them as the matter out of which a new value is created.

Chapter IX
Privacy:
A Rational Context

The concept of a rational context follows naturally from much of the foregoing discussion. A rational context may be defined as a context the awareness of which is part of the principle of a rational action. The term rational context thus introduces no new concept into the analysis, but simply isolates one aspect of many rational ends and actions. The usefulness of the term is simply that it draws attention to a common aspect of a variety of principles, actions, and ends. Privacy is such a rational context.

In this chapter I analyze the concept of privacy and attempt to show why it assumes such high significance in our system of values. There is a puzzle here, since we do not feel comfortable about asserting that privacy is intrinsically valuable, an end in itself — privacy is always for or in relation to something or someone. On the other hand, to view privacy as simply instrumental, as one way of getting other goods, seems unsatisfactory too. For we feel that there is a necessary quality, after all, to the importance we ascribe to privacy. This perplexity is displayed when we ask how privacy might be traded off against other values. We wish to ascribe to privacy more than an ordinary priority. My analysis attempts to show why we value privacy highly and why also we do not treat it as an end in itself. Briefly, my argument is that privacy provides the rational context for a number of our most significant ends, such as love, trust and friendship, respect and self-respect. Since it is a necessary element of those ends, it draws its significance from them. And yet since privacy is only an element of those ends, not the whole, we have not felt inclined to attribute to privacy ultimate significance. In general this analysis of privacy illustrates how the concepts in this essay can provide a rational account for deeply held moral values.

An Immodest Proposal: Electronic Monitoring

There are available today electronic devices to be worn on one's person which emit signals permitting one's exact location to be determined by a monitor some distance away. These devices are so small as to be entirely unobtrusive: other persons cannot tell that a subject is "wired," and even the subject himself — if he could forget the initial installation — need be no more aware of the device than of a small bandage. Moreover, existing technology can produce devices capable of monitoring not only a person's location, but other significant facts about him: his temperature, pulse rate, blood pressure, the alcoholic content of his blood, the sounds in his immediate environment — for example, what he says and what is said to him — and perhaps in the not too distant future even the pattern of his brain waves. The suggestion has been made, and is being actively investigated, that such devices might be employed in the surveillance of persons on probation or parole.

Probation leaves an offender at large in the community as an alternative to imprisonment, and parole is the release of an imprisoned person prior to the time that all justification for supervising him and limiting his liberty has expired. Typically, both probation and parole are granted subject to various restrictions. Most usually the probationer or parolee is not allowed to leave a prescribed area. Also common are restrictions on the kinds of places he may visit — bars, pool halls, brothels, and the like may be forbidden — the persons he may associate with, and the activities he may engage in. The most common restriction on activities is a prohibition on drinking, but sometimes probation and parole have been revoked for "immorality" — that is, intercourse with a person other than a spouse. There are also affirmative conditions, such as a requirement that the subject work regularly in an approved employment, maintain an approved residence, report regularly to correctional, social, or psychiatric personnel. Failure to abide by such conditions is thought to endanger the rehabilitation of the subject and to identify him as a poor risk.

Now the application of personal monitoring to probation and parole is obvious. Violations of any one of the conditions and restrictions could be uncovered immediately by devices using present technology or developments of it; by the same token, a wired subject assured of detection would be much more likely to obey. Although monitoring is admitted to be unusually intrusive, it is argued that this particular use of monitoring is entirely proper, since it justifies the release of persons who would otherwise remain in prison, and since surely there is little that is more intrusive and unprivate than a prison regime. Moreover, no one is obliged to submit to monitoring: an offender may decline and wait in prison until his sentence has expired or until he is judged a proper risk for parole even without monitoring. Proponents of monitoring suggest that seen in this way monitoring of offenders subject to supervision is no more offensive than the monitoring on an entirely voluntary basis of epileptics, diabetics, cardiac patients, and the like.

Much of the discussion about this and similar (though perhaps less futuristic) measures has proceeded in a fragmentary way to catalog the disadvantages they entail: the danger of the information falling into the wrong hands, the opportunity presented for harassment, the inevitable involvement of persons as to whom no basis for supervision exists, the use of the material monitored by the government for unauthorized purposes, the danger to political expression and association, and so on.

Such arguments are often sufficiently compelling, but situations may be envisaged where they are overridden. The monitoring case in some of its aspects is such a situation. And yet one often wants to say the invasion of privacy is wrong, intolerable, although each discrete objection can be met. The reason for this, I submit, is that privacy is much more than just a possible social technique for assuring this or that substantive interest. Such analyses of the value of privacy often lead to the conclusion that the various substantive interests may after all be protected as well by some other means, or that if they cannot be protected quite as well, still those other means will do, given the importance of our reasons for violating privacy. It is just because this instrumental analysis makes privacy so vulnerable that we feel impelled to assign to privacy some intrinsic significance. But to translate privacy to the level of an intrinsic value might seem more a way of cutting off analysis than of carrying it forward.

It is my thesis that privacy is not just one possible means among others to insure some other value, but that it is necessarily related to ends and relations of the most fundamental sort: respect, love, friendship, and trust. Privacy is not merely a good technique for furthering these fundamental relations; rather without privacy they are simply inconceivable. They require a context of privacy or the possibility of privacy for their existence. To make clear the necessity of privacy as a context for respect, love, friendship, and trust is to bring out also why a threat to privacy seems to threaten our very integrity as persons. To respect, love, trust, or feel affection for others and to regard ourselves as the objects of love, trust, and affection is at the heart of our notion of ourselves as persons among persons, and privacy is the necessary atmosphere for these attitudes and actions, as oxygen is for combustion.

Privacy and Personal Relations

Before going further, it is necessary to sharpen the intuitive concept of privacy. As a first approximation, privacy seems to be related to secrecy, to limiting the knowledge of others about oneself. This notion must be refined. It is not true, for instance, that the less that is known about us the more privacy we have. Privacy is not simply an absence of information about us in the minds of others; rather it is the control we have over information about ourselves.

To refer, for instance, to the privacy of a lonely man on a desert island would be to engage in irony. The person who enjoys privacy is able to grant or deny access to others. Even when one considers private situations into which outsiders could not possibly intrude, the context implies some alternative situation where the intrusion is possible. A man's house may be private, for instance, but that is because it is constructed — with doors, windows, window shades — to allow it to be made private, and because the law entitles a man to exclude unauthorized persons. And even the remote vacation hideaway is private just because one resorts to it in order — in part — to preclude access to unauthorized persons.

Privacy, thus, is control over knowledge about oneself. But it is not simply control over the quantity of information abroad; there are modulations in the quality of the knowledge as well. We may not mind that a person knows a general fact about us, and yet feel our privacy invaded if he knows the details. For instance, a casual acquaintance may comfortably know that I am sick, but it would violate my privacy if he knew the nature of the illness. Or a good friend may know what particular illness I am suffering from, but it would violate my privacy if he were actually to witness my suffering from some symptom which he must know is associated with the disease.

Privacy in its dimension of control over information is an aspect of personal liberty. Acts derive their meaning partly from their social context — from how many people know about them and what the knowledge consists of. For instance, a reproof administered out of the hearing of third persons may be an act of kindness, but if administered in public it becomes cruel and degrading. Thus if a man cannot be sure that third persons are not listening — if his privacy is not secure — he is denied the freedom to do what he regards as an act of kindness.

Besides giving us control over the context in which we act, privacy has a more defensive role in protecting our liberty. We may wish to do or say things not forbidden by the restraints of morality but nevertheless unpopular or unconventional. If we thought that our every word and deed were public, fear of disapproval or more tangible retaliation might keep us from doing or saying things which we would do or say if we could be sure of keeping them to ourselves or within a circle of those who we know approve or tolerate our tastes.

These reasons support the familiar arguments for the right of privacy. Yet they leave privacy with less security than we feel it deserves; they leave it vulnerable to arguments that a particular invasion of privacy will secure to us other kinds of liberty which more than compensate for what is lost. To present privacy, then, only as an aspect of or an aid to general liberty is to miss some of its most significant differentiating features. The value of control over information about ourselves is more nearly absolute than that. For privacy is the necessary context for relationships which we would hardly be human if we had to do without — the relationships of love, friendship, and trust.

Love and friendship, as analyzed in Chapter Five, involve the initial respect for the rights of others which morality requires of everyone. They further involve the voluntary and spontaneous relinquishment of something between friend and friend, lover and lover. The title to information about oneself conferred by privacy provides the necessary something. To be friends or lovers persons must be intimate to some degree with each other. Intimacy is the sharing of information about one's actions, beliefs or emotions which one does not share with all, and which one has the right not to share with anyone. By conferring this right, privacy creates the moral capital which we spend in friendship and love.

The entitlements of privacy are not just one kind of entitlement among many which a lover can surrender to show his love. Love or friendship can be partially expressed by the gift of other rights — gifts of property or of service. But these gifts, without the intimacy of shared private information, cannot alone constitute love or friendship. The man who is generous with his possessions, but not with himself, can hardly be a friend, nor — and this more clearly shows the necessity of privacy for love — can the man who, voluntarily or involuntarily, shares everything about himself with the world indiscriminately.

Privacy is essential to friendship and love in another respect besides providing what I call moral capital. The rights of privacy are among those basic entitlements which men must respect in each other; and mutual respect is the minimal precondition for love and friendship.

Privacy also provides the means for modulating those degrees of friendship which fall short of love. Few persons have the emotional resources to be on the most intimate terms with all their friends. Privacy grants the control over information which enables us to maintain degrees of intimacy. Thus even between friends the restraints of privacy apply; since friendship implies a voluntary relinquishment of private information, one will not wish to know what his friend or lover has not chosen to share with him. The rupture of this balance by a third party — the state perhaps — thrusting information concerning one friend upon another might well destroy the limited degree of intimacy the two have achieved.

Finally, there is a more extreme case where privacy serves not to save something which will be "spent" on a friend, but to keep it from all the world. There are thoughts whose expression to a friend or lover would be a hostile act, though the entertaining of them is completely consistent with friendship or love. That is because these thoughts, prior to being given expression, are mere unratified possibilities for action. Only by expressing them do we adopt them, choose them as part of ourselves, and draw them into our relations with others. Now a sophisticated person knows that a friend or lover must entertain thoughts which if expressed would be wounding, and so — it might be objected — why should he attach any significance to their actual expression? In a sense the objection is well taken. If it were possible to give expression to these thoughts and yet make clear to ourselves and to others that we do not thereby ratify them, adopt them as our own, it might be that in some relations, at least, another could be allowed complete access to us. But this possibility is not a very likely one. Thus the most complete form of privacy is perhaps also the most basic, since it is necessary not only to our freedom to define our relations with others but also to our freedom to define ourselves. To be deprived of this control over what we do and who we are is the ultimate assault on liberty, personality, and self-respect.

Trust is the attitude of expectation that another will behave according to the constraints of morality. Insofar as trust is only instrumental to the more convenient conduct of life, its purposes could be as well served by cheap and efficient surveillance of the person upon whom one depends. One does not trust machines or animals; one takes the fullest economically feasible precautions against their going wrong. Often, however, we choose to trust people where it would be safer to take precautions — to watch them or require a bond from them. This must be because, as I have already argued, we value the relation of trust for its own sake. It is one of those relations, less inspiring than love or friendship but also less tiring, through which we express our humanity.

There can be no trust where there is no possibility of error. More specifically, man cannot know that he is trusted unless he has a right to act without constant surveillance so that he knows he can betray the trust. Privacy confers that essential right. And since, as I have argued, trust in its fullest sense is reciprocal, the man who cannot be trusted cannot himself trust or learn to trust. Without privacy and the possibility of error which it protects that aspect of his humanity is denied to him.

The Concrete Recognition of Privacy

In concrete situations and actual societies, control over information about oneself, like control over one's bodily security or property, can only be relative and qualified. As is true for property or bodily security, the control over privacy must be limited by the rights of others. And as in the cases of property and bodily security, so too with privacy, the more one ventures into the outside, the more one pursues one's other interests with the aid of, in competition with, or even in the presence of others, the more one must risk invasions. As with property and personal security, it is the business of legal and social institutions to define and protect the right of privacy which emerges intact from the hurly-burly of social interactions. Now it would be absurd to argue that these concrete definitions and protections, differing as they do from society to society, are or should be strict derivations from general principles, the only legitimate variables being differing empirical circumstances (such as differing technologies or climatic conditions). The delineation of standards must be left to a political and social process the results of which will accord with justice if two conditions are met: (1) the process itself is just, that is, the interests of all are fairly represented; and (2) the outcome of the process protects basic dignity and provides moral capital for personal relations in the form of absolute title to at least some information about oneself.

The particular areas of life which are protected by privacy will be conventional at least in part, not only because they are the products of political processes, but also because of one of the reasons we value privacy. Insofar as privacy is regarded as moral capital for relations of love, friendship, and trust, there are situations where what kinds of information one is entitled to keep to oneself is not of the first importance. The important thing is that there be *some* information which is protected. Convention may quite properly rule in determining the particular areas which are private.

Convention plays another more important role in fostering privacy and the respect and esteem which it protects; it designates certain areas, intrinsically no more private than other areas, as symbolic of the whole institution of privacy, and thus deserving of protection beyond their particular importance. This apparently exaggerated respect for conventionally protected areas compensates for the inevitable fact that privacy is gravely compromised in any concrete social system: it is compromised by the inevitably and utterly just exercise of rights by others, it is compromised by the questionable but politically sanctioned exercise of rights by others, it is compromised by conduct which society does not condone but which it is unable or unwilling to forbid, and it is compromised by plainly wrongful invasions and aggressions. In all this there is a real danger that privacy might be crushed altogether, or, what would be as bad, that any venture outside the most limited area of activity would mean risking an almost total compromise of privacy.

Given these threats to privacy in general, social systems have given symbolic importance to certain conventionally designated areas of privacy. Thus in our culture the excretory functions are so shielded that situations in which this privacy is violated are experienced as extremely distressing, as detracting from one's dignity and self-esteem. Yet there does not seem to be any reason connected with the principles of respect, esteem, and the like why this would have to be so, and one can imagine other cultures in which it was not so, but where the same symbolic privacy was attached to, say, eating and drinking. There are other more subtly modulated symbolic areas of privacy, some of which merge into what I call substantive privacy (that is, areas where privacy does protect substantial interests). The very complex norms of privacy about matters of sex and health are good examples.

An excellent, very different sort of example of a contingent, symbolic recognition of an area of privacy as an expression of respect for personal integrity is the privilege against self-incrimination and the associated doctrines denying officials the power to compel other kinds of information without some explicit warrant. By according the privilege as fully as it does, our society affirms the extreme value of the individual's control over information about himself. To be sure, prying into a man's personal affairs by asking questions of others or by observing him is not prevented. Rather it is the point of the privilege that a man cannot be forced to make public information about himself. Thereby his sense of control over what others know of him is significantly enhanced, even if other sources of the same information exist. Without his cooperation, the other sources are necessarily incomplete, since he himself is the only ineluctable witness to his own present life, public or private, internal or manifest. And information about himself which others have to give out is in one sense information over which he has already relinquished control.

The privilege is contingent and symbolic. It is part of a whole structure of rules by which there is created an institution of privacy sufficient to the sense of respect, trust, and intimacy. It is contingent in that it cannot, I believe, be shown that some particular set of rules is necessary to the existence of such an institution of privacy. It is symbolic because the exercise of the privilege provides a striking expression of society's willingness to accept constraints on the pursuit of valid, perhaps vital, interests in order to recognize the right of privacy and the respect for the individual that privacy entails. Conversely, a proceeding in which compulsion is brought to bear on an individual to force him to make revelations about himself provides a striking and dramatic instance of a denial of title to control information about oneself, to control the picture we would have others have of us. In this sense such a procedure quite rightly seems profoundly humiliating. Nevertheless it is not clear to me that a system is unjust which sometimes allows such an imposition.

In calling attention to the symbolic aspect of some areas of privacy I do not mean to minimize their importance. On the contrary, they are highly significant as expressions of respect for others in a general situation where much of what we do to each other may signify a lack of respect or at least presents no occasion for expressing respect. That this is so is shown not so much on the occasions where these symbolic constraints are observed, for they are part of our system of expectations, but where they are violated. Not only does a person feel his standing is gravely compromised by such symbolic violations, but also those who wish to degrade and humiliate others often choose just such symbolic aggressions and invasions on the assumed though conventional area of privacy.

The Concept of Privacy Applied to the Problem of Monitoring

Let us return now to the concrete problem of electronic monitoring to see whether the foregoing elucidation of the concept of privacy will help to establish on firmer ground the intuitive objection that monitoring is an intolerable violation of privacy. Let us consider the more intrusive forms of monitoring where not only location but conversations and perhaps other data are monitored.

Obviously such a system of monitoring drastically curtails or eliminates altogether the power to control information about oneself. But, it might be said, this is not a significant objection if we assumed the monitored data will go only to authorized persons — probation or parole officers — and cannot be prejudicial so long as the subject of the monitoring is not violating the conditions under which he is allowed to be at liberty. This retort misses the importance of privacy as a context for all kinds of relations, from the most intense to the most casual. For all of these may require a context of some degree of intimacy, and intimacy is made impossible by monitoring.

It is worth being more precise about this notion of intimacy. Monitoring obviously presents vast opportunities for malice and misunderstanding on the part of authorized personnel. For that reason the subject has reason to be constantly apprehensive and inhibited in what he does. There is always an unseen audience, which is the more threatening because of the possibility that one may forget about it and let down his guard, as one would not with a visible audience. Even assuming the benevolence and understanding of the official audience, there are serious consequences to the fact that no degree of true intimacy is possible for the subject. Privacy is not, as we have seen, just a defensive right. It forms the necessary context for the intimate relations of love and friendship which give our lives much of whatever affirmative value they have. In the role of citizen or fellow worker, one need reveal himself to no greater extent than is necessary to display the attributes of competence and morality appropriate to those roles. In order to be a friend or lover one must reveal far more of himself. Yet where any intimate revelation may be heard by monitoring officials, it loses the quality of exclusive intimacy required of a gesture of love or friendship. Thus monitoring, in depriving one of privacy, destroys the possibility of bestowing the gift of intimacy, and makes impossible the essential dimension of love and friendship.

Monitoring similarly undermines the subject's capacity to enter into relations of trust. As I analyzed trust, it required the possibility of error on the part of the person trusted. The negation of trust is constant surveillance — such as monitoring — which minimizes the possibility of undetected default. The monitored parolee is denied the sense of self-respect inherent in being trusted by the government which has released him. More important, monitoring prevents the parolee from entering into true *relations* of trust with persons in the outside world. An employer, unaware of the monitoring, who entrusts a sum of money to the parolee cannot thereby grant him the sense of responsibility and autonomy which an unmonitored person in the same position would have. The parolee in a real — if special and ironical — sense, cannot be trusted.

Now let us consider the argument that however intrusive monitoring may seem, surely prison life is more so. In part, of course, this will be a matter of fact. It may be that a reasonably secure and well-run prison will allow prisoners occasions for conversation among themselves, with guards, or with visitors, which are quite private. Such a prison regime would in this respect be less intrusive than monitoring. Often prison regimes do not allow even this, and go far toward depriving a prisoner of any sense of privacy: if the cells have doors, these may be equipped with peepholes. But there is still an important difference between this kind of prison and monitoring: the prison environment is overtly, even punitively unprivate. The contexts for relations to others are obviously and drastically different from what they are on the "outside." This itself, it seems to me, protects the prisoner's human orientation where monitoring only assails it. If the prisoner has a reasonably developed capacity for love, trust, and friendship and has in fact experienced ties of this sort, he is likely to be strongly aware (at least for a time) that prison life is a drastically different context from the one in which he enjoyed those relations, and this awareness will militate against his confusing the kinds of relations that can obtain in a "total institution" like a prison with those of freer social settings on the outside.

Monitoring, by contrast, alters only in a subtle and unobtrusive way — though a significant one — the context for relations. The subject appears free to perform the same actions as others and to enter the same relations, but in fact an important element of autonomy, of control over one's environment, is missing: he cannot be private. A prisoner can adopt a stance of withdrawal, of hibernation as it were, and thus preserve his sense of privacy intact to a degree. A person subject to monitoring by virtue of being in a free environment, dealing with people who expect him to have certain responses, capacities, and dispositions, is forced to make at least a show of intimacy to the persons he works closely with, those who would be his friends, and so on. They expect these things of him, because he is assumed to have the capacity and disposition to enter into ordinary relations with them. Yet if he does — if, for instance, he enters into light banter with slight sexual overtones with the waitress at the diner where he eats regularly — he has been forced to violate his own integrity by revealing to his official monitors even so small an aspect of his private personality, the personality he wishes to reserve for persons toward whom he will make some gestures of intimacy and friendship. Theoretically, of course, a monitored parolee might adopt the same attitude of withdrawal that a prisoner does, but in fact that too would be a costly and degrading experience. He would be tempted, as in prison he would not be, to "give himself away" and to act like everyone else, since in every outward respect he seems like everyone else. Moreover, by withdrawing, the person subject to monitoring would risk seeming cold, unnatural, odd, inhuman, to the very people whose esteem and affection he craves. In prison the circumstances dictating a reserved and tentative facade are so apparent to all that adopting such a facade is no reflection on the prisoner's humanity.

The insidiousness of a technique which forces a man to betray himself in this humiliating way or else seem inhuman is compounded when one considers that the subject is also forced to betray others who may become intimate with him. Even persons in the overt oppressiveness of a prison do not labor under the burden of this double betrayal.

As against all of these considerations, there remains the argument that so long as monitoring depends on the consent of the subject, who feels it is preferable to prison, to close off this alternative in the name of a morality so intimately concerned with liberty is absurd. This argument may be decisive; I am not at all confident that the alternative of monitored release should be closed off. My analysis does show, I think, that it involves costs to the prisoner which are easily overlooked, that on inspection it is a less desirable alternative than might at first appear. Moreover, monitoring presents systematic dangers to potential subjects as a class. Its availability as a compromise between conditional release and continued imprisonment may lead officials who are in any doubt whether or not to trust a man on parole or probation to assuage their doubts by resorting to monitoring.

The seductions of monitored release disguise not only a cost to the subject but to society as well. The discussion of trust should make clear that unmonitored release is a very different experience from monitored release, and so the educational and rehabilitative effect of unmonitored release is also different. Unmonitored release affirms in a far more significant way the relations of trust between the convicted criminal and the society which he violated by his crime and which we should now be seeking to re-establish. But trust can only arise, as any parent knows, through the experience of being trusted.

Finally, it must be recognized that more limited monitoring — for instance where only the approximate location of the subject is revealed — lacks the offensive features of total monitoring, and is obviously preferable to prison.

The Role of Law

This evaluation of the proposal for electronic monitoring has depended on the general theoretical framework of this whole essay. It is worth noting the kind of evaluation that framework has permitted. Rather than inviting a fragmentation of the proposal into various pleasant and unpleasant elements and comparing the "net utility" of the proposal with its alternatives, we have been able to evaluate the total situation created by the proposal in another way. We have been able to see it as a system in which certain actions and relations, the pursuit of certain ends, are possible or impossible. Certain systems of actions, ends, and relations are possible or impossible in different social contexts. Moreover, the social context itself is a system of actions and relations. The social contexts created by monitoring and its alternatives, liberty or imprisonment, are thus evaluated by their conformity to a model system in which are instantiated the principles of morality, justice, friendship, and love. Such a model, which is used as a standard, is of course partially unspecified in that there is perhaps an infinite number of specific systems which conform to those principles. Now actual systems, as we have seen, may vary in respect to how other ends — for example, beauty, knowledge — may be pursued in them, and they may be extremely deficient in allowing for the pursuit of such ends. But those who design, propose, and administer social systems are first of all bound to make them conform to the model of morality and justice, for in so doing they express respect and even friendship — what might be called civic friendship — toward those implicated in the system. If designers and administrators fail to conform to this model, they fail to express that aspect of their humanity which makes them in turn fit subjects for the respect, friendship, and love of others.

Finally, a point should be noted about the relation between legal structures and other social structures in establishing a rational context such as privacy. This context is established in part by rules which guarantee to a person the claim to control certain areas, his home, perhaps his telephone communications, and so forth, and back this guarantee with enforceable sanctions. These norms are, of course, legal norms. Now these legal norms are incomprehensible without some understanding of what kind of a situation one seeks to establish with their aid. Without this understanding we cannot grasp their importance, the vector of development from them in changing circumstances (such as new technology), the consequences of abandoning them, and so on.* What is less obvious is

* It is a tenet of some forms of positivism that this statement is wrong insofar as it suggests that without appreciation of the context we have no understanding of the meaning of legal norms. This tenet seems wrong for a number of reasons. Legal norms are necessarily phrased in open-ended language, and their specification in actual circumstances needs the aid of the context — that is, the reason for the norm — to determine the appropriate application. This is obviously so when there are changed circumstances and recourse must be had to

that law is not just an instrument for bringing about a separately identifiable and significant social result: it is a part of the very situation that it helps to bring about. The concept of privacy requires, as we have seen, a sense of control and a justified, acknowledged power to control aspects of one's environment. In most developed societies the only way to give a person the full measure of both the sense and the fact of control is to give him a legal title to control. A legal right to control is control which is the least open to question and argument, it is the kind of control we are most serious about. Consider the analogy of the power of testamentary disposition. A testator is subject to all sorts of obligations, pressures, and arguments; certain things are so outrageous that he would scarcely dare to do them. Yet, within very broad limits, in the last analysis he is after all free to do the outrageous. And both the fact that certain dispositions are outrageous, immoral, wrong, and the fact that the testator is nevertheless free to make them are *together* important to define the autonomy and personality of a person in the particular situation. In the same way the public and ultimate character of law is part of the definition of the rational context of privacy.

---

the principle of the norm. It is less obvious in so-called "central" or "paradigm" cases, but I suggest this is less obvious only because the context is so unproblematic as to require no explicit attention.

Part Three
Life and Death

Chapter X
Life Plans
and Mortality

An examination of the ends men pursue leads finally to questions about life and death. Moralists have tended to consider these questions primarily by reference to the dramatic cases of suicide and murder, where a person deliberately seeks his own or another's death. I shall have little to say about these cases. I shall be concerned with the more pervasive questions: when is it rational to risk death for one's own ends, and when is it morally permissible to impose the risk of death on others? The issue of risk is pervasive because every choice affects, however slightly, the probability of death. For every choice there can always be found some alternative which is more — and some alternative which is less — likely to result in one's own death or the death of others. This is as true of social as of individual choice.

I am concerned with the question of risk of death not only because it is more pervasive than the traditional issues surrounding deliberate killing, but also because I find the notion of deliberate killing a difficult and elusive one. I am not sure how to define deliberate killing so as to set it off clearly from cases of imposing risk. It is thus also my purpose to clarify indirectly the issues surrounding deliberate killing by becoming as clear as I can about risk of death and leaving it to others to determine how — if at all — deliberate killing requires a different analysis.

I shall treat the question of when and to what degree an individual or society may impose the risk of death as a question of morality, justice, and fairness, as those concepts are elaborated in Chapter Four. I reject, therefore, a utilitarian analysis which would view this question as one of determining how individual and social choices may — in this respect, as in all respects — maximize the sum of utilities. I assume, instead, that life, or freedom from danger to life, is a good, which like all goods must be justly distributed, and in respect to which persons must deal fairly with each other. But the general concepts of morality, justice, and fairness cannot be applied to this special good — the good of life, or of safety — without regard to its special nature.

To accord with the general concepts of morality and justice, we must determine what constraints rational men would accept and impose on each other in respect to risk of death. It becomes necessary therefore to determine how rational, moral men view death and the risk of death, to determine whether the life plans and preference structures of rational men have any common general features respecting death. For if the concepts of rationality and the life plan do entail such common general features, then the constraints respecting risk of death that moral men would accept and impose on each other must reflect these common features. For this reason, in this chapter I shall inquire into the significance of mortality in the formation of individual life plans. If any constraints can be discovered about the relation of death to the life plans of the individual rational man, they will determine in part when and to what degree it is morally justified to impose risk of death on others. These latter questions I consider in the last two chapters of this book.

Before proceeding to determine whether rational life plans take the fact of death into account in some generally similar way — that is, whether the concept of the life plan entails some common general strategy in respect to death — it is necessary to say more about the life plan than was said in Chapter Six.

It has been established only that the life plan is the ordering that a rational person imposes as between his various ends. That ordering is a rational life plan if it is an ordering which the person in some sense implicitly or inchoately accepts as his own, in the way that he accepts his particular ends and values as his own. The forms of this ordering are determined in part by the particular ends a person has. Thus ends like love or justice entail certain long range patterns of behavior, structuring a large number of particular ends and actions into a system. These ends, however, entail only a partial ordering. But the life plan is determined also by the tendency or desire for system, coherence, or harmony as such. And some degree of this coherence, it was argued, is a necessary aspect of the concept of human personality. We must now proceed to define further what the characteristics and forms of those orderings may be.*

Life plans must deploy ends in time. Even apart from the fact of mortality, there are a limited number of things that a person can do and experience simultaneously. Moreover, as was shown to be the case with the elements constituting a particular end, the order in which items are arranged affects the nature of the total arrangements. So also the order in which ends are arranged affects the kind of life or life plan a person has. Mortality means that time is a scarce resource. Thus not only is it important how ends are arranged in time, but whether any and how much of the scarce resources of time are allocated to a particular end. A full account of the concept of the life plan would deal with the allocation of all other significant scarce resources as well. No such complete elaboration will be attempted, however. And indeed I shall not even present a full elaboration of life plans in respect to time, but rather I shall concentrate on those aspects of time which are specially related to death.

* It should be recalled that this inquiry is different from but in no way inconsistent with decision or utility theory, which also considers a rational man's ordering of his values — his preference structure. Utility theory takes a person's ends and their relative importance as given, and seeks only to describe or prescribe a degree of consistency in their ordering in terms of a limited number of very general rationality assumptions: — for example, transitivity of preferences, independence of irrelevant alternatives. Robert Nozick points out, "it may always be possible to produce a gimmicky real-valued function such that its maximization mirrors one's moral views in a particular area." And so also it may always be possible to present a life plan or a preference structure in terms of utility theory. The analysis in this essay, however, takes neither ends nor preference structures as given, but seeks to determine what are the ends and preference structures of rational moral persons.

Time and Identity

There is a conception of the future which is the corollary of the means-ends model developed in Chapter One. By this model the only relevant moment is the present moment, and choices are rationally made so as to maximize the value of the present moment. Future moments are relevant only as they bear on the valuation of the present, and the future can bear on the present only as the present contemplation of the future itself leads to the lesser or greater enjoyment of the present moment. On this model the only relevant question is the psychological one of how much present expectations as to the future affect present satisfaction. This question is often expressed in terms of the concepts of the time horizon or time discount. The discount is the rate at which present values would be traded for comparable future values, and it is assumed that the discounting of the future is more and more extreme as the future becomes more remote. The purpose of mapping the rate of discount is to determine at a particular moment what the optimum arrangement of values through time should be in order to maximize satisfactions.

Now it is inevitable that the time discount is determined in accordance with present tastes and preferences. If the sole relevance of the future is how our present contemplation of it bears on our present enjoyment, then weighting the discount more and more heavily against the future is intuitively appealing: we are presently distressed by the prospect of future pains and elated by the prospect of future pleasures with decreasing intensity as those pains and pleasures are more and more remote. The notion is closely akin to the utilitarian notion of sympathy, whereby we are affected by the pains and pleasures of others with decreasing intensity as those others are more remote from us in time, place, and similarity of circumstance.

But of course we do not consider our future and postpone present enjoyments only because we thereby alleviate a present pain; just as we do not govern our conduct toward others simply so as to produce in ourselves vicarious pleasures and pains by sympathy. On the contrary the concern we feel for our future selves, just as the sympathetic joys and sorrows we feel for others, are more the product of a sense of responsibility for these future selves and

for others. We do not provide for ourselves in the future only because we would be uneasy now if we did not. Rather we are uneasy
now about our future selves because we conceive of our future
selves as continuous with our present selves. In short, the sense of our
own continuity is an organizing principle of our emotions, of our
attitudes, of our beliefs, and the anxieties we feel are an expression,
and not the cause, of our sense of responsibility for our future
selves.

Of course the shape of persons' time discounts can be a matter
for empirical inquiry, but there is also a rational inquiry, a philosophical inquiry that can take place. According to the philosophical inquiry we may conclude that discounting the future as such is
irrational, or rational only on a conception of ourselves which
must be characterized as aberrant. If the satisfactions of a future
self are equally important as the satisfactions of a present self, then
of course it is irrational to discount the future in favor of the present. For what would it mean to somehow prefer one's present
self? Is my future self less important to me, less myself? To justify
a preference for the present one may refer to very important factors
such as the increasing uncertainty that a future self will be alive or
otherwise capable of enjoying a satisfaction, or perhaps uncertainties about my own future tastes and preferences. But these factors
are only quibbles with the simplifying assumption by which the
value which is or may be discounted is truly the same at both times,
present and future. (In due course it will be appropriate to drop
this simplifying assumption, and to examine the way in which uncertainties of various sorts and changes in tastes and preferences
are to be taken into account.) The other possibility is to disclaim
the identity of present and future selves. This disclaimer would
mean that in caring for myself and valuing what I value I may
yet care less or not at all for my future self, and this implies a lack
of sense of identity between my present and future self.

This lack of identity cannot be denied a priori. There is no a
priori reason why bodily continuity or continuity of memories and
the like should entail the identity of the selves so related in time.
Yet if we deny this identity, a whole complex of related concepts is
left without a foundation. Any end whose realization is extended
over time can no longer be the end of a person without a continuous identity over that time. Nor is it sufficient to assert that a

person may have such time-extended ends and emotions while lacking identity over time, if only we are prepared to treat the memories of the past and the anticipation of the future as part simply of the feelings, beliefs, and attitudes which define his present self. For what must then be explained is why memories of the past and anticipations of the future have the bearing they do on a present self. And any account of this bearing of past and future on the present entails a systematic connection between the experiences of past persons and the anticipated experiences of future persons, a connection that is expressed in terms of the concept of identity. In the end, we may conclude that the concept of identity is a way of accounting for the special relation a present self has to past and future selves. If we are considering persons who have certain ends, attitudes, emotions, and relations, then it follows that those persons at least must be considered in terms of continuity of time, as selves who persist over time.*

This analysis of identity over time also permits some conclusions about the senses in which a person may rationally be committed or constrained in his choices by his past self. There are three kinds of commitments to be considered. First, the past obviously constrains the present and the future in that past actions and choices influence the options subsequently open. One need only say as to this that not only is it inevitable, it is a necessary corollary of the proposition that it is rational in the present to so constrain the future.

Second, our past actions involve commitments to others, which it is rational and moral to honor. Promises are one example, the begetting of children another. This second kind of commitment is different from the first, in that it can be disregarded. In this sense, it is a true commitment while the first is not. This second commitment once again calls into question the issue of identity over time, for one might ask why am I bound to honor the commitments which a past self has made any more than I am bound to honor those of a stranger, a near relative, or a friend. The answer to this

* The form of the argument is analogous to that in Part One, where it was not asserted that the moral relations of one person to others could be demonstrated a priori, but only that persons conceived in a certain way, having certain ends, emotions, and so forth, must be conceived as related by certain principles to other persons. Here it is argued that they must be conceived as related to past and future selves according to the concept of identity.

issue of identity is, of course, similar to that made just previously. The identity of a present and past self cannot be demonstrated a priori. Rather this identity is a necessary implication of certain moral relations between persons. To refuse responsibility for the promises and actions of a prior self is to disable one's present self from entering into moral relations with others. To be a moral person today means among other things to accept responsibility for one's past self. And so we see here, as in regard to the future, that identity over time, now back into the past, is a concept that emerges from and is necessary to the kinds of ends, relations, and emotions that characterize us as human. That we must honor our past commitments, that our past binds us in this sense, is a part of this complex.

We are brought then to the third sense in which the past may commit us. Are we committed by our own life plans? Is a life plan, that is, the form of coherence we impose on our systems of ends, a commitment to oneself that is as exigent as our moral commitments to others? In short, are we free to change our minds? Even where no obligations to others are involved, the very notion of a life plan precludes too frequent and too rapid changes, for it is absurd to conceive of a life plan which always operates only for a short period immediately after its adoption. And a person who never carries out his plans will eventually cease to believe in himself as a person capable of coherence, just as a person who constantly betrays trust will in the end not be trusted. But is this a commitment? I believe that one cannot say more than this: *while* one adheres to one's plan, the present and the future are in fact committed by the past, but no more than the past is determined by the future. It is the plan itself which is the commitment. To make this point by the analogy to a piece of music, it is true only in a sense that subsequent moments of the music are determined by the prior moments. For the prior moments may as well be seen as determined by the subsequent one. In truth the whole piece is determined by the score, the plan, which is then expressed in time. To the plan itself there is no commitment, and the fact that in the past it was adopted and formulated is not a basis for commitment. Nor is it a basis for commitment that if one time and again fails to adhere to one's plans the conclusion becomes inescapable that such a person is incapable of coherence — that is just a fact about a particular sort of person. There is, then, no commitment to a life plan, but rather the life plan itself is a commitment to a certain course of action. The conclusion is that one is entirely free to change one's mind and change one's plan at any and every moment.

The coherent life plan is a peculiarly rational strategy for dealing with time. By treating time as a dimension in which various elements are arranged according to a plan, certain aspects, one might almost call them claims, of time are denied. For it is quite natural to look on time as a one-way stream, where the past is the cause of what follows, and the future is viewed as all effect. The life plan allows the future to determine the past as much as the past determines the future.

Change and Uncertainty

Apart from the most general fact that life plans must be realized in time, these plans have another temporal dimension: they must take into account the circumstance that persons change over time. As they acquire more knowledge and experience their judgments change; so also do their tastes and preferences. Moreover, judgments that were perfectly rational on the basis of guesses about the future must be revised on the basis of new information. The process of aging makes new factors relevant and old ones relevant in different ways. These factors may be divided roughly into three categories, but with no thought that the categories are completely distinct. First, there is the category of resolving uncertainties about external circumstances. A person is forced to plan with regard to external factors which at the time of choice are uncertain. As time passes these uncertainties may be resolved, and may be resolved otherwise than the actor had expected. The rationality of a new response is, of course, strictly entailed on the assumption that the individual's system of tastes and preferences has not changed.

Second, there are changes in the person himself; some of these like aging are more or less inevitable, others like debilitating illnesses or serious accidents are more uncertain. These differ from the first category because they affect a person's tastes and preferences in a way that external circumstances do not. The growth in skill and mastery which comes with maturity affects a person's notion of the range of satisfactions and relations open to him — being able to do more, he wants to do more. Similarly with the loss of physical vigor the range of what seems important is affected in various ways.

Third, there is the circumstance that persons do, and — depending on the degree of the change — do quite often, change their life plans. This third circumstance obviously is closely related to the second, but still should be distinguished from it so far as possible, even if the distinction will only be a matter of degree. In the second category the change in tastes and preferences is accounted for in the life plan. Thus a rational person may arrange his life so as to allow him to utilize fully the potentialities of each stage of his life cycle. He will understand that as a youth he may desire adventure while his tastes as an old man may be for tranquillity and comfort, and so he might channel his youthful adventuresomeness into means that may yield the security he will desire in his old age. Education and career plans often show this kind of continuity and "sympathy" for one's future self. This approach thus seeks to subserve within the master plan even radical changes of taste and preferences. It asserts the continuity of the person through such changes, and, as it were, subordinates changing taste and preferences to the master taste or master preference which is the rational life plan.

The third sort of change bespeaks a radical discontinuity in the life plan. This discontinuity can be manifested in a number of ways. A person may proceed to act upon a new plan, dishonoring the commitments implicit in the old one. He may feel resentment and bitterness about constraints which he has imposed on himself pursuant to an old life plan. He may, as in the case of persons who become insane or amnesiac, adopt a new life plan without any sense of the old life plan which is being abandoned.

The conception of a rational life plan has implications for the responses that persons having such a plan make to the facts of the human life cycle. In general the most significant fact about the life cycle is that it entails changes of various sorts, and the issue might be put as the attitude toward change entailed by the conception of the rational life plan. The attitudes entailed by this conception of rational coherence is that of internalizing within the plan the external constraints upon it. In this way the obvious irrationality of planning as if nothing would change when it is known many things will change is avoided. Further, major impinging circumstances are accepted not only as limitations but as correspondingly major elements in the coherent system of the plan.

The question arises what is a rational strategy to adopt toward the circumstance that changes in life plans are always possible. This question is susceptible of a logical argument, for whatever strategy is adopted — whether of closedness or openness, that is, of making commitments, making changes harder in the future, or of keeping options open — is a strategy to control the future, and thus a kind of life plan. Further, a strategy of complete openness is logically impossible. While a strategy of selective openness — keeping certain kinds of options open — implies a judgment about the various options at various stages in the life cycle. But this is the kind of judgment of which a life plan consists. Finally, a bias in favor of openness can only mean a bias in favor of the widest range of choices at subsequent times, but at some point it becomes irrational not to make the choices, trying only always to keep options open. And if one decides which choices should be made at which times, which options closed at which points, this is in fact a very detailed life plan with very sharp constraints and commitments.

Thus the concept of a life plan means that it is not possible to make systematic provisions for changes in life plans, for any such provisions makes the subsequent change not a change in the life plan but rather a step in accordance with a more or less detailed life plan already adopted. Putting this point differently, one might say there is no way to avoid the total wrench which a true change in life plan means for a rational person.

It does not follow at all from the foregoing that provisions cannot be made for the other two aspects of the life cycles set out above, change in external circumstances and change in tastes, preferences, capacities, and the like. On the contrary a rational life plan must make provision for these things. It must make provision for changes in tastes and preferences even though tastes and preferences provide the perspective from which life plans are chosen. For the life plan is correlative with the sense of personal identity, and, just as that identity, is perceived to persist in spite of such changes. As was said above, the life plan becomes a kind of master taste or master preference. Now exactly what weight should be given to tastes and preferences we do not now have is another question. The question is analogous to the question of the weight we should give to the satisfactions of future selves. In general in both cases the answer, which I shall elaborate below, is to arrange the satisfactions over time according to the plan of a coherent whole.

We must also consider the effect on this scheme of the circumstance that ends are pursued not only in time and in changing conditions, but also under conditions of uncertainty. Not only do we know that there will be changes over time, and we must provide for them, but also we know that we are uncertain what those changes will be.

It will seem that what must be done is to conceive of the life plan not just as providing a plan incorporating change and prescribing a response to change, but also as incorporating a plan (perhaps better called a strategy) prescribing alternative responses to depend on which of two or more uncertain events take place. This entails the possibly surprising conclusion that there is no such thing as failure in a life plan. For just as a life plan succeeds if it properly orders circumstances as they are, so also it succeeds if it properly estimates and makes provision for uncertainty. To be sure a person will regret that one rather than another uncertain outcome eventuates, but this regret is not in principle different from the regret that the life plan must be formulated under known and inevitable external constraints. Thus one might say that a life plan incorporates and overcomes uncertainty just as it incorporates and overcomes time and change. True failure comes when one must recognize either that he has not been faithful to his life plan, or that he has chosen what now seems the wrong life plan.

This response to uncertainty is related to what has been said about time and change in another way. The concept of a coherent life plan as correlative to the notions of a coherent personality, and the concept of responsibility for past and future as well as present selves, are significant also in respect to uncertainty. For what has been said about responsibility and certainty over time and through change holds as well for persistence and responsibility in the face of uncertain change. A person's sense of his own continuity and his continuity as a single coherent person for others depends on his having a life plan, which accounts for and absorbs uncertainty, a life plan which does not change even though circumstances change, and which is certain although circumstances are uncertain. Of course, it should be plain that a consistent life plan does not entail an unchanged response to changing circumstances.

Death

All life plans are bounded: this is the most obvious relation of death to the structure of human life plans. A plan for an infinitely long series might well have a very different form from one which is necessarily bounded. The influence of mortality on life plans is so pervasive that it is indeed hard to think of plans for infinitely long series of events. Examples might be plans of social units, such as nations and churches, with a time extension which, while not clearly infinite, usually has no clear end point.* In general we might say that it is a feature of rational life plans that they have a beginning and end.

A further general point, which is perhaps quite obvious but needs to be made explicit, is that the bounded character of life plans must be accepted and used. As is the case with every inevitable constraint on life plans, regrets about these necessary limitations are out of place. It is the function of rational life plans to order the possibilities of human life, and these possibilities are defined by, among other things, the fact of mortality. This is part of the raw material, the substance, which the life plan must order.

Any attempt to develop an account of the significance of life and death choices in the organic structures of life plans must, however, be grounded in a general account of the conception of life plans and of the role that various elements play in them. The conception of life plans was put forward in Chapter Six, in which the general end of coherence was developed. The issue of death shows the need for a greater elaboration of this conception in many directions. Death is the end of all choice, of all action and, at least as far as this world goes, all possibilities. Moreover, death is inevitable and grows more likely with the passage of time, other things being equal. These circumstances about death — or about life, if you will

---

* The example is troublesome since it might be said that the time plan of a nation is really the plan of its then living citizens, and therefore no different in this regard from the life plan of individual persons.

— immediately suggest two limiting cases of life projects: one is instant and immediate death at the first possible moment of choice (let us call this the null plan); and the other is the prolongation of life by all means at any cost. One may disregard both for closely related reasons. There is no significant loss of generality if the concept of rational person is limited to those creatures who have life plans with some content, that is, whose life plan is not simply to realize no possibilities whatever during their lives. So also one may exclude — though perhaps less uncontroversially — those who would accept only ends which maximize the chance of the longest possible life, and who choose whatever they choose for that sole end. Put colloquially it might be said that we are considering as rational persons only those whose life plans involve some use of their lives.

In general, then, life plans are formulated not only against the necessary background of temporal sequence, but against the necessary background of what may be called the human life cycle. Thus we may conclude at this most general level that the fact of mortality gives to life a very specific quality. Life is something which must be used up, and therefore the potentialities within it must in some sense be economized. Every moment of life is valuable, and every capacity is valuable because of death (although for other reasons too). Once used up or passed by it is irrevocably past. Life is a scarce resource. In a rather special, perhaps strained sense, then, death has a positive effect on life plans. It makes life precious.

There is another closely related sense in which death is a positive element of life plans. By being willing to risk death — or even confront the certainty of death — for the sake of a particular end, we can show the value which this goal has for us, we can assign it that value by paying the price of life itself for it. It should be clear by now that I do not mean that there is something artificial about such a gesture, that it is "for show," but rather that death is a resource — like the edge of a painting, the end of a piece of music, the final couplet of a poem — which can be used to give a special meaning to the other elements in the total ensemble that are placed in relation to it. It is not just that one "proves" the sincerity of his love for another by facing death for that person; facing death for another *is* a manifestation of love.

A further related way in which death becomes a resource in life plans is perhaps more familiar and less noble. Death, in a sense, allows one to cut one's losses. It is possible to imagine cases where a person would prefer death to some other consequences as a cost of pursuing an end. Thus he might perform an act of heroism entailing certain death, where he might not perform that act if the cost were a life with drastically diminished possibilities: a life as an invalid, or as a prisoner. The fact of death, in such cases, might be seen as a positive advantage and inducement. Death thus allows us to do things we would not do otherwise.

Now it may be objected that there is a certain absurdity about viewing death as a factor giving life plans their distinctive form. In particular, Sartre has objected to the views put forward in the preceding pages. He argues that since death is the end of the conscious person whose life plan is thus "completed," the life plan ought to be said to cease to be that person's just when it is completed. In other words, whatever it is that death completes, it cannot be my life plan as my plan, but if at all only as it is viewed by others, who alone still exist to respond to the events and impressions constituting the completed life plan. Since death spells the end of a particular person, nothing about death, according to Sartre's objection, can be of significance to that particular person.

This objection is unacceptable, for if it were taken seriously a rational person would treat his death as a wholly extraneous, irrelevant matter, which is of no concern to him whatever. And on this assumption, persons should not rationally be concerned with what takes place after their death; they should, for instance, not be concerned with the welfare of future generations. Nor should they be concerned to arrange their lives so that obligations they presently have might be fulfilled after their deaths. Also on this assumption, the riskiness of a venture cannot rationally be taken into account; it is not rational to prefer safer to riskier alternatives or to prefer quick death to a life of severe and burdensome incapacity. Yet people do take death into account in all of these ways, and indeed, it is hard to know what a system of rational decision would look like that systematically excluded the factor of the agent's death from consideration.

It may be that in arguing against the notion of death as a resolving chord Sartre is objecting to a certain sentimentality and imprecision inherent in that notion. Admittedly in saying that death lends form to life plans, it is not proper to suggest that the actor expects to contemplate the completed whole after death, as he might a completed work of art. But the form of a life plan is experienced while it is being lived and not necessarily when it is completed. Indeed the subsequent contemplation of *any* completed rational action is not the end of that action; rather its end is the successful performance itself.

Another objection which Sartre makes touches this argument. He is much impressed by the uncertainty of death, and from this argues that to conceive projects as deriving their form in part from the boundary of death is irrational. If one could be sure of death from old age or from some other circumstance at even an approximately determinate time, it would make some sense, he concedes, to shape one's projects accordingly, and to conceive of them as shaped by this, but because the time of death cannot be anticipated, one may be unable to complete his projects or may outlive them. This objection too is inconclusive. The concept of a life plan is adequate to take account of uncertainty, and indeed a fully rational life plan includes a strategy for coping with the full range of uncertainties. Thus, if Sartre's objection is to have any force it is necessary for him to show that the uncertainties associated with death are in some way different from other uncertainties which must be taken into account in life plans. And he does not do this. What he does show is that death has a peculiar significance for life plans, which our present discussion does not deny. The task, therefore, of a rational person is to formulate a life plan which takes this limiting factor into account and does so in terms of the probabilities associated with its uncertain occurrence.

The Shape of the Life Plan

Thetis, the mother of Achilles, was allowed to choose for her son between the short, glorious life of a hero and a life of long, obscure serenity as a shepherd. The choice, I would say, was between two life plans, two different ways of using up life. What can we say, now that the relevance of time, change, uncertainty, and death have been canvassed, about the shape of life plans, about the ways in which life is used up and those general constraints acknowledged by rational men? Is the choice for Achilles one that confronts all men in some form, or is one particular solution to be preferred a priori?

I have said that the concept of personal identity over time entails a veto on discounting the future as such: other things being equal, we may not prefer a present to a future end just because it is a present end. So also we may not prefer the future because it is the future. In short, while the present is a trustee for the future it is not the future's slave. This does not mean, however, that we may not prefer the present to the future where the present is more certain, or that we may not prefer to postpone present gratifications for future weightier ends. These further, open questions must be resolved to the extent that we seek a conception of the shape of life plans over time.

The issue of intertemporal ordering is strikingly reminiscent of the questions surrounding interpersonal fairness. Utilitarians assert that maximizing the sum (or the average) of utilities over the relevant population does give force to the value of equality, if a unit of pleasure (whatever that is) from one person is accorded exactly the same weight as a unit of pleasure from any other person. The Kantian-Rawlsian conception of justice, by contrast, demands a more radical recognition of equality in that there must be equality (or a version of it) in the actual distribution of benefits and burdens. On this latter view not only the sum of benefits and burdens matters, but also the way in which it is distributed.

This analogy to the interpersonal case forces us to consider whether to press for equal treatment of all periods — present and future — and whether that equality is satisfied by a utilitarian type rule. Such a rule in the intertemporal case would hold that a rational life plan dealt "fairly" with all life periods by maximizing the sum of utilities over a lifetime, while treating utilities, from whatever life period they come, as equal. A complete analogy to the Kantian-Rawlsian position would require that each life period be treated equally (or that if one life period is to be less well off, still that worst-off life period must be better off than on any alternative life plan).

Now a strict application of the Kantian-Rawlsian rule in the intertemporal case is absurd. It would mean dividing one's life into an infinite series of points, no one of which could be denied any amount of an equal share of gratification and fulfillment for the sake of a greater gratification at some other time. We would be disabled both from saving now for the future and from spending now and paying in the future. This accords neither with common sense nor with the thesis of Part One that many ends are time-extended, for it would be impossible to say to which one of this infinity of selves a particular time-extended end belongs.

The Kantian-Rawlsian rule of interpersonal justice and its rejection of utilitarianism do raise an important issue for the life plan, for the problem of intertemporal ordering: Is the way in which the realization of ends is distributed over time of independent significance in the intertemporal case (as the Kantian-Rawlsian rule says the shape of the distribution is of independent significance in the interpersonal case)? The intuitive answer is affirmative. It would seem that persons are not indifferent as between a lifetime in which all satisfactions are bunched in one period, the rest being dull and empty, and a lifetime in which one enjoys significant satisfactions in many periods of one's life. It is possible, of course, to account for a preference for the latter distribution by some notion of decreasing marginal utility of satisfactions when they bunch up together, or by reference to pains such as the pain of boredom.

Such arguments are probably quite valid, but it is not clear that arguments in that form can account fully for the preferred distribution over a lifetime. More important, notions such as declining marginal utility in life periods that are crowded with satisfactions, or the pain of tedium in empty periods, do not really explain why we prefer a particular distribution over a lifetime. They do not explain a preferred form of life plan because they are just another way of stating that a distribution of a particular form is preferred. Boredom as a pain, for instance, just means that we do not like empty life periods (that we prefer a life plan that avoids such empty periods). To recognize such a pain or disutility means that in addition to our preferences and priorities regarding particular ends, we also have preferences about the way in which these ends are distributed over life. And to this extent the analogy to the Rawlsian concept of justice is valid: the rational man not only has ends and a system of priorities in respect to those ends, he also cares what the shape of his life plan is, how these ends are deployed in time.*

What shape — or shapes — then will the life plan have? I would begin by applying the concepts of Chapter Six to this problem. The life plan must be coherent in several ways. It must reflect the coherence implicit in the major ends and relations. It must permit and exhibit love for other persons. Ends and priorities must be arranged in certain ways if there is to be the development and exercise of competence in matters of knowledge and art. But the life plan also must exhibit coherence and rationality as ends in themselves.

This last means that there is a disposition to order one's life and ends into a coherent whole, a system where the parts are chosen and arranged so as to display the greatest possible richness and unity. It means that ends are chosen and arranged in such a way that they contribute to each other and interrelate in more complex systems. To the greatest extent possible, actions should become ends in themselves, which are related to other ends not as means but as independently valuable units which are also constituent parts of larger ends, rather than simply means to the attainment of later ends. If one imagines actions at times T_1, T_2 ... T_n, then so far as possible the whole series should be conceivable as an integrated unit, the elements of which are related as part to whole rather than as means to end. In this way the action at T_1 attains a value which it would not have simply as a means to the end at T_n, nor even as an action which was simply an end in itself. Thus, for instance, an activity such as learning a subject is not to be viewed simply as a means to the attainment of the capacity which this learning brings. Rather learning is itself the exercise of a capacity, and further the series consisting of learning and then the exercise of a skill learned may be viewed as a single coherent whole. Training to do X and then doing X are drawn together, with the result that training to do X attains a significance commensurate to that of doing X.

In this way the ordering of the life plan not only attains the greatest richness in coherence, but it gives some meaning as well

---

* Once again I insist that this more complicated structure, whatever it turns out to be, can be presented in a way that is consistent with utility theory. I doubt, however, whether such a presentation is helpful or interesting.

to the notion that my present self and my future selves are all equal parts of me, and all equally the concern of my life plan. For to the extent that an activity at T_i is not regarded simply as a means to an end at T_j, and activities at both times attain value by virtue of being constituent parts of a larger end, then the self at T_i is not sacrificed to the self at T_j, and vice versa. Whether each is given *equal* weight cannot be said. Neither self, however, is a means alone (to paraphrase Kant), but is an end as well.

The repertoire of human ends and capacities may be seen as the material out of which a rational person fashions a coherent and rich life plan, and thereby chooses a self. The constraints on the shapes of the life plan, therefore, derive from the disposition to coherence as such, which I have already discussed, but they derive as well from the constraints implicit in the "raw materials" of the life plan. Such raw material includes the character of human relations like those of love and trust, or ends like knowledge, art, and the instinctual ends, and the various natural facts about men: that they require food, that they are mortal, that they have certain senses, and so on. In short we may say that the life plan is constrained by natural facts about man, like the facts of the life cycle and mortality, and by his dispositions and capacities.

Some ends and capacities are more or less specific to a particular stage in the life cycle. Ends related to play of a certain sort are associated with childhood, those associated with learning of skills pertain to earlier stages than those associated with the exercise of skills, reproduction is specific to only a segment of the life cycle, and ends requiring physical stamina and strength tend also to be thus localized. Finally there are — as will be argued in Chapter Twelve — certain ends and capacities which are related directly to the end of the life cycle, the period before death.

Other ends are serial but not local. Learning a skill must precede exercising it. First love may come at any of a number of points in the life cycle but must precede second love. Facing a near certainty of death may occur at any point in the life cycle, but it is unlikely to occur more than once and is likely to be the last experience of the person.

Other potentialities exist constantly or at many points in large segments of a lifetime, as for instance relations of love, friendship, and trust. There are varying possibilities for overlap in ends and capacities. Normally a person will be engaged in realizing several at least long-term capacities at the same time. The more narrowly conceived the action the more exclusively it will occupy the time segment allotted to it. A person may learn a subject and conduct a love affair at the same time, but not read a book and make love at the same time.

These general features of the life cycle must be incorporated into the coherent system of the life plan. This additional set of constraints on the life plan means that the determination of the end and capacity appropriate to a particular point in the life cycle must be a function not just of the significance of that end — however determined — nor a function just of its compatibility with a rich life in future periods. It is also to an important degree a function of the extent to which it specifically furthers subsequent ends and capacities. Thus let us take three ends competing for time T_i: E_1, E_2, and E_3. E_1 involves more risks than does E_2 for the completion of ends at T_j. E_2 is safer; there is less chance of getting killed or incapacitated related to its pursuit. Other things being equal it seems that E_2 is to be preferred. But E_3, while it is as dangerous as E_1 or more dangerous, has the quality that if it succeeds it will make possible the further pursuit of important ends at T_j. I would argue that E_3 though more dangerous than E_1 or E_2 is the preferred alternative because of its possible carry-over to a later period. This preference expresses not only the value of coherence in a life plan; it expresses also a preference for ends — though risky — which can be related to other portions of the life cycle. Thus education is a valuable end not just because it realizes a present capacity, nor just because it allows the exercise of capacities at a later stage, but for the additional reason that it does both at once. The combination is more valuable than its constituent parts. Thus also the sexual capacities are significant in that they bring into being and support relations — between husband and wife and between parent and child — which extend into periods of the life cycle where those capacities may have a diminished importance.

The significance of the moral relations — justice, love, trust — also determines the shape of the life plan, the risks one will take, what one will die for. The capacity to enter into these moral relations is not specific to any particular stage in the life cycle, although the substance of these relations may vary with the progress of one's own life cycle and of the life cycles of those one is related to. The conception of the moral relations put forward in Part One suggests that it is rational to adopt a weighting in one's life plan that gives a considerable preference to the realization of a present capacity for love as against possible future periods of life that would be jeopardized by that realization.

The capacity for love is realized in actions which take as their principle unobliged generosity, so that to fail to seize the appropriate occasions for such acts is to leave the capacity unrealized. The conceptions of love and friendship I have developed entail, for instance, that there will be situations in which a large sacrifice may be appropriate.

An example would be where a person must risk his future life so as to be able to develop relations of love and friendship at all. Such situations at first might seem quite rare — limited to prisoners of war and persons in other extreme conditions — but on reflection it appears that the case in less dramatic form is common, indeed universal. For we all might arrange to live far more secure lives, did we not wish to hold ourselves open to the claims and complications which relations of love and friendship involve. And this implies the solution in the case where the sacrifice is made not to create a relation but because of a relation of love and friendship that already exists. To let the occasion for sacrifice pass by, even for the sake of a longer life and further relations of love, will not do. To love is to make the sacrifice, so that a person who fails to make this sacrifice in order that he may live and love in the future is in fact thwarting the present relation and — unless he repents and reforms, that is, changes his plan and ordering — he will not love in the future either.

The foregoing shows how elusive is the question raised above about the boundaries of a capacity or a period in the life cycle. Surely one need not at every moment be pursuing relations of love and friendships and sacrificing all other ends to them. But how long a period deprived of these relations are we talking about, an hour, a day, a week, or a year? Once again the point can only be made by reference to the notion of coherence. A man who works hard and long at a given task in part to help support his family pursues several complementary ends in the same time period.

Friends may value each other in part because of the capacities each has and because of the disposition each has to realize those capacities. For this reason both ends and life cycle periods are only partly determined by external constraints. To a certain extent the shape of these units is a function of the particular life plan.

The final constraint on the shape of life plans is the fact of death. Death is that fact about life that makes our decisions peculiarly poignant and peculiarly urgent. As I have suggested, if we are to incorporate all that is significant about our lives into the life plan, it behooves us to make creative use as well of the fact of death. Relating this to the conception of coherence and richness as the forms of rationality in a life plan, we can see how the mere prolongation of life is not consistent with these general criteria. Life is to be used up in the best possible way. This means that a rational life plan will not sacrifice significant ends for the sake of prolongation of life as such, but only for life of which some use can be made. It is often not worth many sacrifices to assure oneself of living to a great old age, for there are fewer capacities (and a risk of almost no capacities) associated with great old age. Beyond this commonplace, we can see also why a shorter, more concentrated life (concentrated in terms of the realization of capacities) is seen as the equivalent of a longer life with the same attainments. Given this equivalence and given also the frequent circumstance that the longer life can only be attained by forgoing certain risks and thus the opportunity of realizing some ends, we can see why the Achilles option is a rational one.

Another concrete feature of life plans that emerges is the stronger (though perhaps more dubious) one that one prefers time T_i to T_j even if there are ends proper to both, because a life plan of the form (1) T_1, T_2 . . . T_i, with each period having a realized end associated to it, is preferable to a plan of the form (2) T_1, T_2 . . . T_i, T_j, where T_i is a blank — it is deprived of its proper end or any significant end — even though form 2 is a longer life. The conclusion expresses the notion that a life plan is not only a way of maximizing the number of capacities realized but of giving a richness and realization to each period of life.*

* This argument does not conflict with the basic premise that it is irrational to discount the future just because it is the future. The reason for the discount I argue for here is that the person at T_i is risking life itself at T_j. This is not

This discounting of the future is stated only as a discount and not as an absolute preference for the present. If the preference were absolute it would mean that any risk at all of death and therefore of loss of $T_j \ldots T_n$ would be justified for the sake of T_i. This seems too strong in two ways: there may be a large number of fruitful subsequent periods sacrificed (T_j, $T_k \ldots T_n$) so that by an absolute rule one would sacrifice no matter how much future life to preserve a prior capacity and end. And also an absolute rule might require that a great risk be taken in respect to subsequent ends to avert a small risk of loss to a prior end or capacity. For these reasons the preference for the prior time period can only be expressed as a trade-off weighted in favor of the prior period and its ends.

But finally we simply must choose. We must choose the shape of our life plans, and thus who we are. To be fully human we must be moral, we must love and trust, and these things define partially the shape of our life plans — as do the other major ends, and the general disposition to make of our lives rich and coherent wholes. But the choices all this leaves open are not only infinite, but highly varied. There is great variety among moral, loving, fully coherent human persons. The variety of life styles, of ways in which moral and coherent persons choose to use up their lives, correlates exactly with the variety of life plans and attitudes to death. In the end we are all faced with the choice Thetis made for Achilles.

The Concept of the Risk Budget

The previous section has shown in a general way how ends are ordered over time and trade-offs set between ends at various points in the life plan. I have not sought to give an account of rational choice in general, but rather only of choice in respect to death and risk of death. In this regard a person's life plan establishes the magnitudes of risk which he will accept for his various ends at various times in his life. Though I have been at pains to argue that the relative significance of particular ends and periods cannot be established by some simple measure such as pleasure or utility, it is true that once the plan is established — however that is done

a discounting of the future as such, but only a recognition of the fact that one can be alive at T_1 and dead at T_j, but not the other way round.

— each end and life period will end up being "worth" some risk of death. And it is this risk of death appropriate to each unit as well as to the plan as a whole, which makes up what I shall call the person's risk budget. The life plan will imply other budgets too — of time, money, energy, and the like. Thus the allocations by the risk budget should not be taken to imply a measure of their overall worth relative to each other. A particular unit may be worth more risk of death, but perhaps worth less of some other scarce life resource.

The notion of the risk budget is a probabilistic one. A person in making a life plan and establishing a risk budget does not choose the moment at which he will die. He chooses levels of risk. This does, to be sure, imply something about the moment when he shall die. Again the legend of Achilles illustrates the point. Thetis may be thought of as choosing a life plan and thus a concomitant risk budget for her son — the life plan of a hero involving a risk budget with large allocations to early stages in the life cycle where the capacities of a warrior-hero are located. But this — in a nonlegendary world — is to choose risks not certainties. It is to choose a life plan and risk budget by which one stands an unusually high risk of not living past, say, twenty-five. But one does not thereby — except in rare instances — choose to die at twenty-five. As to a large number of persons choosing this type of risk budget the probability distributions will, however, cluster around that age. Indeed, life insurance companies might write insurance policies in relation to life plans — heroes would pay high premiums through age thirty, and then the premiums would decrease.

If many persons in a society choose roughly similar risk budgets because their life plans are similar (and this because capacities and other constraints are similar), then there should emerge for that society a notion of the "average" life expectancy. This life expectancy would be more than just the average in fact in that society; it would be an average implied by similarities in the risk budgets of the life plans that were being chosen. I would venture a guess that most middle class Americans have roughly similar risk budgets. It may be that in other societies there is less homogeneity, and even apart from external constraints there are varying roles to be chosen with widely varying risk budgets.

To illustrate some of these concepts let us consider a very simple series of actions: a person driving to a store to buy a magazine for light reading. It is perfectly clear that by venturing out into the streets in an automobile the actor is taking some risks. It may well be that an actuary could indicate approximately the increased risk of death in driving, say, one mile in city traffic. Let us posit that the risk is 1 in 1,000,000. Is the end in view worth that risk? If we simply observe the actor's behavior, and the behavior of other actors, we will conclude that the end is worth the risk, but how may we conclude that it is for a rational man? The end in view is evidently a trivial one. The actor could easily go without the magazine, turning to a book or television for entertainment. Why then is it rational for him to take any risk, even a .000001 risk? Can we indeed be sure that this particular actor — rational man or not — would take such a risk if he were fully aware of its magnitude?

The concept of rationality cannot be specified so closely as to yield a conclusion on a discrete end of the sort put in this example. Nor need it be. Let us just say that the end in view is itself a rational end, but that it is trivial. A consequence of saying that a .000001 risk is excessive would be that such a risk would also be excessive for any other end of the actor of an approximately similar degree of triviality: a mile's drive for a pack of cigarettes, a walk involving crossing several busy intersections, and so on. Any one of these acts could be forgone on a particular occasion without changing the picture of the life the actor leads, so that nothing significant might appear to be at stake. Yet if a person were to give up all trivial ends involving even a slight risk of death his life would indeed be very different. Although a particular trivial end is just that, trivial, the capacity for engaging in trivial ends in general — entertainments, comforts, and quirks — is an important aspect of human personality.

One need only consider the tone of life that would emerge if this were not so. It would be intolerably and unrelievedly earnest. The willingness to spend for this kind of thing is one expression of freedom and individuality. The constraints and concerns of the weightier interests have a large aspect of the social or of the objective and external, and they have to do with the needs of others or the demands of objective evidence, as, say, in the pursuit of scientific truth. The class of minor concerns I am talking about now are viewed by contrast as quite arbitrary, one's own entirely, not susceptible of and needing no larger justifications. By giving them some weight, and thus by being willing to accept some risks for their sake, one gives oneself a measure of breathing space and asserts in a radical way one's autonomy. Though in themselves trivial ends are not important — indeed it is of their essence to be unimportant — a rigid denial of any life resources to them has significant consequences.

Erving Goffman in his study of "total institutions," *Asylums,* has shown how important it is to the sense of one's autonomy and worth to have some such area of arbitrary and trivial concerns reserved to oneself. He shows, for instance, how the stultifying atmosphere of certain convents comes in part from a rigid exclusion of any attention to these ends. The imposition is the more insidious in such a context just because of the great emphasis placed on the major interests and potentialities of the person. An inmate of such a convent might perhaps feel free — or at least justified — in asserting herself against authority on some great matter of principle, but she is stifled because to rebel over what appears, and in single instances clearly is, a triviality must seem unworthy to her. But since the minor and idiosyncratic has a place in rational life plans, to assert one's right to give it a place is also a matter of principle, and a principle whose importance transcends any particular use of the freedom granted. Indeed one might be willing to undergo considerable risk to establish one's general right in this regard, and this would be rational even where anything like the same risk for the sake of some particular end within this area would be irrational to the point of insanity.

Thus we may conclude that in a sense an act like driving down the street for a magazine has an aspect of significance for a rational person. Now these rather vague observations may be formalized further to bring out the relation between a particular trivial act and the general notion that a rational life plan has room, significant room, for the class of trivial ends. It is of the nature of trivial ends that they may be postponed or varied, that eschewing the act on any particular occasion is of no significance. This, however, does not mean that on a particular occasion a trivial end should be eschewed because it entails some risk of death, since such a risk will be entailed by pursuit of such an end on *any* occasion, and it is significant that such ends be pursued on some occasion.

What level of risk is appropriate to particular trivial ends? Can it in fact be quite high, since one would be acting rationally and justifiably in taking a great risk to assure one's general freedom to act in the area of trivial ends? That conclusion, of course, does not follow, since there is a difference between waging a battle to secure one's freedom to pursue a whole bundle of ends and taking a risk in respect to one member only of that bundle. The confusion arises from the circumstance that the occasion for asserting that freedom may be presented by some obstacle to the pursuit in a particular instance, which once removed opens the way for a long time to come. Thus learning to fly a private plane might be quite a risky undertaking, while flying for pleasure once trained may be relatively safe, and a trained pilot would not on any particular occasion take the same risk (say due to weather) that he would while he was still training.

Although it is unlikely that anything convincing can be said directly about even the approximate level of risk appropriate to some highly specific trivial ends — driving down the street for a newspaper — when this specific end is seen as part of a class of ends firmer conclusions may be possible. The *capacity* to engage in trivial ends is, as we have seen, a significant one, for which significant risks would often be taken. How big a risk, though, is a significant risk? And how is the capacity to be subdivided?

I shall not attempt further specification of these problems of trivial ends nor of problems relating to ends or the life plan in general. It has not been my purpose in this chapter as a whole and in the preceding discussion to present a fully elaborated structure for life plans and a technique for making calculations in life plans. Rather I have sought to show how the general concepts of Part One, and particularly the concept of the life plan, when applied to the person's choices relating to his death and the risk of death, yield general but nonetheless significant constraints upon rational choice. Orderings with respect to death and risk of death can take many forms, but not any form whatever. I have sought to show that the ordering in a life plan results in a risk budget in respect to risk of death, and that therefore the general forms of life plans will entail general forms of risk budgets.

Now many points about the life plan and risk budget have been left vague. It is my hope that the general concepts, however have been specified sufficiently to permit me to make the arguments I wish to make in the next chapters about the imposition of risks on others. It is my purpose in the two following chapters not only to elucidate the principles governing risk imposition in social contexts, but also to fill out and make more concrete the account, first sketched here, of the risks and plans a rational person assumes for himself.

Chapter XI
Imposing Risks
on Others

The General Theorem

Every choice a person makes has some effect on the risks of death he confronts; so also it has some effects on the risks confronted by others. What moral considerations govern choices involving the risk of death for others? The general theorem advanced in this section is built on the proposition that the justifications for imposing this risk on others are analogous to those governing the rationality of imposing the risk on oneself. Evidently the pursuit of ends other than the prolongation of life involves a sacrifice of that single end, both for oneself and others. Perhaps one may imagine some persons single-mindedly devoted to prolonging the lives of others (never mind for the moment how the benefits of their devotion would be distributed), but, unless the rest would then be bent on other pursuits, we would have a collective version of the madness of the life plan whose sole purpose is to prolong life. One might say that just as it is rational to use up our lives, so it is moral to use up each other's lives. The question is, on what basis do we use up each other's lives. In putting the issue in this form I intend to conflate problems of act and omission, right to act and liberty to forbear from acting, since these distinctions must be derived from and justified by more general principles. I consider it an open question, therefore, not only whether I am morally justified in doing that which endangers another, but also whether I am morally justified in ever pursuing some end other than that which will actively contribute to the greatest prolongation of another's life.

It is obvious that to deny to everyone the right to use up the lives of others in the broad sense intended here is to restrict their liberty and to deny the human ends and capacities of all. To deny this right to some but not to others is to deny their humanity in respect to those others. What is needed, then, is a principle distributing this resource, which is the lives of all, among all those who would use and use up this resource. We may carry over here the arguments of Part One against egoistic and maximizing principles of distribution. The two serious issues are (1) whether a principle of equal right is the appropriate principle here as in other cases of competing claims between persons, and (2) what such a principle could mean as applied to this situation.

Turning to the first question, the most plausible alternative or qualification of the equal right principle would be some view that a person is bound by the principle of equal right only when he is actively increasing the risk of death over what it would be if he did not act at all. As to actions which might decrease the risk for others, he is not morally accountable at all, or at least much less stringently so. This view presupposes a bench mark, a level of risk above which one's actions must rise before (full) moral accountability begins. But this bench mark must be established somehow and according to some moral principle. This brings us back to the principle of equal right. What is possible is that the principle of equal right does establish such a bench mark, which indicates the place at which full moral accountability begins. This is a possibility we must pursue in detail. But the existence or moral soundness of such a bench mark cannot be assumed a priori. Nor have we been given any reason to reject the general validity of the principle of equal right. Thus, the qualified version of the principle of equal right, which would say that this principle only takes effect for choices past some assumed bench mark, begs the question. So far we have been given no reason to qualify the principle of equal right (the principle of morality) in this way.

Turning to the second question as to what the principle of equal right might mean for this class of question, the notion of a bench mark past which full moral accountability takes over may in fact be derived from the principle of equal right and may be necessary to give it meaning.

Summarizing, then, the general theorem which I put forward for consideration is that persons are justified in imposing risks of death upon each other by reference to the principle of equal right, that is the principle of morality. This would mean that all persons may impose risks of death upon each other for the ends and to the extent that all other persons may do so. This, then, would be a special case of the Kantian principle of right, that a person is entitled to the fullest amount of freedom compatible with a like freedom for all other persons according to general laws. Applied to this situation the Kantian principle would mean a person has the fullest freedom to impose risk of death upon others compatible with an equal right on the part of others to impose risks of death upon him according to universal laws.

What does it mean to have this kind of a moral right to impose risks of death upon others? Roughly, it means that the necessity for action, for the pursuit of ends and the exercise of capacities, requires a certain freedom to impose risk of death on others, and that we are justified in imposing that degree of risk on others which we would all agree to so that we would have the maximum degree of freedom to pursue our ends and exercise our capacities. This, as has been said, is a specification of the Kantian principle of right. The Kantian principle of right, however, speaks only of general freedom, and not freedom to impose the risk of death upon others.

In order for the principle of equal right to apply we must assume that the freedom to impose risk of death upon others constitutes a discrete category of freedoms, discrete, that is, from the freedom to impose upon the liberty of others in general. This does not mean that there are no trade-offs between the freedom to impose the risk of death and the freedom to impose on others in other ways, but only that there are identifiable and universal patterns of such trade-offs admitting conclusions of general validity as to the imposition of the risk of death. The point might be illustrated thus: if, as a matter of fact, to impose the risk of death on others is commensurable with all other impositions on others for each person and, moreover, the trade-off functions vary randomly and widely among all persons, then no general conclusions about freedom to impose risk of death on others would be possible, and the question would be remitted to some general formula ascertaining the appropriate level of freedom to impose on others generally. It is for this reason that in the previous chapter we have developed the principles by which rational persons would accept the risk of death for themselves. By doing this we are able to see whether there are indeed any general principles indicating the relation of risk of death to other ends. To the extent that we have uncovered such general principles for all rational persons, these may now be carried over to our inquiry into the meaning of the principle of equal right in this regard. To the extent that all rational persons have trade-offs in respect to the risk of death of a certain general sort, we are enabled to derive a moral trade-off in terms of which we may ascertain the risk of death which one person may impose on others.

The argument for this is as follows. Impositions of all sorts on other persons are morally justified because any rational person would agree to permit such impositions upon himself as a price for his freedom of action, provided that the imposition he was permitting to others assured him the maximum degree of freedom compatible with universal laws to impose upon others in the pursuit of his own ends. If a person knows that he and all other persons would accept for themselves in the pursuit of their own ends a certain degree and kind of risk of death in particular circumstances, then it is rational to assume that those persons would allow others to impose that degree of risk of death upon them when the others are engaged upon those certain ends. In this way each person's impositions on others in the pursuit of those ends would be justified. Moreover, were a man to withhold the title to other persons to impose the risk of death upon him in the pursuit of those specified ends, he would not have that same title to impose on them, and therefore would be restricted in the pursuit of his own ends and capacities.

Now this argument does suggest an equality of a sort between the right to impose the risk of death on others and the willingness to accept the risk of death for one's self. Through the principle of equal right this equation is perfectly appropriate. By granting the right of others to impose upon him, he does, of course, increase his own risk of death. However, he grants this right and increases this risk of death as a way of purchasing, as it were, the right to pursue his ends and capacities, and in so doing to impose risks upon others. Presumably he would purchase this right only where the ends and capacities justify accepting a certain level of risk. The only trick is that he accepts the level of risk of death in the pursuit of his ends and capacities not directly, but by granting to others a title to impose this risk upon him. Once again, it must be emphasized that this argument will only work if some rough equation of the trade-offs of all rational persons can be made.

This, then, is the general theorem, and the arguments for it. The next step in our discussion will be to consider how the arguments made in the previous chapter about a rational person's trade-off function in respect to risk of death would work to specify a principle of equal right in respect to risk of death.

The Concept of the Risk Pool

In Chapter Ten, there was put forward the concept of the risk budget, by which a rational person determines the allocation of risks in his life plan. The largest part of the actual determinations in the risk budget cannot be specified beforehand — they are intuitive judgments about the level of risk appropriate to discrete actions such as crossing a street or climbing a ladder. It was possible to be more concrete about the relation of such discrete actions to general classes of ends, and about the concept of a class of ends itself. This in turn permitted some more concrete judgments about discrete actions: that substitutability and postponability did not mean that no risk was rational. Moreover, as ends became less substitutable and postponable, or as a discrete end tended to absorb the whole of a general end or capacity, a higher level of risk was appropriate. Finally, this apportionment of risks to ends through time was related to the changing pattern of ends in a life plan for a life cycle. In this section these notions must be transferred to the interpersonal level.

The most obvious correlate to the notion developed in Chapter Ten is the notion of reasonableness, as embodied in the law of negligence. By that notion a person is held to have acted negligently, to have been at fault, when he has caused an injury or loss to another by taking an unreasonable risk; and this means that given the ends for which he was acting, he imposed a greater degree of risk on others than was justified. Negligence, then, is a function of these two variables, the significance of the end and the degree of risk; this is quite clear in the law.

The situation in the law of negligence is revealing for our purposes. In a way quite analogous to what was said concerning the risk budget, the solution to the problem of reasonableness in negligence (that is to say the solution to the equation consisting of the function of the two variables of risk and end pursued) has not been closely specified in the law. On the contrary, in each particular case where the issue arises it is a matter for the jury, under very general directions, to determine whether or not the conduct of the defendant was negligent. There are, to be sure, numerous rules of law constraining and impinging upon this very general determination. These rules of law sometimes arise out of specifiable, recurring circumstances, but sometimes they are analogous to the general constraints on the concept of a rational risk budget which emerged from the consideration of the form of such risk budgets.

Although the appeal to intuition in the law by the very vague concept of reasonableness has the same form as the appeal to rationality, it must be shown what the general aim of this vague concept is. In the intrapersonal case, the degree of risk was measured against the seriousness of the end pursued. In the interpersonal case the situation will be somewhat more complex, because person A may be pursuing a serious end and impose risks on person B who at that time is pursuing a trivial end. For instance, a fire engine may be going to a fire traveling the same road as someone driving on a Sunday outing. The concept of reasonableness in negligence law would hold that the Sunday driver could not complain if the fire company imposed a higher risk on him than he was entitled to impose on the fire company. If we consider the justification for imposing risks on others set forth in the first section of this chapter, it will appear why this is perfectly appropriate. On the assumption that each individual in society has a risk budget having at least the same very general contents and constraints, then, it has been argued, it is a corollary concept that it is rational to take risks in order to pursue one's own ends and that it is justified to impose the risks on others and accept the imposition of risks from others in the mutual pursuit of ends.

This general theorem does not entail any need for a correspondence at any particular time between the risk imposed and the end pursued. That is, there is nothing in this concept to require that a risk of a certain level may be imposed on others only when those others are themselves imposing risks of that level. Rather, the general notion of a lifetime risk budget would suggest that at various times risks of various degrees will be imposed for ends of varying degrees of seriousness, and if those risks have ends roughly corresponding to each other the liberty of all will be maximized if the risks may be properly imposed and accepted. Applying this to the Sunday driver and fire engine, the point would be that although the Sunday driver's house may not be the house that is on fire at the moment, his house might have been on fire at some other time or may be on fire in the future, or some other significant corresponding risk may be appropriate at some time, and this makes the imposition upon him of this serious risk appropriate. Nor would it be correct for him to argue that he is entitled to impose the same degree of risk on the fire company when he is out on his Sunday drive that they are entitled to impose on him as they go to a fire, since he is not at that point pursuing an end which in his risk budget, or the risk budget of a rational person, has a degree of risk attached to it of that seriousness.

The notion that emerges I would characterize by the concept of the risk pool which is the interpersonal correlate of the risk budget. This notion holds that all persons by virtue of their interactions contribute, as it were, to a common pool of risks which they may impose upon each other, and on which they may draw when pursuing ends of the appropriate degree of seriousness. Now the case of the Sunday driver and the fireman indicates some problem in that one may argue that an actor may simply decide to draw very heavily on his contribution to the risk pool in respect to an end which other actors might consider quite trifling. There are several reasons why this kind of strict "consumer sovereignty" is not followed out in the law. The most obvious reason is administrative: by judging the seriousness of the occasion in terms of generally accepted estimates, there is some control over whether an individual is in fact withdrawing more than his share from the risk pool. If an individual were indeed allowed to allocate whatever degree of risk he wished to whatever end he wished, the problem of determining what balance he was maintaining in the risk pool would be intolerable. The correlate in morality of this legal administrative argument is the notion that not only should persons be fair — and the risk pool is an aspect of fairness — but also that it is important that persons have a degree of confidence that others are being fair. This confidence could scarcely be maintained if persons could draw on their balance in the risk pool ad lib.

There are, no doubt, also paternalistic reasons for denying this kind of full consumer sovereignty. By such reasons the unwillingness to allow a person to assign to a particular end any degree of seriousness that he wishes is related to a judgment that to exceed certain limits would be so irrational that society should not go along with that assignment, and thus, however indirectly, society puts a degree of pressure on the individual not to take what are conceived of as irrational risks. To be sure, the individual can (except in extreme cases) avoid this pressure if he takes the risk himself and does not impose it on others. That is to say, a person may take foolish risks in respect to his own safety, and society often will not interfere.

Finally, in addition to administrative and paternalistic reasons against full consumer sovereignty relative to the risk pool there is a complex reason about the coordination of activities. The point is that by assuming that persons' risk budgets are similar, we each know what to expect from each other and we each know approximately what kind of risks will be imposed upon us in various situations. If persons were allowed to impose wildly anomalous degrees of risk for anomalous ends, even though their total withdrawal from the risk pool was not excessive, this kind of coordination of expectations would be considerably impaired. In a sense this might be urged simply as a reason for saying that a person taking a high risk for an anomalous end imposes even higher risk on others than might have at first appeared, and reduces his balance in the risk pool by a correspondingly higher amount than might have first appeared. The point is strong enough made even in that way, but I believe that the importance of coordination and the importance of allowing persons to form some notion of what risks might be imposed upon them in certain situations, so that they might plan whether or not to get into those situations, makes the imposition of a degree of uniformity of judgments particularly pressing. However, whether this argument ends up giving determinative weight to this degree of uniformity or only a very great weight, to be traded off against other values, I cannot say.

Ordinary and Grave Risks

The concept of the rational risk budget allows for a number of cases where certain ends will loom so large as to justify the actor in taking very high risks of his own death to attain them. Does the concept of the risk pool mean that one is justified in imposing on others whatever risk we would be rational in accepting ourselves? Is there no difference between the imposition of a risk on another, and the acceptance of a risk for oneself? I have not shown that as a purely formal matter the general theorem is inconsistent with a notion of the risk pool by which persons may never impose a risk of more than a certain magnitude upon each other, though they may accept much larger risks for themselves. I have only shown the necessity of some pooling of risk at some level.

What reasons would all rational persons have for preferring a principle which places a lower limit on the degree of risk they are willing to have imposed on them by others — and therefore may impose on others — than on the degree of risk they will impose on themselves? In answering this, it should be recalled that in the individual risk budget high risks become more appropriate as they are necessary to more significant ends and capacities. Now if the right to impose risks on others were truly symmetrical with the risk budget, then as a person approached the point of critical need for his own purposes, he would be entitled to sacrifice not only his own life but that of another person. There are a number of reasons why this symmetry is unacceptable, but they all derive from the single point that sacrificing another for one's own purposes must be viewed as different from sacrificing oneself.

In sacrificing myself for some grave end of my own I am using up my own life in a way that I choose; that choice is a manifestation of my life plan and of my commitment to it. As such it is also a manifestation of my self-respect, for that concept might well be specified in terms of the seriousness with which I take my own ends. In short, because my ends are important to my life plan, in a sense because I *am* my system of ends, it is rational for me to use up my life for those ends. Does it follow that therefore I can use up another person's life? The argument why it might follow is that by acknowledging this right in myself I acknowledge a similar right in others, and by acknowledging this right in others I use up my life indirectly — that is I open myself up to its being used up — for a purpose of my own. But when I stand prepared to sacrifice my own life, I do it when *I* choose, and in specific conjunction with a crucial aspect of my life plan. If another person does this to me, the sacrifice will have no specific connection with some crucial end or capacity of mine. I may well be cut off in an entirely random way, relative to my life plan, and the only comfort would be that I had lost a gamble which I had made in order to allow myself to impose at some point greatly on others. Thus while the grave risks I would take for myself will be tied specifically to a crucial end, the grave risks imposed on me would be random over my life cycle.

This, I would suggest, is a result we should not accept. Rather we should accept a certain lesser freedom in accomplishing our ends (a lesser freedom, that is, to impose on others) in return for a greater security that we will not be exposed to grave risks by others at random points in our life cycle. This more cautious principle allows me to retain a greater measure of control over my life. It allows me to limit the grave risks to which I am exposed to cases where crucial ends are at stake.

This same point can be made another way. By denying myself the right to impose grave risks on another I am showing him respect; I am forgoing an advantage of my own because I cannot know that I shall not cut him off at a particularly inopportune point in his life cycle. (If I know that I shall, the argument is even stronger.) This is, of course, the exact complement of the point made above about my self-respect.

What is presented here can only be an argument of degree. It cannot be allowed to prove too much. It cannot be allowed to prove that we may not impose and should not accept the mutual imposition of some degree of risk. This would make all action impossible. What is being argued is that there is a certain level of risk — let us call it the ordinary or background level of risk — which is necessary to allow ordinary activity to take place. Moreover, within this there may be some modulations: not every legitimate activity will justify the same level of risk. This ordinary level is mutually imposed and accepted. Beyond this ordinary level one may accept risks for ends of his own, but may only exceptionally impose them on another, unless that other also accepts the risk as part of what might be considered a joint venture.

Now there is the obvious (though not for that reason less difficult) problem of drawing the line on what is after all a continuum between the ordinary and the extraordinary. One may wish to say that this is a difficult problem only until one has resolved to solve it by being somewhat arbitrary or by saying that the two concepts shade into each other at their boundaries. Yet there is a complexity which renders this strategy difficult. Let us say that the boundary exists at the range .5 – .6, or whatever other range one chooses. There will surely be some point, p, clearly within the area of ordinary risk and some point, q, clearly within the area of extraordinary risk. The difficulty is that one can always create p out of q, by discounting q by some other risk, r (for example: $p = .08$, $q = .8$; then if $r = .1$, $p = q \cdot r$). This being the case do we say $q \cdot r$ is an ordinary risk? To deny it would seem irrational. Yet if we admit it, can we rule out q as extraordinary in the rare (.01) case in which it comes up?

If $q \cdot r$ are taken together instantaneously then they are simply equivalent to p, and that is all there is to it. But if one has first faced r and then one faces q, the fact that one has already faced r seems irrelevant. What one faces is q, which is clearly an extraordinary risk. This would seem to mean that what is relevant is the size of the risk one actually faces at a particular moment. The person who has driven with great care and at a low rate of speed all his life should not thereby purchase any greater right to continue at what may otherwise seem quite a safe rate of speed when a child darts out in front of his car.* But we will see in the next section that this simple conclusion will not always obtain.

* To be sure there will be cases where a risk of ordinary level p can be analyzed into a risk r of a risk q, where $p = r \cdot q$, and p is less than q, but if once r occurs we are powerless to turn back, to avoid risk q. But if we are

Obligations

There are cases in which the past history of the situation is generally thought to make a difference, varying the level of risk one may impose on others. Ordinary prudence and care require that a person be prepared and willing to stop short — say within 100 feet of first seeing a hazard — if by so doing he can avoid death or injury to another person. Let it be conceded also that a person need not in general take an action sacrificing his own life in order to avert a grave risk to another. Now let us imagine the case where A loads his truck with heavy steel pipe in such a way that if he stops short it will shift forward and is very likely to crush him in the driver's cab. A, thus laden, sees B drive out of a side road into his path. If A stops short he will avoid hitting and perhaps killing B, but he will also risk being killed by the pipe stacked in his truck. It would seem that A had the right to impose no more than a certain level of risk on others in venturing out on the highway in pursuit of his ends. If he stays within that level and there is an accident — something goes wrong — he is not at fault. If he stays within that level and something goes wrong, he need not sacrifice his life to avoid taking the life of another person who is involved in the encounter. But since he ventured out bearing this particularly heavy and dangerous burden he forfeits that right.

This argument makes the rightfulness of A's conduct depend on choices made and risks taken on some distinct, earlier occasion. We can see this if we contrast A's situation with that of C, a hitchhiker who is a passenger in the cab of A's truck. C is not constrained to risk his life to save B. If A in a fit of cowardice had leapt from the cab leaving C at the controls, we feel that C would be justified in not stopping short. Yet at the moment of the crucial option — to stop or not to stop — the choice of risks presented to A or to C would be exactly the same. This must show that A's prior action in loading the truck in some way obligated him to drive so as to avert danger to persons in B's position, even at the risk of his own life. It is this obligation that I wish to explore.

powerless to take the risks r and q into account separately, then it is proper to consider them in combination, and in combination they are perfectly proper. After r occurs and we are faced with q, about which we can do nothing but hope, we may feel horror, but should not feel either regret or guilt.

Let us consider the most obvious case of an obligation. This is a case where I have promised to some person that I will accept a certain rather high risk to save him if he should get into peril, in return for his agreement to do the same for me. If circumstances turn out so that I am called upon to risk my life to save that person, one would say that here is an obligation to take the higher level of risk than would otherwise be required. It is the past history which creates the obligation here.*

As we have seen, the obligation of promises is simply one sort of obligation. The general obligation of fairness, which is the obligation to do one's part in compliance with a scheme which one has voluntarily entered, or from which one voluntarily has derived benefits, is the more general case. And this more general obligation of fairness will apply in respect to the question of accepting and imposing risks as well. Even if there have been no explicit promises, therefore, if a person involves himself in a situation where persons accept and impose levels of risk upon each other on the understanding that others will abide by the limits set by these levels, then there is an obligation to do one's part when one's turn comes to accept burdens.

Applying this to the truck case, we may say that a person who ventures out on the highway is taking advantage of a general societal scheme in terms of which persons accept and impose levels of risks of a certain sort on each other. It is one's obligation to stay within those levels. But the driver of the truck can only do so by applying the brakes and risking being crushed by the pipe with which he has loaded his truck. If the lives of the people in a car with which he might come into a collision are at stake there would seem to be no excusing circumstance, and his obligation would be to make that sacrifice. In general we might say that the

---

* A standard gambit in dealing with this sort of a moral problem is to treat the security of promises in the future as one of the forward-looking considerations which bind me to keep my promise. But that gambit can be readily blocked by further positing a situation in which my failure to keep my promise will not become known. It should be readily apparent that this is simply a standard case of the moral requirement that one fulfill obligations of fairness, of which obligations under a promise are an example, even though no utility maximizing considerations would compel us to do so. The structure of this argument is fully developed in Part One. We have here nothing more than a special case in which the burden we must take up in fulfillment of our obligation is a burden which involves the acceptance of risk.

person has no right to excuse himself from the performance of an obligation because he himself has for his own purposes made the performance of that obligation more onerous than it need have been. Indeed, we may specify the concept of the risk pool further by recognizing that liberty is maximized if persons are allowed to do things such as loading their trucks in the way the driver in our hypothetical case has done, provided only that if an emergency arises they are willing to accept the consequences of their action and not shift them on to others. The driver of the truck who refuses to stop short, arguing that it is unreasonable to make him sacrifice his life, is in the position of somebody who voluntarily determines that he will not insure his house against fire, because he prefers to save the premium and use it in some other way, and then claims when a fire occurs that the fire has cost him so much money that he should be compensated by the insurance company anyway.

In all these situations we must consider not only the last moment of choice but the context, the history of the circumstances, since these might create an obligation to act in a certain way and may determine what that obligation is. And this conclusion requires us to revise to some extent the argument in the preceding section which held that the past history is irrelevant.*

These arguments lead to a rather surprising conclusion. Let us posit that the reasonable level of risk in driving is a function simply of speed. And let us posit further that the rate of speed corresponding to reasonable care in the risk pool is 50 miles an hour. Suppose that last week I drove for a time at 75 miles an hour without mishap. One might suppose that the fact that the risk did not

---

* The complex bearing of the past history of an event on our present rights in effecting withdrawals from the risk pool is well illustrated by legal doctrines and distinctions. The person who has himself created the hard choice between his own life and that of another will in law only be able to defend his taking of the other life if he did not create that situation improperly or on the assumption that he would take the consequences. An assailant who initiates a deadly attack on another cannot then hide behind the defense of self-defense if his victim in defending himself threatens the assailant's life. A driver who has negligently proceeded to cross the tracks when he should have seen an approaching train cannot complain if the engineer will not endanger the safety of his passengers by stopping abruptly to avoid a collision. Persons who employ dangerous instrumentalities (such as railroad engines or escalators) have a special obligation to come to the aid of persons injured by those instrumentalities even though it is conceded that they were free of fault in respect to the accident.

eventuate should make that bit of misconduct irrelevant; I should not have to drive less than 50 miles an hour during the next week in order to "make up" for it.

Consider, however, that if I plan my driving for two weeks, driving one week at 75 miles an hour and the other week at 50 miles an hour, then my plan of conduct is in the aggregate gravely more risky than that of a person who plans to drive 50 miles an hour during both weeks. And if I plan to drive one week at 75 miles an hour and the second week at 25 miles an hour my conduct may be about as risky as a person who drives at a steady 50 miles an hour. But if I drive during that first week at 75 miles an hour and nothing happens (or something does happen and I pay), is not the only question before us, how risky should my conduct be in the next week? And is not the only rational answer that I should drive at 50 miles an hour, no more no less?

The answer to this last question is no. If I made an explicit bargain with the other members of the public that I will drive 75 miles an hour one week and 25 miles the next, then surely if I get through the first week I should not be able to go back on my bargain. To do so would be to withdraw more than my share from the risk pool. Now one would be tempted to say that the only question would be what risks will I impose in the future. One would be tempted to say that risks in the past are like dreams from which we have awakened; they have no further reality. But we can see that this argument for escaping from one's obligation to drive at 25 miles an hour the second week is really the same thing exactly as an argument on the part of a person, who is called upon to fulfill a promise, that utility would be maximized overall if now that his turn has come to fulfill his promise, he did not do so. Such conduct would be unfair, and if generalized disastrous. Nor at this stage should we be impressed by the argument that the unfair, undutiful conduct may not in fact be an example to others, may not in fact be generalized, for that is beside the point.

This point may be illustrated by another example. Let us imagine that parking spaces are rationed by the use of parking meters. If I come to a meter and find I have no change, perhaps I should still be allowed to park there. This is equivalent to driving 75 miles an hour during the first week. But should it be open to me to argue that when I next have the chance I can simply forget about the money that I would have put into the meter? Should I not on some future occasion put twice as much into a meter? Or should I not accept a system of sanctions by which I pay a reasonable fine which is nevertheless a very large multiple of the money I would have put into the meter, on the assumption that the cost of the fine discounted by the probability of my being tagged is about the equivalent of the money I would have paid? Surely if every time it was inconvenient to put money into a parking meter there were no consequences at all in the future, the scheme for rationing parking spaces by parking meters would break down. Further, my obligation to the scheme is an obligation of fairness, so that I must make my contribution regardless of the probabilities that my delinquency will or will not in fact contribute to its breakdown.

Is the situation as to risks truly analogous to this example? Might it not be argued that in the case where I park at the meter and do not pay I have (let us assume there is a genuine scarcity of parking spaces) deprived somebody else of the convenience of parking at that meter, but where I have driven 75 miles per hour during the course of the week and injured nobody it would seem that no harm has been done, no costs imposed on others. It seems somewhat metaphysical to equate the palpable disutility of being deprived of a parking space to the disutility of having been subjected to a risk. And yet the equivalence is there, and must be taken seriously. If a large number of drivers drive on alternate weeks 50 and 75 miles an hour the highways will be a good deal less safe, and there will be an appreciably larger number of accidents than if all drivers drove 75 miles an hour and 25 miles an hour on alternate weeks.

It would seem then that we have here a rather different principle for decisions under uncertainty when we consider the interpersonal case than when we consider decisions under uncertainty where an individual is making choices only for himself. If a person acts unreasonably in relation to his own personal risk budget, but gets away with it, it does not make any sense to insist that he has an obligation to "pay back" in the future. At most what he must do in reflecting on his past deviations is to assure himself that it was, indeed, a deviation and not in fact the assertion of a rival risk budget in a rival life plan. But once he is assured that his conduct was truly an anomaly, that he will be true to his risk budget, it is hard to see what sense there could be in his imposing on himself a penalty in the future. Yet such penalties in the future because of past conduct are just what we have argued for in respect to the interpersonal case under the concept of the risk pool. The closest one can come to such an argument for the intrapersonal case is the argument of self-discipline.

Should the argument be allowed to lead to the conclusion that the person who drove particularly carefully last week is entitled to drive more heedlessly of the safety of others the next week? And more generally, should we conclude that the risk pool furnishes a certain stake for each participant in the pool upon which he might draw as he chooses so long as he does not exceed the total amount of his share? Some objections to an analogous notion have already been adduced: in particular it was pointed out that such a prin-ciple would in practice be utterly unadministerable. The argument from administrative convenience is not, I should say, an insub-stantial or merely legalistic one. The fairness of a scheme depends on the confidence the participants have that others are abiding by it, and an unadministerable scheme would be unstable because it could not create that confidence. Obligations of the risk pool arise out of the principle of fairness, and persons are not as clearly bound by fairness to schemes which are easily evaded and difficult to administer.

It must be recognized that these objections must overcome the argument that where possible a person should be able to arrange his withdrawals from the risk pool in any way he likes. It is not clear that they do overcome the argument. After all that argument has working for it the presumption in favor of liberty. But it is our intuition that a person who has been more careful than necessary in the past is *not* thereby entitled to impose greater risks on others, even apart from problems of administration. And we feel this even though we may come to agree that a person who has been careless in the past is thereby obliged to make a kind of restitution by being particularly careful for a time in the future. This asymmetry, I would suggest, is an aspect of the principle about the special status of grave risks. The point has been made that the concept of the risk pool puts a ceiling on the risks we may properly impose on others which is lower than the ceiling on the risks we would be willing to take ourselves. This argument might be extended to the issue before us now. By allowing the past to vary the social risk ceiling only in one direction, we say that no matter how careful we have been in the past, we may not on any particular occasion deliberately withdraw more than a certain amount from the pool. In less abstract terms this would mean that we may not deliberately confront others with a grave risk of death so long as we have any choice in the matter.*

Some Further Limitations on the Risk Pool: Kidney Banks and Life Rafts

The principle of the risk pool imposes a standard which is not an efficiency standard but one of justice and fairness: the hazard of no individual is used to increase the benefits to others, but all share equally in the benefits and burdens of the system. Now this conception might seem to lead in two specific cases to conclusions that are offensive to our moral intuition. (1) A person who, after a shipwreck, had the "good luck" to find a spar big enough to support only one might have to submit to a lottery if subsequently another survivor approached the spar. Or if a person is in the

* This argument should not, of course, be taken to state too much. It should not be taken to state that where there is a small risk r of a grave risk q, and the product of r and q is a risk of reasonable proportions, we may not take the risk $r \cdot q$ where, should r occur, we would be powerless to turn back. Rather, the argument states at most that once r has occurred and we can turn back from confronting risk q we should do so. Imagine that I have sent a salesman on a trip in a one-engine plane in summer to the south. I know there is a certain chance of his being killed by a tornado, and yet all things considered this may not be an unreasonable risk. If I learn as he is underway that there are twisters in his vicinity, I should warn him to turn back. But if the twisters develop and there is nothing I can do, then I should be blameless. Indeed one of the factors that leads us to characterize the original decision as reasonable is the assurance that, in the class of case where I can instruct him to turn back, I will do so, thereby reducing the ex ante total risk involved in the decision. But if I can do nothing subsequently, the potential partitioning of the risks is irrelevant. What one might well ask, however, is whether it is permissible to create deliberately the situation where one cannot turn aside from the grave risk q, in order to save the possible addititonal resources? If one may not so bind the situation deliberately in advance, and if one is not entitled to be less careful later because one has been more careful in the past, is not all incentive gone to be specially careful? If I am right about this asymmetry of the bearing of past history, then instances of extra care in the past are like gifts: one need not make them, but once made we cannot demand payment after all,

desert with food only sufficient to sustain one life, he would have to flip a coin if he comes upon a traveler lost without food. (2) The state, if it did so on a truly random and equal basis, might be justified in compelling individuals to donate a kidney or other vital organ — where the donation is not fatal — to save lives in an emergency.

These cases raise the question about what resources (using the term resources in its broadest possible extension) a person may in justice be required to share, and therefore what the extension of the claims made upon a person by the risk pool notion are. We might ask analogous questions where what is at stake is not life but other aspects of well-being. For instance, do we wish to say that persons with a greater appreciation for natural beauty, or persons with a happy disposition, or persons enjoying a happy marriage should pay taxes at a higher rate, on the theory that they lead happier, richer lives, and that their surplus over the happiness of others is something that in justice they might be required to contribute to the general societal pool? Or to take another example of this type of problem, Rawls assumes that, although the higher compensation paid to more talented persons is justified only insofar as it inures to the benefit of all, these more talented persons are indeed morally entitled to the additional income: they cannot be *compelled* to contribute their extra talents to the general societal pool gratis.

Now it may be said that the answer to these questions depends on the existence of an explicit societal scheme to which all contribute and from which all may withdraw benefits. This answer would suggest that only because there is no societal scheme at work in the shipwreck or desert explorer cases there is also no obligation to submit to the equalization that society could and should impose. But this answer is unconvincing. We could, after all, easily imagine informal customs, equivalent to societal schemes, to cover such cases. Moreover, even where the problem occurs in the context of a fully elaborated societal setting, the difficulties remain. A societal rule compelling the contribution of organs could be imagined, and perhaps even enforced. And still the intuition remains that no such demand can in justice be made of persons. Indeed, the existence of an explicit social scheme is neither a necessary nor a sufficient condition for the obligation to contribute to a general pool. The organ transplant case shows that it may not be sufficient. That it is not a necessary condition emerges from the shipwreck or desert explorer cases, where good arguments might be advanced on an analogy to the principle of justice even though an explicit societal scheme does not obtain.

What is needed, it would seem, is some set of principles which do not rely on the existence of explicit social schemes, that would yet indicate what the appropriate contributions to the risk pool should be. What is needed is a bench mark indicating where contributions must begin and where in some coherent sense a person may regard certain attributes as his own, which he is not morally obligated to share with others, but may share or not as he chooses.

The solution to this problem depends on two related components. First, the argument for equalization in the shipwreck situation is not as convincing as it may seem at first sight. To be sure a lottery between the two survivors as they confront each other over the plank does give each an equal chance at that moment, but what is missing is any argument for making that moment determinative. Why, it can be argued, is not the finding of the plank a sufficiently random circumstance to allow the conclusion that the two survivors in question had equal opportunities in respect to it? And if that is a plausible point, then to make the fortunate survivor undergo a second lottery would be unfair to him. This can be seen even more clearly if we postulate a third survivor arriving on the scene at the conclusion of the lottery between the first two. What this shows is that as to certain advantages and disadvantages, at least as seen at a particular moment in time, either no scheme of randomization obtains, or one may view the actual inequality as simply the outcome of some acceptable scheme for randomization.

Now these two interpretations are not quite equivalent. There is a moral difference between acting in a way which equalizes in the absence of a scheme, and adopting an explicit equalizing scheme and then acting in pursuance of it. I would not wish to suggest that where some equalizing scheme is readily apparent for a situation, so that any moral person would arrive at the conclusion that such a scheme existed, that still he would not be bound by the scheme unless he explicitly adopted it. On the contrary, in such a case the scheme is directly binding morally on all. An example of this sort of a directly deducible moral obligation is the obligation of beneficence, that is the obligation to render aid to another person when that person's need is great and the burden on the actor is small. The force of this principle of beneficence does not derive, as some might think, from the great disparity between the burden imposed and the benefit conferred, but rather from the directly intuitable nature of the obligation, requiring no mediation by explicit arrangement.

I do not wish to argue that there might not in the shipwreck example be devised explicit schemes which would randomize and equalize the benefits and burdens in that sort of situation better than letting the burdens fall where they may. Customs of the sea, customs of travelers in the desert, and the like, which are quite explicit even though they are customs, are examples of such equalizing arrangements. My argument is, rather, that in many situations in the absence of some explicit arrangement to which all involved parties have consented to be bound, there may be no better approximation to equality than the rough and ready randomization entailed by the principle of letting the loss lie where it falls. This point may be seen if one considers the felt moral oddness of the survivor swimming toward the plank, and arguing to the person holding on to the plank that some better randomizing principle than plain luck would have this or that form, according to which the person on the plank must either give it up entirely or submit to a lottery. The point is that such schemes and the obligations deriving from them are only binding if one from the outset has accepted an equal chance in respect to them. In a sense the person making this suggestion in midocean is, as it were, changing the rules of the game in midstream.

I pass now to the second class of case, in which the question is raised whether persons could in justice be compelled for equality's sake to contribute to society certain natural advantages, like superior talent, good health as represented by two functioning kidneys, a happy disposition, and so on. The answer in this case depends on rather different considerations. Certain advantages, indeed certain attributes, are so intimately associated with the concept of personality that a strong argument can be developed that they provide a kind of bench mark from which equality is to be measured. This might be put in another way. We are talking about the equality or the equal right of persons, and persons are entities which have certain attributes making them this person or that person. We therefore should not require that they divest themselves of their claim to these attributes in creating equality of persons, but rather that equality of persons be an equality of entities defined as including this certain intimate bundle of attributes. Put yet another way, one might say that when we speak of equal right or impartiality of right between persons as moral entities, we are speaking of persons as three-dimensional objects having certain concrete attributes, rather than as dimensionless points to which attributes are then allocated and distributed according to some plan of fair distribution. There are two problems with this assertion: first there is the problem of isolating the attributes which will be assigned this special status; second there is the related problem of justifying any such special status for such attributes or indeed any attributes. These two problems are sufficiently similar that I shall proceed to deal with them together.

The working criterion for the principle of morality, the principle of equal and impartial right, has been to ask what would a rational person who did not know of his particular circumstances agree to as included within morality. Since the notion of rationality is quite general, this criterion is in fact a criterion of unanimity on the part of rational, hypothetical persons. Now why should rational persons who do not know what their attributes may be agree that certain of these attributes will be counted as theirs, with the consequence that they will not be required to contribute them to the societal pool for purposes of equalization? Why should they legitimate beforehand possibly very large inequalities of benefits and burdens between persons, when there is no way of knowing that these benefits and burdens are likely to be distributed by (what Rawls has called) the natural lottery in any roughly equal way?

I contend that some such inequality is preferable to the acquiescence in possible equalizing schemes. This means that in an initial position persons would prefer the risk of dying because a kidney transplant could not be demanded; they would prefer the risk — now moving to the general case — of suffering the deprivations arising from being born without talents and into a society where talents can be obtained from the more talented only by compensating them therefore; and would prefer the risk of being less happy without being able to demand compensation from those with a sunnier disposition. This preference rests on the assumption that all rational persons would find that their liability to contribute to such equalizing schemes would be so deadly an assault upon their personal integrity that the benefits that might accrue from such schemes, should they happen to be at the less fortunate end of the initial natural distribution, would not be sufficient to make this assault upon their integrity seem worthwhile.

As has happened at a number of points in this study, it is not possible to give an unassailable argument for this conclusion. Rather the form of the argument must be that certain attributes — for instance one's bodily organs, one's talents, the effort one is willing to make, one's disposition and mood — are so closely related to a conception of one's self, that to make them available for trading-off in a scheme of morality would be, as it were, to gain the world and lose one's own soul. Less metaphorically, a rational person in an initial position would feel that to purchase benefits at the risk of having to make a contribution of these most intimate attributes is to purchase benefits at the risk of having to become another person and thus to commit a form of suicide.*

Perhaps we can also see why such things as happiness, effort, capacity for appreciation, cannot be demanded as of right by the moral community from any individual. The reason has to do with the primary importance to the concept of personality of control over self. If effort, disposition, powers of appreciation, were distributed to individuals only provisionally by the natural lottery, subject to redistribution in order to attain equality, then it is hard to see that anything would be left of the notion that human persons have a natural right, deriving from the concept of personality itself, to control who they become, what they are. And therefore acceptance of possibly very great inequality in this regard is a necessary condition of considering one's self a human person.

* Yet another way of making this point is to say that in the initial position, in which the principle of morality is specified and its corollaries derived, persons may be viewed as dimensionless points, but that does not mean that these dimensionless, attributeless points are unaware of the fact that real persons have attributes which are necessary to the conception of an actual person. Thus when one is considering moral principles from a standpoint of equality and impartiality, one need not prescind from the knowledge that the entities to whom these moral principles apply, and among whom they establish a kind of equality of right, are human persons, and that human persons exist inextricably associated with certain attributes.

If that is so, then the argument has some plausibility that in an initial position any rational person would agree to the existence of such inequalities.

Now talents, efforts, and forsooth even kidneys are things which a person in relations of love might quite rationally choose to yield to another. But it is of the essence of relations of love or friendship that the gifts we make in those relations are gifts which are freely given. Indeed, when I argue that moral title to absolute control of these attributes is a necessary condition of the notion of personality, I would argue also that by making gifts of these advantages to others one makes one's self a certain sort of person.

Finally, we might ask whether there are not limits even here on what of himself a person might be permitted to sell or give away. Mill would not allow a man to sell himself into slavery. Should one be permitted to give away his eyes or his heart while he is still well? I shall not attempt a resolution of this problem.*

I readily concede that the class of attributes which are exempted from contribution to the risk pool by this argument is left entirely vague. Why should we tolerate a draft in war time, while balking at the notion of compelling the contribution of talents generally? Is it really so clear that persons should not be compelled to contribute to a blood bank? And if they might, why not a sperm bank, a kidney bank, or an eye bank? Perhaps, after all, the boundary of the class of inherent attributes is conventional, so that what is important is that society observe whatever constraints such conventions impose. But I shall not elaborate this argument further.

---

* Should we allow a person to sell a kidney or blood or sperm, as we allow him to sell his talents? If so, then the arguments of distributive justice would seem to require that at least poorer persons be subsidized by some health insurance scheme in their purchase of organs for transplantation, as they are subsidized in their purchase of, for instance, education from the more talented members of society. Is this simply a fiscal substitute for forced contributions to the societal pool? I think not for two reasons. First the more talented person or the donor of the kidney receives his full compensation, and contributes to the societal pool only by virtue of being a higher-income bracket taxpayer — higher because of his sale of a capital asset. Second, the person selling his inherent attribute is not compelled to do so, and if the society is a just one generally with a proper prior distribution of income, financial need will not compel him to sell his talents or his body.

Chapter XII
The Value
of Life

The Problem of Statistical Lives

A problem of rational choice in respect to life and death that has recently received attention from writers with an economist's point of view — for example, Calabresi, Raiffa, Schelling — is the problem of statistical lives. These writers have considered the apparent anomaly that we are prepared to expend far greater resources in saving the lives of known persons in present peril, than we are prepared to devote to measures that will avert future dangers to persons, perhaps unknown and not yet even in existence. The anomaly arises insofar as a consistent policy favoring the expenditure of resources for persons in immediate peril can be shown in the long run to lead to a smaller number of lives saved with the same or perhaps even a larger long-run expenditure of resources.

An example which is often adduced is that of the mining enterprise which will spend vast sums in rescuing a few men trapped in a mine shaft, while no equivalent sums, even appropriately discounted, would be spent on safety measures to prevent such incidents, even if many more lives would in the long run thereby be saved. The field of medicine provides many examples. A hospital with limited space may discharge many appendectomy patients one day earlier than optimally desirable in order to make room for a few heart surgery patients, who will require many weeks of hospitalization, even though the mortality among the many appendectomy patients thus discharged is larger than if the relatively few patients requiring heart surgery were simply turned away with the near certain knowledge that they would soon die without the surgery. A developing nation may devote large resources to general medical facilities, when public health measures would reduce the death rate more efficiently.

An example pointing the other way — toward economic "rationality" — is the following. Persons admitted to a hospital with a certain grave disease may receive treatment a or b. The state of knowledge about a is fairly complete and the chances of success are p. Very little is known about b, except that so far the rate of cure is q, which is lower than p. It is quite clear that if in all such situations, there is no recourse to treatments of type b (that is, treatments which are less successful but not fully explored), medical knowledge will not advance nor new cures develop as rapidly. It appears that some hospitals will systematically "experiment" with treatment type b, on the view that a patient coming to a hospital with such a strategy has a better overall chance of cure than in a hospital which only uses treatment a.

The following is a hypothetical example of the same "rational" or maximizing strategy. Let us imagine a fatal infectious disease, for which a serum is available. Let us further hypothesize that this serum, administered undiluted, will cure the patient. Diluted one part in 10,000 the serum is an entirely effective vaccine against the disease. Let us imagine there is a fixed amount of the serum, and that that amount is clearly insufficient to treat the number of persons who have come down or will come down with the disease. Finally, this disease is highly infectious and is transmitted by a person to others before the infected person has any symptoms. In such a case it would seem rational to deny the serum to persons suffering from the disease and to reserve it for purposes of vaccination.

The economist's instinct in all such cases is to say that the only rational strategy is that which maximizes the numbers of lives saved at the least sacrifice of other ends. More precisely this view analyzes the problem intially into two components: life-saving and all other ends — opera, trips to the moon, whatever. Life will have a value relative to those other ends. What that relative value is represents the trade-offs between life and other ends, and these trade-offs may be quite complex — we value life more highly relative to some ends than others; or as the risk of death increases we may require an even greater increase in the chances of attaining some competing end. The trade-offs between life and other ends then expresses exactly what is the value of life. In the economist's view rationality requires that resources be allocated in such a way between life saving and competing ends as to attain the highest possible level of welfare as defined by these trade-offs. But in determining the appropriate allocation of resources to live saving one thing is clear on this view: the allocation is determined on the assumption that the resources allocated to live saving will be spent so as to maximize the number of lives saved or minimize the number of lives lost. The maximizing view may be summarized thus: how we have allocated resources between life saving and other ends is a judgment about the relative worth of human life which can be made in many different ways, but what makes no sense is to use the resources allocated to life in any other way than that which saves the greatest number of lives.

Familiar moral and legal intuitions may not correspond to this model of rationality, although the issue is rarely faced in such starkly abstract terms. The mining company which refuses to spend money on saving the trapped men may be liable not only civilly but criminally for a wrongful omission to save one toward whom they stand in a special relation of duty. This may be so even though the mining company has invested large amounts in safety equipment which substantially reduces the risk of disasters occurring, and even though such a rule of liability forces the mine to allocate resources away from such safety measures with a long-run net increase in the number of lives lost in the mine. So also a doctor who used treatment *b* might be guilty of malpractice. The distinctions made by some moralists between killing and letting die, acts and omissions, direct and indirect agency, could be seen as instances of the same or related "irrational" and "sentimental" attitudes. These arguments are often encountered in discussions of the treatment of civilian populations in time of war. Finally, the same issue arises not only in respect to questions of life and death. We may choose between alleviating the poverty of a few persons today or spending those same resources on education, thus alleviating the poverty of many more at a later time. Is it not sentimental to be moved by the palpability of the immediate case?

Some Entailments of Maximizing

There are several arguments for the preference for the immediate over the statistical which must be dispensed with at the outset. None of them is invalid. But at the same time none of them is sufficient to justify a preference for the immediate over what I call the economists' maximizing strategy which puts known lives in present peril on an exact parity with statistical lives in statistical perils. Rather what these arguments show is that a preference for the immediate under most conditions is what the maximizing strategy requires. These arguments do not, therefore, operate at all to justify a preference for the immediate when such a preference conflicts with the maximizing strategy.

The rational maximizing strategy will often make some provision for cases of immediate, actual peril — let us call this rescue — and such a strategy will mean the withdrawal of resources from measures designed to avoid such peril ever occurring, that is, measures of prevention. Whether and to what extent this is true will depend on the expected yield of rescue and preventive measures; and this will depend on such circumstances as the nature of the peril, the available means for rescue and prevention, the information available about the present and the future, and the like. Thus if safety measures in mines are expensive and not very effective while emergency rescue operations are effective and not ruinously expensive, this would argue for the rationality, in terms of maximizing efficiency, of standing ready to rescue when peril occurs but devoting few if any resources to preventive measures. So also in the serum example, circumstances may be imagined where the most efficient course is to hold all of the serum available for persons who have contracted the disease and to reserve none for inoculations, or to fix some proportion of the serum to be used for curative (rescue) and for vaccination (preventive) use. In general, the effectiveness of saving lives by a rescue or a prevention strategy or both may decrease per unit of resource devoted to them, in which case the maximizing strategy would require a mix of rescue and prevention to obtain the most efficient solution — that is, the one in which the greatest number of lives are saved over the long run.

A perfectly natural argument for rescue over prevention, for the immediate over the statistical, is that it is foolish to refuse to give help now which we know will be effective in order to help persons in the future, when we do not know they will need our help. Thus would we not feel foolish if we refused the serum to dying patients, reserving it for vaccinations against an epidemic which never materialized? Or perhaps we use up our present stock of serum on patients because we believe some other help may be available when the epidemic strikes. More serum may become available, or some other cure may be discovered. These arguments do have, to be sure, some quality of awaiting a deux ex machina, but they should not be dismissed out of hand because they can be expressed in a way which makes them a rough and ready approximation of a perfectly valid point under the maximization strategy: what is being maximized is the *expected* number of lives saved, and that is all that can be maximized. This means that in deciding between a rescue or a preventive strategy it is not only valid but necessary to discount future lives that might be saved, by the uncertainties that the peril to them would ever arise or that these resources would be needed to avert it in the future. Indeed these discounting factors, which justify, even on the maximizing view, a "bird-in-the-hand" bias in favor of taking such measures as one can to save persons presently in peril, are analogous to the factors justifying a rational man's general relative discounting of the more remote in favor of the less remote time period.

Moreover, a maximizing strategy does not lead you to say: we have only budgeted a certain amount this year to rescue operations or to rescue operations in this type of disaster, and since there is less than the necessary amount left in our budget, we will not attempt this rescue. Such an interpretation would mean that we would never know what to do until the last day in the year. Instead the budgets established by a maximizing strategy would relate to expenditures per man to be rescued in each identifiable type of accident. This figure would be a function of the probabilities of an accident of the specified type occurring, the cost of rescue operations and their likelihood of success as the amount spent on them is increased. With the budgets fixed in this way, though in a given year we may exceed our optimum budget, if we have estimated our probabilities correctly, the long-run allocation will be correct.

Furthermore, such a strategy would, by hypothesis, never lead you to refuse to press a rescue operation to its successful completion, if this is the sort of accident in which your overall plan has prescribed that there should be rescue operations at all, and if your budget was made up with an accurate estimate of the probable costs of rescue, and if all the information you will ever have to go on is available at the start of operations. (The case where you acquire further information as operations proceed is considered below.) This point is, indeed, an analytical truth. The determination that a particular kind of accident is "worth" rescue operations entails that even if rescue operations are pressed to completion without regard to expense in the particular case, in the long-run rescue operations for this type of accident will average out to the budgeted amount per man per accident. The grim side of this argument is the entailment that our overall strategy will decree that no rescue operations at all be mounted in certain types of accidents. A good example of such accidents would be astronauts caught in a permanent moon orbit or a submarine lost at the bottom of the ocean.

The foregoing does assume that the domain of accidents is necessarily divided between those in which rescue will and those in which it will not be attempted. In the first class rescue will be pressed forward in the particular case, regardless of cost; in the second no attempt at rescue whatever is to be made. This dichotomy runs contrary to our sense that in most cases it is rational to spend some resources but not to be prepared to spend whatever is necessary. That sense is correct for situations in which we cannot firmly identify at the time of the initial occurrence of a particular accident the type of accident that has occurred. Miners are trapped in a mine, but we do not know whether they are trapped at twenty feet or two hundred feet, in an air pocket or near a pocket of poisonous gas. A person is brought to a hospital, and we do not yet know if he has suffered a heart attack, a stroke, or a concussion. A plane is lost, and we do not yet know where, in what terrain, and under what circumstances it went down. These cases comprise a large part, probably the largest part, of the cases in which we must consider whether to go forward with rescue operations. In such cases the anlysis is somewhat more complicated in that it is rational to expend some resources on discovering what subclass in the more general class of accident has in fact occurred. Having spent those resources we may then decide according to our budget that it is or is not worth going forward with rescue operations.

How much resources we will expend on this inquiry and in what cases is of course, like our response once we have the information, fixed by the general maximizing plan. Moreover, this process of gaining information may itself coincide with the rescue measures appropriate to a subclass of accident. One way of finding out whether the men are trapped at twenty feet is to tunnel down that far. Having done so, whether we go down further will depend not on how much we have spent already but on how much more we must spend to go down another twenty feet and what the chances are of such an additional expenditure leading to success. This calculation of the worth of the additional expenditure may or may not justify proceeding.

It is possible that this accretion of marginal decisions may lead us to tunnel two hundred feet to rescue one man, at a cost far in excess of what we would have been prepared to spend at the outset had we known that only this could succeed. But this is only an apparent anomaly. If each of our marginal decisions to proceed along the way was based on an accurate estimate of the chances of success by expending a further not excessive amount, then the number of cases in which we end up spending more to rescue a man than we would have had we known at the outset what we knew at the finish will be balanced by cases in which we spend less. In the long run we will have spent just the right amount. Once more this is an analytical truth, and indeed it is but a more elaborate version of the analytical truth proposed above concerning completion of rescue. For present purposes it is important to see that here too we will rescue in some cases and decide not to rescue in others (though the decision is made later in time) depending on the allocation fixed by the maximizing strategy.

Finally, it is true that in many cases (strictly speaking, in all cases) the occurrence of an accident or its nonoccurrence should lead us to revise our estimates (perhaps only to a negligibly small extent) of the probabilities of that event and a large class of other events as well. But this too does not justify any preference for a rescue strategy as such. The revised estimate may entail a smaller not a larger allocation to rescue (for example, because we now believe that successful rescue operations are more expensive than we had thought). But in any case our revised estimates will go into the fixing of a new allocation to rescue, and this new allocation — like the old one — is governed by the goal of maximizing the numbers of lives saved at the least cost.

The important general point about all these arguments is that they may on occasion justify a preference for persons in peril — for a rescue strategy — but they do so entirely in terms of maximizing the expected number of lives saved. And nothing in these arguments shows that the present peril is entitled to any special consideration as such. So far as these arguments are concerned if the expected value in terms of lives saved is maximized by totally ignoring rescue, by ignoring persons in present peril, that is the course to be followed.

Some Invalid Arguments

A point that has on occasion been raised in discussion of this problem is that persons do in fact display a bias toward present peril and that they do so in a way and to a degree that suggests they would not correct this bias if it were shown that in a particular class of situation it does not maximize the expected number of lives saved. Whether this is so is, of course, a matter of empirical demonstration. But what conclusions follow from this fact, if it is a fact? Perhaps that the behavior described is rational, but in terms of more complex value premises than have so far been considered. This possibility will be explored at length below.

A more sweeping claim is sometimes made that this bias discloses a disbelief in statistics, or a recognition of the "fact" that our information is so incomplete that it is misleading to speak in terms of statistics at all. This argument must be rejected. A statistical or probabilistic approach is just an approach to rational decision in the face of incomplete knowledge. When this argument is put forward it is put forward as if there were a difference in kind between the incomplete knowledge formalized and formulated by statistics —

such as life expectancies and industry accident statistics — and the incomplete knowledge about the outcome of rescue operations for a person in some rather special and rare kind of peril or the incomplete knowledge about how safe it is to cross a particular street at a particular time. The argument builds on this asserted difference in kind to justify a bias in favor of the immediate where no actuarial statistics are available or even easily imaginable. The argument is fallacious. I take it to have been abundantly demonstrated that no rational case can be made for the existence of such a difference in kind. In all the situations considered there is only a difference in the amount of information presently available. But availability of information in itself has no bearing on our estimation of the probabilities of the occurrence of an event. Incompleteness of information as to the future does not relieve us of the need to plan for the future on the basis of whatever knowledge we have.

Another argument that might be made is that in many situations, such as mine disasters, epidemics, storms at sea, it is justified to expend resources to the utmost because such emergencies call forth unexpected reserves of energy, resourcefulness, courage, and willingness to sacrifice. Of course this argument may be nothing more than a misleading form of the argument in favor of making provision for a future in which new resources may become available. New resources may become available because of efforts stimulated by the exhaustion of resources, or they may become available independently of prior decisions. But beyond that, anyone charged with responsibility for such matters must try to foresee as precisely as possible what the reserves of energy, courage, and the like available in an emergency will be, and to calculate accordingly. If only the emotional claims of immediate peril are sufficient to call forth certain extraordinary efforts, if as a matter of fact such zeal would not be available for preventive measures which — though less dramatically appealing — were more likely to save lives, then rational planning must take this into account.

But taking it into account need mean no more than taking into account in the allocation of resources to rescue and preventive measures that certain resources are available only to rescue operations. It still must be decided at the outset whether these resources will be utilized. For instance, should provision be made before any peril occurs to have rescue equipment available in an emergency?

And if it appears at the planning stage that in the zeal of the moment of crisis there would be irresistible pressures to expend too great resources on rescue operations, then it would seem correct to make sure at the outset that such pressures could be resisted, even to the point in extreme cases of deliberately planning not to have means available at the time which this zeal could make use of. In short if the allocation of resources to life-saving is correct, and the allocation of life-saving resources between rescue and preventive measures is also correct, then it cannot be improper to assure at the outset that the allocations are adhered to even in the pressure and excitement of an emergency.

A related argument holds that in cases like that of the mine disaster, although the whole society or the government may not be required to devote unlimited resources to rescue, still the mining company — which stands in a special relationship — should be required to do everything in their power to rescue the men that they "sent" down into the mine. Even if there were no problem of defining these special relations in a way that did not beg the question, the argument is fallacious. If coal mining were a state enterprise and rescue operations a state responsibility — as air and sea rescue operations are now — a limit would be set on rescue operations in terms of the relative value of life and other ends. But if coal is produced by a number of small firms instead of one large firm, which is the state, there is no reason for a different social judgment as to the relative value of life and other ends — including the price of coal. Moreover, this last-ditch argument is not as generous as it seems at first, since it is only the particular employer who must exhaust his resources on rescue. This implies a limit in fact on the amount so spent, and a limit which will vary with the fortuity of the actual resources of that firm.* Those urging the significance of

* There is a version of this last-ditch argument which is not invalid in all cases. In the case of a one-shot undertaking (for example, to scale a particular mountain, to recover a wreck on the ocean floor), there may be two kinds of risks. The first is the risk of an accident causing sudden and immediate death. The second is the risk of an accident which presents some chance of rescue after its occurrence if further resources are expended. The expected value of the ends to be achieved, of the costs of those ends, and of rescue may be such that it is worth embarking on the undertaking, but only on the assumption that if an accident of the second type occurs, the available resources will be diverted to rescue and the enterprise abandoned.

special relationships may, however, be concerned with relations of love and friendship. That issue is considered below.

Finally, there is the argument — considered by both Calabresi and Schelling — that in showing some preference in the case of the person in immediate peril, we demonstrate the value we place on human life. Let us call this the symbolic value argument. First it is necessary to get straight what we mean by this argument. Presumably if it is valid in any circumstances, it must be valid as a general policy adopted beforehand, that is, before either preventive measures might be undertaken or an emergency arises calling for rescue. What would such a general policy look like? The notion of symbolizing the value of life by spending an amount on rescue in addition to that dictated by a maximizing strategy can have only two interpretations: (1) that our total life-saving budget remains the same, with the necessary entailment that this "symbolic" increment which we add to rescue has been withdrawn from prevention; or (2) that we do not decrease the prevention subbudget of the total life-saving budget when we add this symbolic increment to the rescue subbudget, with the necessary entailment that an amount corresponding to the symbolic increment has been withdrawn from some or all of the other ends competing with life-saving in general for scarce resources. In short this symbolic increment to the rescue subbudget must come from somewhere. Now if, as in the first interpretation, it comes out of the prevention subbudget — which was set it must be recalled by a maximizing strategy — then it follows we are spending our total life-saving allocation in a way that will *not* lead to the greatest saving of lives in the long run. If, on the other hand, the amount is withdrawn from other substantive ends, this means that the amount allocated to those ends is less than optimum. More lives are saved, but less is accomplished.

With this clarification one must ask what exactly it is that this strategy symbolizes. The answer that must be made is that our concern for human life is symbolized. But surely it is odd to symbolize our concern for human life by actually doing less than we might to save life. This leaves the second interpretation, that we symbolize our concern for human life by spending more on human life than in fact it is worth. That alternative is also unacceptable, since what we wish to do is to symbolize the value of human life as what it is, that is, one value out of many, having a certain relation to other values. The second alternative misrepresents this value by making it greater than we believe it to be. Moreover, the anomaly is deeper if we consider that the special symbolic amount is added to the rescue subbudget of the life-saving budget, irrespective of whether this symbolic increment does the most good (saves the most lives) by being allocated to rescue. If it does not, we are again in the position of symbolizing our concern for human life by wasting our life-saving resources in a way that does not save the most lives possible.

A variant of this argument would justify the anomaly by saying that the added amount is necessary to educate people who do not understand the force of these arguments about how seriously we take human life. Whether it is necessary, of course, is a question of fact. One would wish to know whether the cost in human lives is worth this educational measure, and whether it is sound policy to educate people by using invalid arguments. Is it not better to train people to think rationally, if this is possible? Moreover, if the education variant is correct, then the added amount, which appears (to the unsophisticated whom we are educating) to be added to the rescue subbudget in a particular case, is really intended as a preventive measure after all, since the purpose of the lesson presumably is to educate people to behave correctly in respect to the value of human life.

Fairness

The most obvious objection to a pure efficiency argument is an argument from fairness. As applied in this context an argument from fairness would hold that it is not sufficient to justify the choice of a particular strategy as to life saving that it leads to the least net expenditure of lives in the long run. It must also be shown that the risk of death is fairly apportioned among the relevant population. What does fairness mean in situations such as those we have been considering in this section? If the victims who are sacrificed in these pursuits are chosen at random this would seem to be all that fairness demands. This does entail that it is intolerable that any particular person or group run a greater risk than another — at least not without some corresponding compensation.

Thus in the epidemic example, whether vaccine or serum is chosen, it must be made available without discrimination between classes of recipients. And this may be a significant constraint, for it may well be that the most efficient scheme requires discriminations which fairness precludes.

Does fairness require more? Is it unfair that one person and not another is the victim of a mine disaster, than one falls victim of the epidemic before the serum is available and another is inoculated in time? Are these instances of bad luck or unfairness as well — assuming of course that it is not the black miners who are chosen for the most dangerous work and the slum dwellers who always fall prey first to disease? To be sure, at any particular point some persons will be better off than others, but if this is the working out of a fair gamble in which all participated, then the losers cannot complain. After all it is assumed that all desire and have an equal chance of sharing in the benefits of the risky enterprise.

The argument thus is that equity achieved by all having an equal chance is as equitable as the more obvious kind of equity where there is an equality of outcome — all get the serum or none get the serum. But it is important to note that for this argument to work there must be a rough equality of the exposure in fact. If we are choosing one man out of five for a dangerous patrol, it will not do to tell the man who is chosen out of spite by his platoon leader that after all he stood a one in five chance of being chosen. He did not. To justify an outcome by reference to a lottery, the dice must not have been loaded — to mix a metaphor. One must actually have enjoyed a chance of winning. A test of this might be whether one could imagine trading on that expectation, spreading the risk, insuring and reinsuring. In this sense certain mishaps relative to a defined segment of the population may be viewed as truly random events, thus insuring fairness in respect to the burden of those mishaps.

Fairness, thus, is an important qualification to efficiency as the criterion for choosing between a preventive or a rescue strategy, for deciding whether and how much in a particular case to prefer persons in present peril. But nothing that has been said about fairness suggests any reason for preferring a rescue strategy. There is no reason to believe that the burden of misfortune will fall more equally if in general we prefer to some degree (not dictated by efficiency) the plight of persons in present peril. Examples of this being so may exist, but so also equity may in other special circumstances require doing more than is "efficient" by way of prevention. Therefore, for the purposes of the present problem of statistical lives, the efficient and the fair solutions do not diverge in any systematic way.

The aspect of fairness I have been considering may be identified with the notion of distributive justice, that aspect of justice which establishes the basic distribution of benefits and burdens throughout the society. Another aspect of justice, corrective justice, requires that a person who has been deprived of his just share (as determined by the canons of distributive justice) be appropriately compensated for his deprivation. Thus a person imperiled by the omission of safety measures which should have been taken in his behalf is entitled not only to the amount of rescue generally allocated by the maximizing strategy to persons in his predicament, but to whatever additional amount is necessary to bring his level of risk down to the norm. This additional amount should be provided by the person at fault or by the persons who benefited by the previous maldistribution.

Finally it is an aspect of fairness to keep faith with the reasonable expectation which a man has knowingly created in others, usually for his own purposes. And respect for this kind of fairness may also sometimes lead to choices that do not obviously square with a maximizing strategy. Thus in the coal mining case or in the case of a ship lost at sea, there may have been an explicit or implicit undertaking to the miners or passengers to make extraordinary efforts in their behalf in the case of a disaster. The principles of fairness and morality developed in Part One dictate that such undertakings should be honored, even if on some view it may in the event be more efficient not to do so. Indeed this is just a special case of the several obligations of fidelity to one's promises and undertakings. It may often be the case that when the time for performance of a promise comes, it may seem more efficient to break the promise. And it may well be the case that in many of the situations where we feel the pressure to do more for some person or class of persons than a maximing strategy dictates, this aspect of fairness is at work.

But we must be careful not to make too much of this argument.

Let us say that "doing more" by way of rescue out of respect for a prior undertaking is similar to keeping a promise; this should not lead to a complete unbalancing of our social accounts. If I have promised to one person to pay him a sum of money, this promise does not qualify my obligation to other persons to pay them what I owe, or to pay my taxes. The extra measure paid out to one person should not be at the expense of what in justice is owed to others. It should be at my own expense. So if the coal company has undertaken to make heroic efforts in respect to one group of miners, the cost of that effort should not be placed on other subsequent miners — statistical miners — by skimping on safety measures for their protection. The extra cost should come out of the company's own assets. To be sure, sometimes the party who made the promise simply does not have enough assets to absorb the extra burden and to do what he should by all others. There is in that case a conflict of obligations. And I would suggest tentatively that the voluntarily assumed extra obligation should yield.

In general, the recognition of the binding force of undertakings is not a qualification of the maximizing strategy so much as it is a recognition of the value of liberty to do what one wishes with one's own uncommitted resources. Perhaps I am under no moral obligation to save another at grave peril to myself, but still I should be able to do so if I choose, and I should be able to make a binding promise to do so — provided the rights of others are not thereby infringed.

We should be careful also not to read implicit undertakings or promises into too many situations. Where there is an express promise, there is usually a reasonable expectation. So also if (1) I make sacrifices or accept risks for your benefit, (2) in the expectation that you will assume a certain obligation to me, and (3) you knew that I was making the sacrifice only on the inducement of that expectation, and (4) you intended me to act thus for your benefit relying on my expectations, then surely all the conditions are present for holding that my reasonable expectations must be honored. But it is not every expectation that deserves this kind of respect. Absent some special basis, the only reasonable expectations that persons have are that they will be treated rightly and fairly. But that may mean no more than that they get what's coming to them under the maximization strategy.

The Personalist Argument

The two arguments I shall consider now grow out of a feeling that after all some basis for preferring the person in known peril survives the series of refutations I have paraded so far. Moreover, in discovering what that basis is, some values in and features of problems of social choice in general may be illuminated. These arguments do not, however, end up justifying a systematic preference for persons in present peril.

The first argument I shall consider grows out of a distinction between personal relations — relations of love and friendship — and the more abstract relations of justice and fairness. This argument I shall call the personalist argument.

I am assuming a particular conception of love and friendship which is not simply descriptive, but is in part theoretical and normative. This conception presents an account of love and friendship which establishes the importance of relations of love and friendship, and the connection between love and friendship on one hand and justice, fairness, and respect on the other. Without repeating the account in Part One, I would recall one conclusion here. There are assumed, first, principles of justice and fairness which allocate benefits and burdens equally in social situations. The willingness to recognize the due entitlements of others under the principles of justice and fairness is defined as the attitude of respect, and the sense of one's own entitlements vis-à-vis others as self-respect. Love and friendship are seen as being built upon a base of respect and self-respect in that in love and friendship a person freely relinquishes entitlements which he believes to be securely his own for the sake of another person. He makes the interests of another his own interests, and invests in their welfare some of the moral capital to which he is entitled under the principles of justice and fairness.

Now the personalist argument holds that some preference for known over statistical lives is justified by virtue of the fact that it is with known lives that we enter into relations of love and friendship, while to the abstract statistical lives we stand in relations defined by justice and fairness. Thus the personalist argument holds that some preference might be given to the situation of the miners trapped in a cave-in or the persons presently suffering from the epidemic disease. The reason for the preference would be that relations of love and friendship are personal relations, in which the parties to the relation are aware of each other as particular persons, as individuals, rather than as abstract persons having only such characteristics as make them the appropriate objects of duties of justice and fairness. And these personal relations are expressed by a greater concern and a greater degree of sacrifice than we show, let us say, to our fellow citizens when we fulfill our obligations of fairness to them by paying our income tax. Relations of love and friendship, by contrast, bring us into concrete, individualized and emotional contact with another person. And, so the personalist argument goes, it is in recognition of the greater urgency of these relations, and of the importance for human beings of being able to realize these relations in significant ways, that it is justified to devote relatively more resources to saving the lives of persons in known peril than to preventive measures benefiting abstract, statistical persons.

An obvious question about this argument is how it deals with the circumstance that in many — probably most — of the situations we are considering, the person in known peril may be identified to the person in a position to help him, but he is otherwise a relative stranger, not a friend or loved one. He may be one's employee in a company employing thousands, or a fellow worker in such a company. Or he may be a stranger whom a doctor sees for the first time when he is brought into the hospital. However, in considering this question, we should realize that apart from close blood relatives, people enter into relations of love and friendship by degrees, starting out as relative strangers. A person is a potential friend if we encounter him in some degree of particularity, as a person with particular, concrete attributes. Thus every stranger we encounter in a situation where personal interaction of some sort is possible — every person who appears to us as a particular person — is a potential friend. What more is needed is an act of choice which will realize that potential. Moreover, the risk situation, the situation in which risks are imposed or dangers averted, may be the very situation that actualizes the merely statistical individual before us as a particular person, and thus as a potential friend.

But must we seize the opportunity, must we treat as a friend the stranger whom we first encounter in such a situation? We might answer no, but consider the consequences. If we say no to the particular stranger we are saying to him that though we can see plainly enough that he is a particular person, not just a statistical, possible person, we refuse to take that particularity into account. We will look through him — or through his individuality, at any rate — as if he were not there, and see only an abstraction. We will refuse to recognize an individuality that is there for us to recognize, and we will do it moreover in a context where that other person's life might be at stake. It is this that seems a horrible thing to do, horrible to contemplate and horrible to experience. An encounter — where a life might be saved or a vital interest served — is an encounter in which we make friends and establish personal, not merely abstract, relations with persons. It would seem that the more crucial the encounter — the more we might do to or for the person — the more the situation cries out for actualizing the potential which an encounter with a particular, concrete individual contains, that is, the potential for a relation of love or friendship. Thus in many of our dealings — as taxpayers, as voters, as public servants, as entrepreneurs — we can only look at our fellow men as abstractions, as statistical persons. But often too we will encounter people as actual persons, and there it seems we have the occasion, the opportunity to show our deeper humanity.

This argument has a great intuitive appeal, and I have tried to put it forward in its most compelling form. But there are two objections to the personalist argument that I believe leave very little of it standing.

First, those in future peril may themselves fall in the class of persons to whom the personalist argument gives preference. I have spoken at times of known lives as opposed to statistical lives, and of present peril as opposed to future peril. But these are not equivalent concepts and each bears differently on the validity of the personalist argument. Thus there is the case of the father of identical infant twins who must decide whether to authorize a kidney transplant to save the life of one twin, but at the cost of impairing the health — that is, increasing the risk of death at some later age — of the healthy twin. Both of the lives in question are identified and as to both there exist similar relations of love. The difference is that the peril to one is a present peril. A similar case is that of the commander of a small force of men, all of whom he knows well and is closely tied to by bonds of affection. He may have to decide whether to risk the lives of several men — for example, by delaying a return to a position of safety or by depleting fuel supplies — to save one in present peril. In such cases the personalist argument does not explain a preference for the person in present peril. Greater weight than efficiency and fairness dictate is given to the person in present peril, and the interests of other persons to whom one stands in exactly the same relation of love and friendship are thereby sacrificed.

Since the specification of the category in terms of present peril does not work, at least not all by itself, let us consider an alternative specification in terms of known as opposed to unknown persons. But this must in turn be further specified: known at the time that the original decision is made, or known at the time the risks eventuate. Thus we may decide to give the serum to persons now suffering from the hypothetical disease because they are in known peril, while the persons who will suffer later when the epidemic strikes and no serum is available are not now known. They are simply a statistically defined sample of the total population. Some may not yet have been born. However, when the epidemic strikes those later victims will be as clearly identified as are the patients now before us. Even if we concede that one can stand in a relation of love and friendship only to a known person, we know now that we will later stand in exactly the same relation to those later sufferers as we stand to these present ones. But if we define the concept of identified person as one who now is or later will be (is likely to be?) identified, we have lost the whole force of the personalist argument as an argument for giving some lives greater consideration than they would receive by virtue of efficiency and fairness alone. And if we seek to escape this result by asserting that it is only lives presently identified and presently in peril we then must somehow deal with the case where no one is yet in any peril and we are deciding how to allocate our resources over the future. Do we, because no one is in peril at the time, plan simply in accordance with fairness and efficiency, and then, when disaster strikes, cheat on the plan, thereby imperiling persons at later times? Or do we in our planning make some provision for the personalist argument? But how can one do that? Only by making a decision at the planning stage that we will have more accidents than "necessary" so as to provide occasions for rescue. Moreover we will prefer accidents with possibilities of rescue to those without it, even though this may result in more fatalities due to unsuccessful rescue attempts. Finally, it should be recognized that to the planner all these lives are equally unknown.*

What this shows is that love and friendship do not justify disregarding obligations of justice and fairness, the beneficiaries of which are, after all, real persons too. The generosity of love and friendship is based on giving up what is one's own, not in depriving a third person of his just and fair entitlements. But if the personalist argument (somehow specified) depends on the relations of love and friendship, it does not therefore justify a preference which in effect robs those who do not stand in those relations. So also it would seem that there is no callousness, no horror in sticking to a fair and efficient life-saving plan in the event. You do not deny the humanity of the persons whom you refuse to favor beyond what the correct strategy dictates. Whatever horror the potential rescuer and the victim read in each other's eyes when the rescuer turns away and does no more is *not* a horror at treating or being treated as less than a person. It is perhaps the horror at realizing the vulnerability and helplessness of persons. But that is a different matter.

Finally, it must be acknowledged that love and friendship do bring forth a sacrifice for another of one's own interests beyond obligation. In the life-saving problem this means the actor — the rescuer or doctor — might take personal risks which he is not in fairness required to take either for persons in present peril or for statistical lives. Such acts of generosity are indeed characteristic of love and friendship. They are not done out of duty. But there is no support here for the personalist argument. Such acts are free and generous. Often they are done for the sake of persons to whom there are pre-existing strong ties of love or friendship. Sometimes to be sure they are done surprisingly and gratuitously for a stranger,

---

* A related thrust would ask just how precisely identified the person in peril must be. Is it sufficient that we know that one out of n number of persons is surely in peril? How large may n be? Is it sufficient that there is a risk p that an identified person is now in peril? What of a risk p as to one of n persons? And if we say the personalist argument holds in cases of less than complete certainty or identification in the present, should we not also include uncertainty about future perils?

and such an act of sacrifice and friendship for a stranger does indeed illuminate something about the potentiality for friendship between all men. But sacrifices of this order can also be made for purely abstract persons, humanity in general, as when medical researchers work for the cure of a disease whose victims are not yet born. The fallacy of the personalist argument is that it either would require these free and generous sacrifices by some obligation in a certain class of case or would remove the generosity altogether by depriving one class of persons of a portion of their just due for the benefit of another class.

Before leaving this range of arguments, it is important to admit the existence of a serious problem to which no definitive answer has been supplied. There is an implication in what has been said in refutation of the personalist argument that a person is never justified in preferring the life of a person to whom he stands in a relation of love or friendship. But surely it would be absurd to insist that if a man could, at no risk or cost to himself, save one of two persons in equal peril, and one of those in peril was, say, his wife, he must treat both equally, perhaps by flipping a coin. One answer is that where the potential rescuer occupies no office such as that of captain of a ship, public health official, or the like, the occurrence of the accident may itself stand as a sufficient randomizing event to meet the dictates of fairness, so he may prefer his friend or loved one. Where the rescuer does occupy an official position, the argument that he must overlook personal ties is not unacceptable. But what if there is no official position and the chances of rescuing the stranger are better than of rescuing the wife? One feels that up to a point the personal tie may still be respected, but only up to a point. This issue and the principles it involves remain unresolved for this discussion. Nevertheless, however this issue is resolved, it should be noted that the resolution does not entail a preference for persons in present peril as such.

How One Dies

The intuitive judgment favoring known lives in present peril may well derive from a sense that not only is it important how many people die, but also what the circumstances of their death are. I shall examine the values involved in how one dies, because they add a needed extra dimension to the consideration of life and death presented so far. An appreciation of these values certainly has a bearing on how we allocate resources, personally and socially, for indeed the recognition of any significant set of values entails some corresponding allocation of time, energy, life, or resources. It will appear, however, that the recognition of these values does not serve in the least to justify a systematic preference for known over statistical lives, a preference for rescue over prevention. Rather these values comprise simply an addition to the total set of values which compete with or complement the claims of the total life-saving budget in various ways.

If some forms of death are preferable to others for all persons, then it is appropriate for society to take this into account in its allocation of resources. To take an obvious example, deaths involving considerable prolonged pain and impairment of capacities are in general less desirable than deaths without such suffering. A rational person, considering the matter beforehand, would be justified in taking this into account in planning his own life, and society therefore is justified in allocating resources in a way that recognizes the importance of avoiding deaths attended by great suffering. It may follow that resources should be allocated away from other ends — including life saving — to the alleviation of suffering. However, there may be a special linkage between life saving and the alleviation of suffering. For instance, if a particular disease has associated with it both a high mortality rate and a painful and lingering death, then there is an additional reason for allocating resources to decrease the incidence of that disease. Alternatively, the value of alleviating pain and suffering might be recognized by shortening or refusing to prolong the lives of persons suffering from particularly painful diseases (although one would probably want to accede to the wishes of a victim who preferred to live). If the value of avoiding pain and suffering is recognized by refusing to prolong the lives of certain persons or by euthanasia, then, of course, to that extent lives are shortened and the value of life is given less recognition. Conversely, if pain and suffering are lessened by avoiding or curing the fatal disease, to that extent the value of life is given greater recognition. However, in giving this greater recognition to the value of life in order to lessen pain and suffering, it is not necessarily the case that the extra resources will most efficiently serve the life-saving functions. That is, these extra resources might very well save more lives or prolong more lives if they were allocated otherwise.

Thus it is clear that the value of reducing pain and suffering affects the allocation of resources to life saving. But there is no reason to believe that this effect is in any way related to the notion of preferring known lives in present peril. Is there a kind of pain and suffering which is specifically related to the condition of being a known life in present peril? The personalist argument suggested a special pain and horror involved in being in mortal peril and knowing that one was being deliberately denied aid that might be available because such aid was not, as it were, budgeted to that account. But my conclusion was that that kind of pain is an inadmissible factor. Since it is no more than the horror of discovering that in a situation of scarce resources what could rightly be made available had run out and one is doomed. Could this point be amended so as to survive that refutation? Is there some special pain entailed by the knowledge that one is presently in a situation of grave peril? If so, then there is a justification in allocating some resources to the alleviation of that pain, or to preventing situations from coming about in which such pain exists.

The argument for a special pain caused by the knowledge that one is presently in grave peril is on inspection ambiguous and full of problems. Any rational person knows that he must die, so that this special pain if it exists must have something to do with a peculiar degree of certainty about death and the imminence of that death.

Would a rational person prefer to be in a considerable state of uncertainty about his death? Most persons, for much of their lives, are in such uncertainty, but is it preferable? A rational person has certain ends that he seeks to attain in his lifetime. Moreover, the general shape that he gives to his life plan and the arrangement of his ends over his life cycle are related to the facts and suppositions about human mortality. To be sure, mortality must generally be taken into account probabilistically. But nothing that has been argued supports the conclusion that a rational man should in principle approach his life plan differently if the time and circumstances of his death were known. On the contrary, it would seem that with greater certainty comes greater control, and thus a correspondingly greater possibility of realizing one's substantive goals.

This attitude toward uncertainty, and particularly uncertainty in the face of death, is obviously idealized. The question arises whether the ideal has any significant relation to reality. The view exists, and has been argued and presented in various traditions and forms, that the more effective, the more rational, indeed the more fully human the person becomes, the fuller is his acceptance of the inevitability of death and the more easily does he live with that acceptance. This is an ideal which is, of course, familiar in Christian literature, where the true wise man is shown as living with a constant and full awareness of the imminent possibility of death. In a rather different tradition the psychoanalyst Erik Erikson has argued that the full acceptance of the inevitability of death is correlative to a full and unreserved commitment to one's own goals in life. In his view the serenity with which one contemplates the inevitability of death is a function of the confidence one has in life, in the goals one has chosen, and one's capacity to realize them. And in classical literature, the archetype of the person who is noble and confident in the face of a death, whose manner and hour he knows, is Oedipus at Colonus. These ideals of rationality and serenity seem to argue that in the issue before us no special consideration is due simply because one is facing a certain and imminent death.

This ideal and rather stoic conception can be challenged in two ways. Either challenge would justify the notion that there is a special suffering, and therefore special consideration due, in the situation where the person faces relatively certain and imminent death.

The most radical criticism would hold that the picture of human behavior presented in this essay, the picture of the human reaction to time, change, uncertainty, the life cycle, and mortality, is at best a partial and distorted one. By this radical criticism the notion is challenged that what is important and characteristic in the structure of human ends is the ends themselves; and the notion is also challenged that therefore a situation of maximum certainty is necessarily preferable — other things being equal — because of the greater control that is accorded in the formulation and realization of those ends. Rational planning is not seen as a necessary strategy to overcome the problems of uncertainty. Rather uncertainty is seen as not only the natural and inevitable condition in which men pursue their ends, but also as a necessary condition for making life tolerable.

By this criticism uncertainty is necessary to the effective functioning of the human person in two ways. First, it constantly introduces elements of novelty, and thus challenges the person and wards off a deadening tedium. Second, and more important, uncertainty creates a necessary distance between the man at any particular instant in time and the misfortunes which he dreads, particularly the misfortune of his own extinction. Perhaps one might say that uncertainty about achieving one's ends is a price one is glad to pay in return for the boon of uncertainty about the misfortunes which may occur and the death which will occur. Excessive certainty of any sort thus is seen as intolerable because the person who is assured of even the most desirable of his goals is thereby reminded of the similar assurance of his own death. On this view the efforts men make to deal with uncertainty, either to reduce it or to adopt rational probabilistic strategies in the face of it, are never entirely wholehearted. They are incomplete and fragmentary, as the life plan is incomplete and fragmentary, not because of any weakness of intellect or will, but because of the necessary ambivalence of human persons to uncertainty. Human persons must seek to overcome uncertainty to a degree if they are to be at all effective, if they are to attain any of their substantive goals, but yet they also flee certainty and require the comfort of uncertainty and indeterminacy.

If this criticism is valid — and I shall not argue against it, but only present it — then one can readily see why the certainty of a present death is radically and tragically painful, and why significant human resources should be devoted to avoiding and alleviating the suffering of persons in that position. To be presented with a certain and imminent death in circumstances where one cannot rationalize or temporize is to be caught finally in a dilemma which one has sought to avoid, and which all men have sought to avoid throughout their lifetimes. The knowledge of certain and imminent death becomes a kind of exquisite and radical torture, depriving a person of the most important support, on which he has relied all his life. And I emphasize the certainty as well as the imminence of the peril, because what is certain but not imminent one may still possibily rationalize away as perhaps not being certain after all.

Although I cannot refute but do not accept the radical pessimism and skepticism of the above criticism, I believe that it contains an element which is true, and from which one may move to an understanding of the problem presented in this section. The radical criticism I have thus considered seems to state as a universal necessity something which is a tendency in all persons. I would affirm the Eriksonian and perhaps Sophoclean ideal of humanity as an ideal, and a possible one — that is, that a mature, rational, human person can live with, accept, and incorporate into his own ends the realities of human existence, including the reality of his own mortality. Therefore, uncertainty becomes simply an element to be dealt with, rather than the necessary element which makes the whole thing tolerable. Although one sees many lives which seem to exemplify the validity of the radical criticism, one sees enough lives exemplifying the ideal to persuade that the radical criticism is not a universal necessity. And if it is not a universal necessity, then the ideal remains possible and relevant. However, the radical criticism does point up an important tendency, and that is a tendency to move away from reality, in order to make life seem more tolerable though less lifelike. The tension, therefore, which one must concede exists, is a tension between an ideal, and a strong temptation to flee reality and move away from the ideal. That temptation, obviously, must be strongest where one faces a certainty of misfortune, and strongest of all where one faces a certainty of death, more or less imminent.

Now the ideal of rationality and humanity which has been presented in this essay is not presented simply descriptively. It is something that is worth attaining, and thus worth helping others to attain. And this being so, it would seem that men have an obligation to each other to lend assistance and support when they are faced with this danger to their dignity and to the integrity of their conceptions of themselves. Thus the person threatened with imminent death is not — on my view — threatened so much by an intolerable dilemma as he is by a radical test of his own humanity. We support others in this situation, lest our general confidence in a person's ability to order and lead a rational and dignified life be undermined. But the consideration to be shown in that situation is not the consideration which would be shown under the radical criticism presented above. Particularly there would be no occasion to seek to avoid such occasions, by in fact shortening the lives of others or indeed shortening the life of the person in that circumstance itself. The appropriate response, rather, is to strengthen persons beforehand against that circumstance and to provide them with human support and comfort when they are in it. To be sure both of these things will involve the expenditure of human resources. Both moral education and moral support and comfort are not cost-free expenditures of energy, but they are the only expenditures of energy which I would admit are appropriate to the particular problem we have been considering, the only ones which are consistent with the conception of humanity and rationality developed in this essay.

Finally, not only are there special pains involved in facing (near) certain death, but also there are opportunities peculiar to that segment of the life cycle. Certainty of death makes irrelevant various factors which a rational person must otherwise be concerned about and permits a degree of concentration on short range and immediate goals. Some vulnerabilities are removed — one need not be concerned, for instance, whether a given undertaking impairs health. In short the certainty of death may permit a clarity of thought and purity of concentration on some ends which otherwise would be irrational. The certainty may, indeed, allow one a rarely disinterested view of his own life and of life in general.

If certainty of death may involve these possibilities, then it is appropriate to recognize here a distinct period of the life cycle with distinct potentialities. And if the general rule of ordering we have adopted is that it is worth allocating resources over a lifetime so that each significant capacity at each stage of life may be realized, then it follows it is appropriate to allocate resources to this stage and its attendant potentialities. What those resources are I cannot say, but there is no reason to believe that they would lead to some systematic preference for saving identified lives in present peril.

The Primacy of the Concrete

In Part One a theory of value was developed, which emphasizes actions, feelings, thoughts, and perceptions as the crucial, primary ends of persons. Among these ends are: learning a skill, exercising that skill, coming to understand a principle, learning about a state of affairs, eating, drinking, sex, the enjoyment of a work of art, the creation of a work of art, acts of kindness and acts of love. I am aware that what were seen as the basic ends and determinants of value have rather moved into the background during much of the analysis in these last three chapters. Now that we are at the end of this essay I should like to restore the proper emphasis by recalling the status of these ends and showing how an appreciation of their appropriate place clarifies and illuminates certain puzzles.

The concept of the risk budget, it should be recalled, is based upon the concept of the rational life plan. The rational life plan is a kind of principle of principles, by which a person orders his various ends, these ends themselves being constituted by ordering, informing principles. In the life plan and its principle there is attained or embodied the end of rational coherence, which is both an end among other ends, and also an end incorporating the other ends. The risk budget is a part of the complex ordering of the life plan.

In describing this more abstract and inclusive order we may to some extent have lost sight of what is being ordered. The life plan, particularly when we focus on that part of it which I have called the risk budget, takes on the aspect of a timeless mathematical function in which the various elements are weighted and summed and a value assigned to the whole. Especially it is a way in which that which has not yet occurred and might not occur may be assigned a value and compared to those things which are in the process of occurring. But it should not be forgotten that it is not the plan alone which has value; the value of the plan derives from the elements which it orders, the rational actions which it orders. In this a rational plan might be analogized to the principle of justice. The principle of justice is a principle of ordering among individuals, but it is an ordering which is intended to express the primacy and sovereignty of individual persons. It is the persons who have value, and the value of the ordering of justice derives from this. In the same way the rational plan is a principle of coherence among rational actions, and derives at least a large measure of its value from the fact that it is an ordering of values.

This point about life plans has in fact been brought out in a number of ways, as in the discussion of commitments in Chapter Ten. But I would like to reassert in a general way the primary position of concrete actions in the life plan which orders them.

What can this assertion of a primary position amount to? Must we not conclude that we grant each action *exactly* its correct position by assigning it its place in the life plan and then adhering to the life plan? I do not know how we can escape this conclusion, but it is interesting that we should want to. The unease we feel with this conclusion derives, I believe, from the possible suggestion that we act and pursue ends not for their own sake, but for the sake of the life plan which orders them. It is as if a utilitarian suggested that we pursue this or that pleasure in order to maximize utility. Indeed I have argued that to some extent coherence in the life plan is pursued as an end in itself among other ends; but it must also be asserted that particular ends are pursued for their own sake, subject only to the constraints of the life plan. Or, to put the point somewhat differently, persons pursue the general end of coherence in a life plan by pursuing particular ends according to its constraints. Once this is seen the primacy of concrete ends and actions need not be viewed as threatened.

Applying this to the problem of known against statistical lives, or to the problem of present against future ends, both these problems may be seen as arising out of the uneasy suspicion that the rationality of the life plan sacrifices specific ends to the plan itself. By pressing the claim of the known life, the present action, the concrete possibility on the verge of actualization, one feels that one is, as it were, heroically championing the claims of the various concrete ends against the claims of rationality, of the life plan itself.

Now this reaction to the claims of the life plan is based, of course, on a fallacy, perhaps a deep fallacy. It is just not the case that the life plan denies the primacy of the ends and actions it orders. What is more, this heroic argument in behalf of the concrete is a game that cannot be won. Presumably the champion of the concrete would argue for some preference for the present, the known, the palpable as against the statistical, the future, the potential. But he would do no more than give these former a preference; he would not give them an absolute status. And this preference can be perfectly well accommodated (if need be) in a rational plan or a risk budget, as a weighted trade-off. Indeed just this was considered in respect to known as against statistical lives. Perhaps there is an argument to be made for such a general weighting in favor of immediate or concrete actions. I do not know of it.

Notes
Index

Notes

Chapter II. *Means and Ends*

A Straw Man

It is highly doubtful that any real philosophical figure of significance corresponds to the straw man. Perhaps it is in the nature of a straw man that no one should correspond to his position; and that if a correspondence is asserted in respect to a particular person, the defenders of that person should deny the correspondence. Bentham is as close as I can come. Consider his dictum: "Prejudice apart, the game of pushpin is of equal value with the arts and sciences of music and poetry." *The Works of Jeremy Bentham,* ed. John Bowring (1843), II, 253.

Kant gives an interesting formulation of the straw man's position in *The Critique of Practical Reason* (pt. I, §3, note 1): "Just as to the man who wants money to spend, it is all the same whether the gold was dug out of the mountain or washed out of the sand, provided it is everywhere accepted at the same value, so the man who cares only for the enjoyment of life does not ask whether the ideas [which he enjoys] are of the understanding or the senses, but only how much and how great pleasure they will give for the longest time." Quoted in Duncker, "On Pleasure, Emotion, and Striving," *Philosophy and Phenomenological Research,* 1(1940): 392–393.

It seems to me that McNaughton in "A Metrical Conception of Happiness," *Philosophy and Phenomenological Research,* 14(1954):172, constructs, using Von Neumann-Morgenstern utility, a metric of pleasure that is quite similar to that implied by the straw man model.

The philosophical literature on pleasure is huge. I shall mention only those works that strike me as particularly relevant to my thesis in this chapter. Plato's treatment of pleasure is to be found principally in the *Philebus*, and, as commentaries such as Reginald Hackforth's (1945) or A. E. Taylor's (1956) show, Plato anticipates much of the later debates about hedonism. For instance, Socrates makes a higher and lower pleasure argument similar to that of Mill, and agrees with Kant that although the pleasures of the mind or thought are higher pleasures, human nature being complex, the good for man is a good that includes sensual pleasure. There is an important discussion of pleasure also in Book IX of *The Republic*.

Aristotle's views on pleasure, especially as an accompaniment to activity, have obviously been very influential for my account. See *Nicomachean Ethics*, Books IX and X, and Urmson, "Aristotle on Pleasure," in *Aristotle*, ed. J. M. E. Moravcsik (1967).

For an interesting analysis of pleasure and related concepts which draws heavily on phenomenological writings and on the speculative psychology of the nineteenth and early twentieth century, see Duncker, in *Philosophy and Phenomenological Research*, 1(1940):391.

The utilitarian critics and exponents of Bentham's concept of pleasure start with Mill in *Utilitarianism* (New York: The Liberal Arts Press, 1957), p. 12f. Bentham himself in *The Principles of Morals and Legislation* (New York: Hafner Publishing Co., 1948), pp. 33–37, 44–63, proposes an elaborate typology of pleasure. Henry Sidgwick's discussion is in *The Methods of Ethics* (1963), bk. I, ch. 4; bk. II; and bk. III, ch. 14. In chapter III of the *Principia Ethica*, G. E. Moore not only gives his own account, but offers a critique of Mill and Sidgwick.

For an attempt to formulate hedonism in the light of modern utility theory, see McNaughton, in *Philosophy and Phenomenological Research*, 14(1954):172. See also Davidson, McKinsey, and Suppes, "Outlines of a Formal Theory of Value," *Philosophy of Science*, 22(1955):140, which does not, however, subscribe to any form of hedonism. For an excellent account of modern utility theory, see R. D. Luce and Howard Raiffa, *Games and Decisions* (1957), ch. 2.

A recent philosophical debate on the concept of pleasure has concerned itself with whether pleasure is best analyzed as a behavior-dispositional term, as is argued by Ryle in the symposium on "Pleasure," in *Proceedings of the Aristotelian Society*, supp. vol. 28 (1954), or sometimes an experience, as is suggested by Gallie, in the same symposium, and by Penelhum in "The Logic of Pleasure," *Philosophy and Phenomenological Research*, 17(1957):488.

For a general introduction to this topic, see Richard Brandt, *Ethical Theory* (1959), ch. XII.

The Complexity of Ends

On the complexity of even the simplest seeming gestures, see Elizabeth Anscombe, *Intention* (1959); H. L. A. Hart, "Acts of Will and Responsibility," in *Punishment and Responsibility* (1968); and A. I. Melden, *Free Action* (1961).

But the most elaborate and, for all its obscurity and complexity, most interesting discussion of the complexity of action is David Schwayder, *The Stratification of Behavior* (1965).

The Concept of Rational Ends

The example of making restitution depends on the acceptance of principles of fair play and respect developed at length in Chapter Four, while the principles in which the concept of a gift are embedded are elaborated in Chapter Five, in the discussion of love and friendship, and in Chapter Nine, in the discussion of intimacy. For an interesting anthropological account of the varying significance of gifts, see Marcel Mauss, *The Gift* (Dennison trans., 1967).

On the relations between the performance and the appropriate gestures see Wittgenstein, *Philosophical Investigation,* for example, §200, and Jonathan Bennett, *Rationality* (1964), pp. 39–40.

There is a discussion very similar to my own of the difference between a random activity (a child throwing clay), and an activity governed by a principle, concept, or rule (a potter at work at his wheel) in R. P. Wolff, *Kant's Theory of Mental Activity* (1963), pp. 121–125.

The notion of what it is to understand and follow a rule is discussed by Wittgenstein, §§142–243. See also Michael Dummett, "Wittgenstein's Philosophy of Mathematics" in *Wittgenstein — The Philosophical Investigation* (George Pitcher ed., 1966).

In general my conception of rational action owes much to the views of David Schwayder in *The Stratification of Behavior* (1965), and Stuart Hampshire, in *Thought and Action* (1959).

Explicit and Implicit Principles

Noam Chomsky's views are formulated clearly in *Aspects of the Theory of Syntax* (1965). For a spirited polemical presentation see Chomsky, "A Review of B. F. Skinner's *Verbal Behavior*" in *The Structure of Language* (J. A. Fodor and J. J. Katz eds., 1964). This anthology contains many items of interest by Chomsky and others. Chomsky suggested in "Linguistic Contributions to the Theory of Mind" (unpublished lectures, delivered at the University of California, Berkeley) that perhaps innate linguistic structures have correlates in morals, in social forms, and elsewhere, but doubts that the existence of any of these correlate structures has yet been successfully demonstrated.

Thomas Nagel considers the implications of Chomsky's theories for philosophical problems such as the possibility of a priori knowledge, innate knowledge, in "Linguistics and Epistemology" in *Linguistics and Philosophy* (Ninth New York University Institute of Philosophy, 1969). See also Collins, "Unconscious Belief," *The Journal of Philosophy*, 66 (1969):667.

The argument that doing arithmetic or performing a dance requires at least implicit or inchoate understanding of principles commits me, inevitably, to a position in the dispute about the relation between knowing "how" and knowing "that." I am arguing that to know how implies an implicit or inchoate knowledge of "that." On this distinction, see Gilbert Ryle, *The Concept of Mind* (1949).

Nelson Goodman's *The Languages of Art* (1968) contains a detailed and extensive discussion of choreographic and musical scores, of the notion of performances according to a score, and of the distinctions between works of art which have a score and those that do not; works that involve performances — whether or not according to a score — and works like novels or poetry or paintings that do not; and works like paintings that are necessarily unique objects, and as to which the concept of a forgery is relevant, and works — whether performed or not — which are not unique objects and which thus cannot be forged. The discussions of scores and performances are particularly relevant to the ideas in this and the succeeding chapter.

The distinction between a rule and a rule formulation, which is made in the text, is also made by Max Black, "The Analysis of Rules," in his *Models and Metaphors* (1962).

Chapter 3. *Rational Ends and Their Principles*

The Rationality of Rational Ends

A striking discussion of the relation between reason and ends is Mabbott, "Reason and Desire," *Philosophy*, 28(1953):113. That discussion ascribes to reason a number of functions such as postponing, suppressing, or establishing an order among desires. I add another: to enter into the constitution of the very object of desire.

R. P. Wolff, in *Kant's Theory of Mental Activity* (1963), pp. 121–125, establishes the distinction between rule governed and non-rule governed behavior, and points out that the activity of rule formulation may itself be an instance of one or the other type.

The classical discussion of varying organizing principles in the visual arts is Heinrich Wölfflin, *Classic Art* (Murray trans., 1952), and *Principles of Art History* (Hollinger trans., 1932). A more recent discussion is E. H. Gombrich, *Art and Illusion* (2nd ed. 1961).

The reference to modernist art and its problems is a capsule reference to the extensive and brilliant writings of Michael Fried, which display in the highest degree not only the immanence of reason in art, but the function of the philosopher-critic in bringing to the surface what that rational structure is. The reference in the text may best be referred to Fried's catalog essay to the exhibition "New York Painting and Sculpture, 1940–1970" (Henry Geldzahler, ed., 1969).

Kinds of Rational Ends

On the complexity of actions, see the references to Anscombe, Hart, Melden, and Schwayder in the notes to the previous chapter. On the complexity of the "act" of seeing, see E. H. Gombrich, *Art and Illusion* (2nd ed., 1961). In large part his work is devoted to this theme. Nelson Goodman quotes John Constable's dictum that "painting is a science . . . of which pictures are but experiments." *The Languages of Art* (1968), p. 33. The experiment is an experiment in the complex act of seeing.

Particular Ends and General Principles

There is an extensive literature on the dispositional interpretation of the concept of having a principle. This is largely concerned with the issue of what it is to hold a moral principle. For a bibliography on that issue see page 245. As to the notion of acting on a principle, see the discussions by G. E. Anscombe in *Intention*, §§9–16, and by David Schwayder in *The Stratification of Behavior*, pt. 2.

Chapter IV. *The Principle of Morality*

The Principle of Morality Introduced

For a survey of the literature on the domain of the concept of morality, see Frankena, "Recent Conceptions of Morality," in H. N. Castaneda and George Nakhnikian eds., *Morality and the Language of Conduct* (1965).

My specification of the principle of morality may be related to several sources. In general, the conception of morality and personality as an expression of impartiality is very similar to that put forward by Thomas Nagel in his forthcoming *The Possibility of Altruism*. It derives, most obviously, from Kant's categorical imperative, for which see generally H. J. Paton, *The Categorical Imperative* (1947), and L. W. Beck, *A Commentary on Kant's Critique of Practical Reason* (1960). Kant does not, however, explicitly confine the categorical imperative to the domain I prescribe for morality. The definitive modern statement of this principle I believe is found in John Rawls's formulation and arguments regarding what he calls the principle of right in his forthcoming work on justice. The concept of right in his scheme of principles occupies the same place as does the principle of morality in mine. Moreover, the principles — justice, fairness, fidelity, and beneficence — are the same in both his and my scheme, and derive from his work.

My formulation raises the issues considered in the modern literature of moral philosophy in respect to the generalization or universalizability principle in ethics. A full discussion and good selective bibliography can be found in David Lyons, *Forms and Limits of Utilitarianism* (1965), to which should be added R. M. Hare, *The Language of Morals* (1952) and *Freedom and Reason* (1963).

The Principle of Morality as the Most General Principle Applicable to Relations with Other Persons

The concept of reciprocal rational principles that recognize the rational capacities of other persons is Kantian. It finds its most succinct expression in the third formulation of the categorical imperative: "Act so that you treat humanity, whether in your own person or in that of another, always as an end and never as a means only." *Foundations of the Metaphysics of Morals* (Beck trans., 1959), p. 47 (429). The correlative concept of respect is also Kantian, see J. H. Paton, *The Categorical Imperative*, ch. V, and L. W. Beck, *Kant's Critique of Practical Reason*, at entries under "Respect" in the index. For a distinguished psychologist's version of this Kantian concept, see Jean Piaget, *The Moral Judgment of the Child* (Gabain trans., 1962).

There is an account of reciprocal recognition of personality, very similar to that I offer, in Nagel, "Sexual Perversion," *The Journal of Philosophy*, 66(1969):5.

The discussion of reciprocal recognition of the principles of a performance as essential to the successful accomplishment of certain performances is important also in the philosophical discussions of meaning. Thus there is the view that a successful linguistic performance involves the utterer's and audience's each having a reciprocal and similar understanding. See Grice, "Utterer's Meaning and Intentions," *The Philosophical Review*, 78(1969):147.

Why Should We Be Moral?

The account I give of the reasons for being moral does not quite accord with the Kantian notion that morality should be chosen for its own sake, but the difference is not great. I argue that in choosing morality one chooses to be a certain sort of person. This is not to say one chooses morality as a means of becoming that sort of person. Indeed to choose morality one can only choose it for its own sake.

The principled aspect of feelings — moral and otherwise — emotions, attitudes, and relationships is the subject of a substantial literature which is discussed in the notes to the first section of Chapter Five. This literature to some extent overlaps with that concerned with whether, and to what extent, a person may at one and the same time claim to accept a moral principle and act contrary to it, since both topics are concerned with the relation between moral judgments and principles and dispositions to behave in certain ways. Writings addressed to the relation between accepting a moral principle and acting on it include: Alston, "Moral Attitudes and Moral Judgments," *Nous,* 2(1968):1; Foot, "Moral Beliefs," *Proceedings of the Aristotelian Society,* 59(1958–59):83; Foot, "When is a Principle a Moral Principle?", *Proceedings of the Aristotelian Society,* supp. vol. 32(1958):279; Gardiner, "On Assenting to a Moral Principle," *Proceedings of the Aristotelian Society,* vol. 55 (1954–55); R. M. Hare, *The Language of Morals* (1952), ch. 2; P. H. Nowell-Smith, *Ethics* (1954), ch. 18; Ryle, "Conscience and Moral Convictions," *Analysis,* 7(1940):31; J. J. Walsh, *Aristotle's Conception of Moral Weakness* (1963). See the bibliography in Walsh on the topic of *Akrasia.* See also Anscombe and Austin in the symposium on "Pretending," *Proceedings of the Aristotelian Society,* supp. vol. 32 (1958); and Herbert Fingarette, *Self-Deception* (1969).

The notion that a person who eschews morality completely may be so unfamiliar as to appear mad is considered in Fingarette, "Responsibility," *Mind,* n.s. 75(1966):58.

Justice and the Obligations of Fairness. The Rawlsian System

My account of Rawls's system as well as many of the arguments I make for it are based primarily on Rawls's extensive work on justice, which is to be published soon and has circulated widely in mimeographed form. The general scheme of that system is presented in "Justice as Fairness," *Philosophical Review,* 67(1958):164, reprinted in F. A. Olafson, ed., *Justice and Social Policy* (1961). A valuable further elaboration of that scheme appears in "Constitutional Liberty and the Concept of Justice," in C. J. Friedrich and J. W. Chapman, eds., *Nomos VI — Justice* (1963). Rawls sketches his views on distributive justice and argues for the maximin principle in respect to the distribution of economic goods in "Distributive Justice" in Peter Laslett and W. G. Runciman, eds., *Philosophy, Politics and Society* (third series), 1967, and "Distributive Justice — Some Addenda" *Natural Law Forum,* 13(1965):51. Rawls sketches his views on individual obligation and the obligation of fairness in "Legal Obligation and the Duty of Fair Play" in Sidney Hook, ed., *Law and Philosophy* (1964), p. 3. In "The Sense of Justice," *Philosophical Review,* 73(1963): 281, Rawls presents his views on the attitudes, moral feelings, and emotions related to his concept of justice in particular and his system as a whole.

For a complete bibliography on the topic of distributive justice, see Nicholas Rescher, *Distributive Justice* (1966).

The best statement of Kant's contractarianism is in *The Metaphysical Elements of Justice* (Ladd. trans., 1965). For a discussion of the defining features of the original position and the persons in it, see Fried, "Natural Law and the Concept of Justice," *Ethics*, 74(1964):237.

In his forthcoming work Rawls develops and documents the relation of his concepts to Kant. For Hegel's critique, see *Hegel's Philosophy of Right* (Knox trans., 1942), pp. 33–34.

On fairness, see Rawls in Hook, *Law and Philosophy*, and the appropriate chapter in Rawl's forthcoming work on justice. See also Fried, "Moral Causation," *Harvard Law Review*, 77(1964):1258.

On the distinction between a contractarian and a utilitarian view of justice, see the bibliography in Nicholas Rescher, *Distributive Justice*.

The distinction between Rawls's Kantian view of individual obligation and a utilitarian view is related to the dispute between rule- and act-utilitarianism. It would seem that a defense in Rawls's terms of a system of obligation is more likely to succeed than the more formal arguments of the rule-utilitarians, whose position often seems arbitrary. Of particular importance in Rawls's scheme is the notion of publicity, that is, that whatever principle is held is one that could openly be taught. This derives from Kant and is discussed also by Harrod in "Utilitarianism Revisited," *Mind*, n.s. 45(1936):137. For a selective bibliography, see David Lyons, *The Forms and Limits of Utilitarianism* (1965). Of particular interest, in addition to the Harrod article, are Broad, "On the Function of False Hypotheses in Ethics," *International Journal of Ethics*, 26(1918):377; Rawls, "Two Concepts of Rules," *Philosophical Review*, 64(1955):3; Smart, "Extreme and Restricted Utilitarianism," *Philosophical Quarterly*, 6(1956):344.

Chapter V. *Love, Friendship, and Trust*

The point of departure for the arguments in this chapter is Rawls, "The Sense of Justice," *Philosophical Review*, 72(1963):281. Two other works that I found particularly helpful in arriving at the conceptions put forward in this chapter are Jean Piaget, *The Moral Judgment of the Child* (Gabain trans., 1962), and Max Scheler, *The Nature of Sympathy* (Heath trans., 1954). Both these works have roots in Kantian and idealist philosophy and in particular in the Kantian teaching regarding respect and moral feelings generally. For an exposition of Kant's views see Paton, *The Categorical Imperative*, and Beck, *Kant's Critique of Practical Reason*.

The subject of moral feelings, emotions, and attitudes and their relation to principles and understanding has received considerable attention in recent philosophical literature. In addition to the works by Alston, Anscombe, Fingarette, Foot, and Gardiner in the notes to Chapter Four, and those mentioned above, the following works are of interest: Alston,

"Feelings," *Philosophical Review,* 78(1969):3; Bedford, "Emotions," *Proceedings of the Aristotelian Society,* supp. vol. 32(1958):261; Chisolm, Brentano's Theory of Correct and Incorrect Emotion," *Revue internationale de philosophie,* 20(1966):395; Duncan-Jones, "The Notion of Conscience," *Philosophy,* 30(1955):131; J. C. Fluegel, *Man Morals and Society* (1955); Stuart Hampshire, *Thought and Action* (1959), chs. 3 and 4; Hegel, *The Phenomenology of Mind* (Baillie transl., 1961), pp. 229–267; David Hume, *Treatise of Human Nature,* bks. II and III; Anthony Kenny, *Action, Emotion and Will* (1963); Perkins, "Emotion and Feeling," *Philosophical Review,* 75(1966):139; Gilbert Ryle, *The Concept of Mind* (1949), ch. IV. J.-P. Sartre, *Being and Nothingness* (Barnes trans., 1966), pt. 3, ch. 3; Charles Taylor, *The Explanation of Behavior* (1964); Thalberg, "Remorse," *Mind,* n.s. 72(1963):545; M. Warnock, "The Justification of Emotions," *Proceedings of the Aristotelian Society,* supp. vol. 31 (1957).

Recent philosophical discussions have not directed themselves specifically to the concepts of love and friendship, which were important subjects for consideration in philosophical and theological writings. References are made to these emotions and relations in much of the writings cited above; I have been greatly influenced by the discussions in Piaget, Rawls, Sartre, and Scheler. Two interesting further works are Martin D'Arcy, *The Mind and Heart of Love* (1945); and Douglas Morgan, *Love: Plato, The Bible and Freud.* On aspects of love and sexuality see Sartre and Scheler, and Nagel, "Sexual Perversion," *Journal of Philosophy,* 66(1969):5.

The discussion of friendship and to some extent love draw heavily on Aristotle, *Nicomachean Ethics,* bks. VIII–IX.

My discussion of trust derives mainly from Piaget, *Moral Judgment of the Child,* and Rawls in *Philosophical Review,* 72 (1963):281. For an interesting psycho-sociological consideration of trust, see Garfinkel, "A Conception of, and Experiments with, 'Trust' as a Condition of Stable Concerted Action," in O. J. Harvey, ed., *Motivation and Interaction* (1963).

Chapter VI. *The System of Ends: The Concept of the Life Plan*

Knowledge as a Rational End

The classical statements of knowledge as an end are in Plato and Aristotle. See, for example, Plato, *The Philebus,* and *The Republic;* Aristotle, *Nicomachean Ethics,* bk. X. For a discussion in terms of psychoanalytic theory of how knowledge might become an end in itself, see R. W. White, *Ego and Reality in Psychoanalytic Theory* (Psychological Issues Monograph no. 11; 1963). There is of course, an enormous philosophical literature on this subject, since almost every major philosopher has addressed himself to it.

Instinctual Ends

In addition to the classical philosophical literature on instincts and the psychological and zoological literature, there has been considerable attention paid to the subject in recent work. To the items in the bibliography given in the notes to the first section of Chapter Five should be added: Brandt and Kim, "Wants as Explanations of Actions," *Journal of Philosophy*, 60(1963):425, and R. J. Peters, *The Concept of Motivation* (1958).

The notion of the incorporation of instinctual ends into rational structures is, I think, at least compatible with Kant's notion of human nature as partially sensual if not actually an expression of his views. My suggestions here owe a great deal to Hampshire, *Thought and Action*; Schwayder, *The Stratification of Behavior*; and Charles Taylor, *The Explanation of Behavior*.

The Concept of the Life Plan

The notion of a life plan as an integrating and ordering of particular ends is in my intellectual history most closely related to a study of Hegel. His difficult and often obscure theses receive a clearer but also sometimes changed expression in J.-P. Sartre, *Being and Nothingness*. A striking, brief, and clear statement of the ordering role of reason is also to be found in Mabbott, "Reason and Desire."

Chapter VII. *The Concept of Society*

To enter the thicket of debate about sociological theories, their substance, their appropriate level of generality, and their empirical potency is a perilous thing to do. Although I would like to imagine that I have done no more than borrowed a convenient vocabulary, remaining neutral in the substantive conflicts of sociological theory, I am sure that my conception of the relation between individual ends and values and social institutions cannot help but be incompatible with some, many, perhaps all major sociological schools of thought. I feel neither competent nor inclined to attempt to document or argue the relationships that might exist. Certainly I feel my point of view has affinities to that of Parsons. But the internal or ethical perspective of this work makes any clear statement of relationship difficult and unfruitful.

In a recent collection of studies of Parsons' theories, Max Black, ed., *The Social Theories of Talcott Parsons: A Critical Examination* (1961), the expositions by Devreux and Williams of Parsons' most general theoretical structure appear to me to draw more heavily on *The Social System* than on any other work. On the other hand, Parsons himself — in a brief exposition of sociological theory — in Parsons, Shils, Naegele, and

Pitts, eds., *Theories of Society: Foundations of Modern Sociological Theory*, 2 vols. (1961), pp. 30–79 — uses a different conceptual scheme from that of *The Social System*, and indicates at p. 30 n. 1 that a full account would require "a rather far-reaching revision of [the] earlier book."

Throughout Part Two I discuss the relation between instrumental institutions, and institutions that are ends in themselves. A classical discussion of how the institutions of bureaucracy become ends in themselves for some of those involved in the institutions, see Merton, "Bureaucratic Structure and Personality," in N. E. Smelser and W. T. Smelser, eds., *Personality and Social Systems* (1963). For the problem generally, see also Y. A. Cohen, ed., *Social Structure and Personality: A Casebook* (1962); and Bert Kaplan, ed., *Studying Personality Cross-Culturally* (1961).

Finally, much of what I say in this chapter is an elaboration of a distinction that H. L. A. Hart makes throughout his *The Concept of Law* (1961), between an external and internal view of rule systems and institutions.

Chapter VIII. *Law as a Means and as an End*

This chapter grows out of a generalized dissatisfaction with the traditional positivist account of the nature of law. This account, which has roots at least as far back as Hobbes, receives its classical expression in John Austin's *Lectures on Jurisprudence* (1879), but it has really been the dominant strain in Anglo-American theoretical thought about law, its tenets propagated in textbooks by such secondary and tertiary writers as John Salmond and E. W. Patterson. Even in the face of the powerful indigenous realist movement, it would seem to me that if most intelligent lawyers or law students were asked to articulate their unstated premises about the nature of law, what would come out would be positivism, tinctured perhaps with some John Chipman Gray and some Holmes. The main characteristics of positivism are its focus on the concept of the sovereign, on the necessity of sanctions, and on the separation of law and morals.

There is very little in positivist theory that takes sides on the question, which is my central concern in this chapter, of the expressive as opposed to the instrumental character of law and legal institutions. Yet the implicit bias is very much in the direction of a purely instrumentalist interpretation. The positivist's insistence on the separation of law and morals suggests that value inheres always in what we may choose to do with law, not in the instrument. The emphasis on the concept of the sovereign and on the necessity of sanctions implies, as Lon Fuller has pointed out, a "from the top, down" conception of law that is also hardly conducive to the view that those subject to the law and legal institutions consider law as intrinsically valuable. These are not, to be sure, necessary implications, and both John Austin and Hans Kelsen admit the existence of other motives for compliance with law than regard for the sanction.

Lon Fuller's thought and writing have been influential in pointing out the aspect of law as a form of social interaction — for example, *The Morality of Law* (rev. ed. 1969), *The Law in Quest of Itself* (1940, 1966) — and in showing how this perspective can lead one to find inadequate the traditional positivist account of law. One conclusion in which I follow him explicitly is the unwillingness to limit the designation of law to the coercive orders of the state in the way that is done by Austin and Kelsen. Fuller has also insisted that law has a moral value as law, and in this chapter I offer a possible interpretation of that claim.

I have also been greatly influenced and instructed by the conception of the legal process developed by Albert Sacks and the late Henry M. Hart, Jr. In their teaching and in their materials — *The Legal Process: Basic Problems in the Making and Application of Law* (1958) — they provide rich illustrations of the conception of law and legal institutions as the structure for a wide variety of social relationships. They also support the notion of the role of the legislator and lawyer as a creative force in the forming of social structures.

Finally, I would draw the reader's attention to the best recent presentation of positivism, H. L. A. Hart, *The Concept of Law* (1961), and to two excellent critiques of this work: Dworkin, "The Model of Rules," *University of Chicago Law Review*, 35(1967):14; and Sartorius, "The Concept of Law," *Archiv für Rechts und Sozialphilosophie*, 52(1966):161. The former work, as a criticism from within positivism, represents a significant departure and a broadening of perspectives and possibilities.

For the classical statement of Holmes's theories, see "The Path of the Law," *Harvard Law Review*, 10(1897):457. See also H. M. Hart, "Holmes' Positivism — An Addendum," *Harvard Law Review*, 64(1951):929.

Expressive Aspects of Criminal Procedure

The knowing punishment of an innocent man is a favorite philosophical debating ground between utilitarians, their revisers, and their critics. For a review of this debate and bibliography, see Richard Brandt, *Ethical Theory* (1959), ch. 19. In addition, see Brandt, "A Utilitarian Theory of Excuses," *Philosophical Review*, vol. 28(1969):337; H. L. A. Hart, *Punishment and Responsibility* (1968); Rawls, "Two Concepts of Rules," *Philosophical Review*, 64(1955):3; Smart, "Extreme and Restricted Utilitarianism," *Philosophical Quarterly*, 6(1936):344.

The more realistic and urgent problem of how certain we must be of guilt to justify punishment has received almost no attention from philosophers. The subject was the occasion for an exchange between Alan Dershowitz and Ronald Dworkin in *The New York Review of Books*, vol. XII, no. 5, p. 22, and no. 10, p. 29.

It is also treated by John Kaplan in "Decision Theory and the Fact-finding Process," *Stanford Law Review*, 20:1165, though, I find, in a misleadingly oversimplified way. Kaplan seems to suggest that various evidentiary rules exist to bring down to an acceptable level the statistical probabilities that an innocent man will be convicted. The view I put forward in this chapter is that many evidentiary rules favoring an accused express other values in the criminal process. The subject will be discussed at length by Alan Dershowitz in a forthcoming book. This subject bears striking similarities to that considered in Chapter Twelve, in respect to the problem of statistical lives. The statistical lives here are those potential victims of an accused who are spared by reason of his incarceration. The known and identified life is that of the accused himself. The reasons for "preferring" the known, identified person in this case, as in those discussed in Chapter Twelve, derive not — as it is often thought — from the fact of his identification but from other values that must be considered in addition to maximizing lives saved or, in this case, public security.

An excellent statement of the function of criminal law and a criminal trial to express moral condemnation is H. M. Hart, "The Aims of the Criminal Law," *Law and Contemporary Problems*, vol. 23 (1958); and Feinberg, "The Expressive Function of Punishment," *The Monist*, 49(1965):397.

For a sense of the dialectic growth of the right to counsel see *Betts v. Brady*, 316 U.S. 455 (1942); *Gideon v. Wainwright*, 372 U.S. 335 (1963); and Kamisar, "The Right to Counsel and the Fourteenth Amendment: A Dialogue on 'The Most Pervasive' Right of an Accused," *University of Chicago Law Review*, 30(1962):1.

Unfortunately no study of comparative criminal procedure that is at once scholarly and illuminating exists. The best work for the general reader is Sybil Bedford, *The Faces of Justice* (1961).

Chapter IX. *Privacy: A Rational Context*

The work of Erving Goffman first made me aware of the intricate structure inherent in small-scale, casual, or intimate and "spontaneous" interactions. These structures seemed to me to be good examples of implicit or inchoate rational principles — see Chapters Two and Three — and thus the fine-grained actions that they structure good examples of rational actions. But it is a formidable task to identify a particular such fine-grained rational end, distinguishing it from the context in which it is imbedded, and to specify it in such a way that it is seen as an instance of something more general. Goffman accomplishes this masterfully, although he is far from explicit as to whether the principles he discovers are what I would call rational principles — that is, principles of the agent rather than theoretical principles — and what if any he believes are the ends that are pursued in these interactions. The way I have chosen to exhibit the principles and rational aspect of these interactions is to consider a principle, privacy, which is implicated in a large array of significant but often quite informal interactions. In this way the principles and rational aspects of such interactions is I hope brought out, although it is not necessary to commit oneself either as to the precise and complete definition of any such interactions or as to their typology. Moreover, as I explain in the text, this enables one to see the special sense in which privacy is intrinsically valuable.

Goffman discusses the concept of privacy explicitly in *Stigma* (1963), ch. 2. In general his works are concerned with the ways in which particular encounters are effected by their social context, and especially the ways in which encounters are defined by their audience, by who is admitted and who excluded from them, and by the terms and moves of inclusion and exclusion. The principal works are: *Behavior in Public Places* (1963); *Encounters* (1961); and *The Presentation of Self in Everyday Life* (1959).

The literature on the topic of privacy is large and growing. An exhaustive and critical review of this literature as well as an excellent discussion of the whole subject can be found in A. F. Westin, *Privacy and Freedom* (1967). A more recent, excellent, and somewhat more specialized treatment is A. Miller, "Personal Privacy in the Computer Age," *Michigan Law Review,* 67(1969):1091. See also the symposium on privacy in *Law of Contemporary Problems,* 31(1966):251–435.

An Immodest Proposal: Electronic Monitoring

For a discussion of actual proposals dealing with electronic monitoring, see Note, "Anthropotelemetry: Dr. Schwitzgebel's Machine," *Harvard Law Review,* 80(1966):403.

For examples of the fragmentary approach to the values involved in privacy see J. McNaughton, "The Privilege against Self-Incrimination: Its Constitutional Affectation, Raison d'Etre, and Miscellaneous Implications," *Journal of Criminal Law, Criminology, and Police Science,* 51(1960):138, and in respect to the right of privacy as recognized in tort law, W. Prosser, "Privacy," *California Law Review,* 48(1960):383. Prosser's approach is criticized in Bloustein, "Privacy as an Aspect of Human Dignity: An Answer to Dean Prosser," *New York University Law Review,* 89(1964):962.

Privacy and Personal Relations

On the general subject of privacy and personal relations see, in addition to the writings of Goffman, Schwartz, "On Current Proposals to Legalize Wire Tapping," *University of Pennsylvania Law Review,* 103(1954):157–58, 161–65.

As for the ways in which the conception others have of us defines in part even our conception of ourselves, see M. Montaigne "De la solitude" in *Essais,* ch. 38, and J.-P. Sartre, *Being and Nothingness* (H. Barnes, trans., 1956), pt. 2.

Erving Goffman has suggested to me in conversation that new methods of data storage and retrieval pose a threat to privacy in that they make readily accessible information about a person's remote and forgotten past. This means a person is unable to change his own and others' definitions of him as readily as once may have been the case.

The Concrete Recognition of Privacy

The relativity of the ways in which different cultures accord the sanctity of privacy is discussed in A. F. Westin, *Privacy and Freedom,* ch. 1. It appears that Gandhi had the idea that not only excretion but ingestion should be private; see Erik Erikson, *Gandhi's Truth* (1969), p. 259.

In *Asylums* (1961), Erving Goffman notes how the deliberate withholding of privacy can contribute to the breakdown of self-respect: "There is another sort of mortification in total institutions; beginning with admission a kind of contaminative exposure occurs. On the outside, the individual can hold objects of self-feeling — such as his body, his immediate actions, his thoughts, and some of his possessions — clear of contact with alien and contaminating things. But in total institutions these territories of the self are violated; the boundary that the individual places between his being and the environment is invaded and the embodiments of self profaned . . . New audiences not only learn discreditable facts about oneself that are ordinarily concealed but are also in a position to perceive some of these facts directly. Prisoners and mental patients cannot prevent their visitors from seeing them in humiliating circumstances. Another example is the shoulder patch of ethnic identification worn by concentration-camp inmates. Medical and security examinations often expose the inmate physically, sometimes to persons of both sexes; a similar exposure follows from collective sleeping arrangements and doorless toilets. An extreme here, perhaps, is the situation of a self-destructive mental patient who is stripped naked for what is felt to be his own protection and placed in a constantly lit seclusion room, into whose Judas window any person passing on the ward can peer. In general, of course, the inmate is never fully alone; he is always within sight and often earshot of someone, if only his fellow inmates. Prison cages with bars for walls fully realize such exposure" (pp. 23–25).

It is just because the privilege against self-incrimination is related to the notion of personal integrity in a way that is at once intimate and symbolic, that criticisms which examine it as a tool for accomplishing some other purpose miss the point.

Chapter X. *Life Plans and Mortality*

Economists have asserted, and reckoned with the phenomenon, that persons tend to discount the future, to prefer present as against future consumption, and to prefer the less remote to the more remote future. Alfred Marshall, *The Principles of Economics* (8th ed., 1890), III, ch. 5, §3, A. C. Pigou, *The Economics of Welfare* (4th ed., 1932), pt. I, ch. II, §3, and Eugen Böhm-Bawerk, *Positive Theory of Capital* (Huncke trans., 1959), II, 268–273, note the phenomenon and moreover distinguish it from a discount based on the uncertainty of the future.

Thus Pigou: "Generally speaking, everybody prefers present pleasure or satisfactions of given magnitude to future pleasures or satisfactions of equal magnitude, even when they both are perfectly certain to occur. But this preference for present pleasures does not — the idea is self-contradictory — imply that a present pleasure of given magnitude is any *greater* than a future pleasure of the same magnitude. It implies only that our telescopic faculty is defective, and that we, therefore, see future pleasures, as it were, on a diminished scale . . . This reveals a far-reaching disharmony. For it implies that people distribute their resources between the present, the near future and the remote future on the basis of a wholly irrational preference."

And Marshall: "If people regarded future benefits as equally desirable with similar benefits at the present time, they would probably endeavor to distribute their pleasures and other satisfactions equally throughout their lives . . . But in fact human nature is so constituted that in estimating the 'present value' of a future benefit most people generally make a second deduction from its future value, in the form of what we may call a 'discount' that increases with the period for which the benefit is deferred."

This censorious tone is present also in W. S. Jevon's *The Theory of Political Economy* (3rd ed., 1888), ch. II, in Ramsey, "A Mathematical Theory of Saving," *Economic Journal*, 38(1928):547, and in Böhm-Bawerk, *Positive Theory of Capital*, all of whom seem quite clear that to discount the future as such apart from its uncertainty is irrational, and a tendency most unrestrainedly displayed by children and "savages." Ramsey, for instance, castigates the discounting of future enjoyments as "ethically indefensible and [arising] merely from weakness of the imagination."

Of great interest is Strotz, "Myopia and Inconsistency in Dynamic Utility Maximization," *Review of Economic Studies*, 23(1955–56):165. Strotz postulates that at a particular moment an individual will devise a plan to maximize his utility over the time span to which it applies. He assumes that this total utility is the sum of the instantaneous utilities at each of the instants in the plan, each instantaneous utility being discounted by some weight. The discounting weight to be applied to future instants may then vary as a function of the distance of the instant from the time at which the plan is devised. The factor by which each time is discounted is then controlled by a function which Strotz calls the discount function. He points out that this discount function can have many, indeed an infinity, of forms. It may be a constant, that is, all instants are weighted equally and not discounted at all. Or the amount of the discount can vary in many ways as the moment grows more remote: for example, it can grow larger at a constant rate, or at some more complicated rate. Strotz then argues that only if the discount function is constant — that is, there is no discounting of the future — or if it has the property of being logarithmically linear, will a person at a future time regard as optimal that plan which he regarded as optimal at some prior time. The result is that in all but those cases, it will be "rational" for a person at a later date to violate a plan which at an earlier date was also "rational," even though his tastes (that is, his instantaneous utility function) have not changed and no new information has been received.

Strotz records two strategies in the face of this pressure for inconsistency. One is precommitment, by which a person at an earlier time forecloses or makes much harder departure from his earlier plan in the light of what the later rationality entails. Examples of this are buying now and binding oneself to pay later, or making a contract or bet that one will adhere to the plan. The other strategy is to take account in the present of this future conception of an optimal plan, and to shape the present plan accordingly. Both strategies involve acting at some time on a plan that is irrational from the point of view of that time, though rational from the vantage of the others. The first strategy allows the past to dominate the future, the second the reverse. For this reason I do not see how either resolves the dilemma created by all but a log-linear discount function. It will be recalled that my argument in the text — in accord with Marshall, Pigou, and Ramsey — calls for no discounting of the future, and thus for a constant discount function of 1, thus leading to no inconsistency by Strotz's proofs. Strotz shows, however that a larger class of discount functions avoids inconsistency. My arguments do not depend on the demonstration of inconsistency. Indeed the crucial point about my conception is that the overall plan only incidentally is formulated at a particular time. It could be thought of as being formulated at any time without a change of its contents.

Strotz's conclusions are worth quoting: "My view is that these questions are difficult to answer mainly because consumer sovereignty has no meaning in the context of the dynamic decision-making problem. The individual over time is an infinity of individuals, and the familiar problems of interpersonal utility comparisons are there to plague us. The interpersonal aspect of the intertemporal problem becomes clear if we think of a similar problem involving a family of brothers where each has a utility functional depending not only on his own utility but upon a weighted sum of the utilities of all of them. Suppose the oldest brother always has the power to allocate the annual proceeds of an estate, but with it being foreknown that each year one brother will die off, the oldest next. The shifting of the discount function of the family head gives rise to the danger of inconsistent planning; and the family head of the moment may consider the alternative strategies of (a) an irrevocable trust, or (b) playing his favorites extra heavily now knowing that they will be out of favor at a later date. What can the detached view of consumer sovereignty be in this context!"

For philosophical literature on sympathy as a basis for concern for others, see the notes to the first section in Chapter Five, especially the reference to Hume.

The concept of personal identity is discussed in Sidney Shoemaker, *Self-Knowledge and Self-Identity* (1963), and P. F. Strawson, *Individuals* (1957). The relevant discussions in Kant are in the *Critique of Pure Reason* (Smith trans., 1929), pp. 218–232; and 365–380.

That in choosing one's life plan and remaining faithful to it one chooses and sticks by a self is a position often argued by Sartre. In addition to *Being and Nothingness*, see *Saint Genet* (Frachtman trans., 1963). See also Fingarette, "Responsibility," *Mind*, n.s. 75(1966):58.

Once again I have been greatly encouraged by the similarity of my views and those of Thomas Nagel in his forthcoming book *The Possibility of Altruism*. In his chapter VIII, "The Interpretation of Prudential Reasons: Identity over Time," he too develops the relation between moral relations to others and the structure of relations to self over time as expressed in the concept of identity.

The concept of the life cycle is developed in the writings of Erik Erikson: *Childhood and Society* (1950); *Identity and the Life Cycle* (1959); *Gandhi's Truth* (1969).

For an excellent elementary presentation of decision theory and the problem of uncertainty, see Howard Raiffa, *Decision Analysis* (1968).

The discussion of Sartre's view refers to *Being and Nothingness*. The resolving chord notion goes back to Hegel's discussion of the end of the world. See J. N. Findlay, *Hegel: A Re-Examination* (1958); Franz Gregoire, *Etudes Hégéliennes* (1958); and especially Alexandre Kojève, *Introduction à la lecture de Hegel* (1947), pp. 336–380. I began my inquiry along these lines as a result of reflecting on John Rawls's lectures on Hegel delivered at Harvard in 1963.

See also Robert Fulton, ed., *Death and Identity* (1965).

For an engrossing sociological and psychological account of attitudes to and behavior in respect to risk, see Goffman, "Where the Action Is" in *Interaction Ritual* (1967). This work contains extensive references to the psychological literature on risk. I wish to thank T. C. Schelling for calling my attention to a number of important problems considered in this chapter.

Chapter XI. *Imposing Risks on Others*

The most persistent issue in the law of torts is the determination of when an actor has imposed excessive risk of harm on another. To be sure there are many cases and doctrines dealing with intentional infliction of harm, but numerically these are insignificant in proportion to the number of situations where an agent is pursuing an end that is quite admissible, but in so doing either risks injuring or fails to lessen the risk of injuring another. The explicit formulations in legal opinions of the criteria for determining when a risk is unjustified tend to be grossly utilitarian. Thus, for instance, in a leading case Judge Learned Hand states that there is negligence if the cost of adequate preventive measures is less than the probability of a harmful event occurring, times the magnitude of the possible injuries if it does occur. *United States v. Carroll Towing Co.*, 159 F.2d. 169 (2d Cir. 1947). Other cases holding similarly are *Beatty v. Central Iowa Ry*, 58 Iowa 242, 12 N.W. 332 (1882); *Williams v. State*, 308 N.Y. 548, 127 N.E. 2d 545 (1955). This analysis leads to two unfortunate results. First, if the burden on the defendant of avoiding the harm would be only slightly greater than the harm itself, the injured party must bear the whole loss, while if the burden would be slightly less than the harm, the plaintiff recovers the full extent of his harm. Second, while it might be argued that the rule economizes overall the total stock of resources, the sole beneficiary of the rule is the particular party in whose favor the balance appears to lie. But one cannot be sure that these utility maximizing formulations would be taken seriously, especially in the face of the large number of special rules defining the rights of parties in particular situations.

Recently writers have urged that considerations of fairness be considered explicitly in formulating standards of liability. See, for example, Keeton, "Conditional Fault in the Law of Torts," *Harvard Law Review*, 72(1959):401. The clearest statement for a fairness standard as opposed to a utilitarian standard is in an excellent unpublished paper by George P. Fletcher, "Non-Reciprocal Risk-Taking — A Synthesis and Critique of the Principles of Tort Liability." Fletcher's thesis differs from the risk pool in that he would require the reciprocal imposition of risk to occur simultaneously, while I argue that the reciprocity may be present if A imposes a risk on B today, while B imposed a risk of similar magnitude on C yesterday, and C will impose such a risk on A tomorrow.

The philosophical literature bearing on the question of justified and unjustified killing is addressed often to issues inherited from theological discussions: the distinctions between direct and indirect killing, or the distinction between killing by act or by an omission. In these discussions the inquiry is whether the direct or the intended killing may be impermissible even if utility maximizing or fairness arguments such as I bring forward here would justify the indirect or unintended killing in analogous circumstances. I offer the suggestion that perhaps a greater clarity about when even the "indirect" killing is unjustifiable might serve to render moot some of the problems this debate has raised. Examples of the literature are G. E. Anscombe, *Intention* (1957); Anscombe, "Modern Moral Philosophy," *Philosophy*, 33(1958):1; Bennett, "Whatever the Consequences," *Analysis*, 26(1966):83; Foot, "The Problem of Abortion and the Doctrine of the Double Effect," *The Oxford Review*, no. 5 (1967):5; H. L. A. Hart, *Punishment and Responsibility* (1968), ch. V. Also of interest is David Daube, *Collaboration with Tyranny in Rabbinic Law* (1965) and Joseph Fletcher, *Situation Ethics* (1966).

The General Theorem

The Kantian principle I refer to is stated in the *Metaphysical Elements of Justice* (Ladd trans. 1965), pp. 35–39. For a more extensive discussion, see Chapter Four.

The Concept of the Risk Pool

For cases considering the right to impose a higher level of risk in an emergency, see *Morris v. Platt,* 32 Conn. 75 (1864); *Town of Mount Dora v. Bryant,* 128 So. 2d 4 (Fla. App. 1861); *Vincent v. Lake Erie Transport Co.,* 129 Minn. 456, 124 N.W. 221 (1910); Keeton, in *Harvard Law Review,* 72:401; *William Prosser, Torts* (3rd ed., 1964), pp. 151–152.

For an excellent discussion of when the law should not honor a person's willingness to have risks of a particular level imposed on him for particular ends, see Gerald Dworkin, "Paternalism," in Richard Wasserstrom ed. *Morality and the Law* (1970).

Obligations

The case of the truck carrying lead pipe is based on *Thurmond v. Pepper,* 119 S.W. 900 (Tex. Civ. App. 1938), in which the driver was absolved of liability. Cases illustrating an increased obligation to others as a result of one's past conduct are *Erie R.R. v. Stewart,* 40 F. 2d 855 (6th Cir. 1930); *Zelenko v. Gimbel Bros.,* 287 N.Y.S. 134 (1935). And see generally W. A. Seavey, *Studies in Agency* (1949), ch. 1.

Another case illustrating this doctrine would be the one in which an unjustified deadly attack could only be repelled by a deadly counterattack. The original attacker would not be justified in killing the counterattacker in order to save his own life. See generally Jerome Michael and Herbert Wechsler, *Criminal Law* (1940), pp. 36–70. The argument runs counter to Hobbes' argument that there is a natural right to kill in order to save one's own life in all cases.

An interesting discussion of the obligation to sacrifice one's life can be found in Michael Walzer, *Obligations: Essays on Disobedience, War, and Citizenship* (1970).

Some Further Limitations on the Risk Pool

The notion that there are limitations on what a man must contribute to the societal pool to be distributed according to the maximin principle (for which see Chapter Four) is related to Rawls's argument that certain fundamental liberties, such as liberty of conscience, are not subject to the maximin principle, but must be guaranteed equally, since they are of greater importance to a rational man than economic goods and would not — at least above a certain minimum level of economic security — be traded-off for economic goods. Rawls presents this thesis in "Constitutional Liberty and the Concept of Justice," *Nomos VI — Justice* (C. J. Friedrich and J. W. Chapman, eds., 1963), p. 98. I extend that argument to other fundamental attributes of personality. For a discussion of the concept of personality, see P. F. Strawson, *Individuals* (1959), ch. 3. For an interesting approach to this question from the standpoint of social psychology, see Erving Goffman, *Stigma* (1963). A contrary view to the one put forward in this section seems to be proposed by Daniel Lyons, "The Ethics of Redistribution," *Mind*, n.s. 78(1969): 427, who appears to argue that every attribute and advantage should be viewed as social property. See also Daube, "Limitations on Self-Sacrifice in Jewish Law and Tradition," *Theology*, 72(1969):291.

For some of the literature relevant to the life-raft problem see the references to Anscombe, Bennett, Daube, Fletcher, Foot, Hobbes, and Michael and Wechsler, above, to which should be added Vivian Walsh, *Scarcity and Evil* (1961), and Lon Fuller's superb "The Case of the Speluncean Explorer," *Harvard Law Review*, 62(1949):616. For an account of some customs of desert travelers, see Wilfred Thesiger, *Arabian Sands* (1959).

The concept of beneficence I put forward here is drawn from Rawls, and is presented in his forthcoming work on justice. There is an interesting literature on beneficence which starts from the difficulty utilitarian theory has in finding place for such a concept. See Feinberg, "Supererogation and Rules," *Ethics*, 71(1961):46; Henry Sidgwick, *Methods of Ethics* (7th ed., 1906); Urmson, "Saints and Heroes," *Essays in Moral Philosophy* (A. I. Melden ed., 1958), p. 198. For a discussion of Kant's views, see Mary Gregor, *Laws of Freedom* (1963), ch. vii.

An excellent discussion of Mill's views and of the problem of paternalism in general may be found in Gerald Dworkin's paper "Paternalism," in Richard Wasserstrom, ed., *Morality and the Law* (1970).

Chapter XII. *The Value of Life*

The term "statistical lives" was coined by Thomas C. Schelling in his provocative paper on this subject, "The Life You Save May Be Your

Own," prepared for the Second Conference on Government Expenditures held at the Brookings Institution, September 14–15, 1966.

Other papers touching on this subject are Calabresi, "The Decision for Accidents: An Approach to Nonfault Allocation of Costs," *Harvard Law Review*, 78(1965):713; and Calabresi, "Reflections on Medical Experimentation on Humans," paper read at the Daedalus Conference on the Ethical Aspects of Experimentation on Human Subjects (1968). For an extensive bibliography as well as considerable enlightenment and entertainment, see Erving Goffman, "Where the Action Is," in *Interaction Ritual* (1967), p. 149. See also M. H. Pappworth, *Human Guinea Pigs* (1967).

The literature relating to rational decision under conditions of uncertainty is that cited in the notes to Chapter X. In particular, the best account is Howard Raiffa, *Decision Analysis* (1968).

It is only recently, in the work of Erik H. Erikson — for example, *Childhood and Society* (1950), *Identity and the Life Cycle* (1959) — that psychoanalytical literature has dealt directly with the problems of aging and death on their own terms and not as symbols of childhood conflicts and perceptions. It appears that Erikson considers the coming to terms with death as a problem proper only to a particular, late stage in the life cycle. In my view, it is a pervasive problem, which colors the whole structure of a person's conception of himself and of his life plan.

A most moving presentation of the encounter with the certainty of approaching death is Leo Tolstoy's story "The Death of Ivan Ilych."

Robert Lifton's account and analysis of the experiences and adaptations of the survivors of Hiroshima, *Death in Life* (1967), shows how disruptive can be the encounter with death if it occurs in a context which does not allow one's developed mechanisms of defense and assimilation to operate. This disruption does not appear to be a function of the certainty or imminence of death, but rather of the compatability of death with the survival of values and valued objects. Erikson makes a similar point in respect to the reactions of Indian peasants forced to witness helplessly the death of their children during famine. *Gandhi's Truth*, p. 273.

Index

Achilles, 169, 177–178
Act, activity, *see* Action
Act and omission, 183, 257
Action: complexity of, 14–18; and ends, 7–19, 34–36; expressive and instrumental, 112–113; moral, 40–41; in Parson's system, 106–107; rational, 17–18. *See also* Ends; Rational action; Rational ends
Aesthetics, *see* Art
Akrasia, 59
Analytic construction, *see* Rawls
Anscombe, Elizabeth, 241, 243, 258
Argument of end or action, *see* Rational principles
Aristotle, 79, 240, 247
Art, 29, 30, 32–33, 34, 90–91; life as a work of, 100; modernist, 242–243
Austin, John, 249

Beliefs, 15–17, 24
Beneficence, 202–203, 244, 259
Bentham, Jeremy, 239, 240
Body, integrity of and personality, 203–205
Böhm-Bawerk, Eugen, 254
Bureaucracy, 249

Cannibalism, 47–48
Capacities, 48–49, 172–177, 179, 181. *See also* Ends; Rational Ends
Change and uncertainty, 162–166
Chomsky, Noam, 21–22
Civic friendship, 130, 151
Civil liberties, 62, 259
Coherence, 32–34, 60, 90–91, 97–101, 114–115, 134–135, 157, 172–176; and art, 90–91; and society, 134–135
Commitment: in marriage, 118–120; and time, 160–162
Complexity, 99–101, 172–176
Condemnation: and criminal law, 128
Constitutions, 24, 62
Context: and rational actions, 137, 139, 141
Contractarian tradition, 162
Crime, 125–126, 128
Criminal procedure, 125–132; adversary system, 130–131; as drama, 131; right to counsel, 131
Cruelty, 50n
Curiosity, 88, 111

Dance, 28–30
D'Arcy, Martin, 247
Daube, David, 258, 259